D0475376

Shopping

in Space

Shopping

in Space

Essays on America's
Blank Generation Fiction

Elizabeth Young and
Graham Caveney

Published by
Atlantic Monthly Press
with Serpent's Tail

First published in Great Britain in 1992 by Serpent's Tail

Published in the United States of America in 1993 by Atlantic Monthly Press with Serpent's Tail

Published simultaneously in Canada
Printed in the United States of America

Library of Congress Cataloging-in-Publication Data

Young, Elizabeth.
    Shopping in space: essays on America's blank generation fiction /
Elizabeth Young and Graham Caveney.
    Includes bibliographical references and index.
    ISBN 0-87113-542-6
    1. American fiction—New York (N.Y.)—History and criticism.
2. Literature and society—New York (N.Y.)—History—20th century.
3. American fiction—20th century—History and criticism.   4. New
York (N.Y.)—Intellectual life—20th century.   5. Postmodernism
(Literature)—New York (N.Y.)   6. City and town life in literature.
7. New York (N.Y.) in literature.   8. Punk culture—New York (N.Y.)
9. Youth in literature.   I. Caveney, Graham.   II. Title.
PS255.N5Y68   1993   813'.540997471—dc20   92-60147

The Atlantic Monthly Press
19 Union Square West
New York, NY 10003

FIRST PRINTING

To my co-author

Contents

Acknowledgements

I am grateful to all the following people for their help and
encouragement:
Dr Patrick Campbell, Lucy Morton, Jenny Turner, Briar
Wood, Kyran Joughin, Bryony Dahl, Michael Hamer, David
Hoffman, John Williams, Stuart Home, Nick Kimberley, Jane
Dickins, Charles Shaar Murray, Charlotte Greig, Tony Peake,
Peter Strauss, Mike Hart and everyone at Compendium
Bookshop, and our editors.

Special thanks to the following writers for their cooperation
and practical assistance: Jane DeLynn, Mary Gaitskill, Lynne
Tillman, Denis Cooper, Joel Rose.

I am indebted to my parents and to Iain and Jane for their
continuing love and support. And to Cha Cha.

My most heartfelt thanks to Peter Mannheim, Mac guru,
for his sympathy and allegiance.

The chapters "On the Road Again" and "Death in
Disneyland" are dedicated to the memory of the late Peter
Lawson (1947–1992).

E.Y.

I am indebted to many people for many reasons, but
particular thanks are due to the following:
For their patience and friendship: My parents, Robert
Houlgate, Rebecca Kidd, James Taylor, Dave Hesmondalgh,
Anita Gyson, Chris Ryding and Richard Brown.
For allowing and encouraging me to write: Nick Kimberley,
Sean O'Hagan, Sam Taylor and Philip Watson.
Special thanks to Duncan Webster for helping me to "deal
with it" when it seemed as though I couldn't quite figure it.

G.C.

Introduction

"Shopping is a feeling."

David Byrne

"Life can never be too disorientating."

Guy Debord and Gil Wolman

American literature has never received a rapturous reception in Britain. Despite the mighty roll-call of the post-war years— Vladimir Nabokov, Saul Bellow, John Barth, William Burroughs, Donald Barthelme—until fairly recently it took some effort to study and research American fiction in a British university. Anyone who formed a passionate adolescent attachment to the writing of Jack Kerouac or Thomas Pynchon could be reasonably sure of remaining out of step with the British literary establishment, probably for the rest of their lives.

This dismissive attitude ensures that when American fiction is published in Britain it is often poorly reviewed by critics. Some writers anglophile in their tastes and attitudes, such as John Cheever or John Updike, have always had an easier ride than others. Otherwise, few critics appear to have an interest in the complexity of the literary movements in America, from the Beat generation and Black Mountain College through the New York Poets and Surfiction group; writers affiliated with any of these broadly experimental areas usually get short shrift in Britain. In the mid-eighties, when the writers derisively known as the "brat-pack" began to be published in Britain, critics were swift to describe them as lightweight and inconsequential without any consideration of the background to their fiction. This response puzzled readers, many of whom found the books entertaining and relevant. They certainly sold in huge quantities.

There is no doubt now that New York underwent a creative renaissance in all the arts during the 1980s. The punk ethos of getting out there and doing something affected not only musicians but also young writers. During the early years of the decade a number of new magazines appeared in New York, many of them initially associated with the vibrant artistic underground of the Lower East Side or "Downtown" area. *Bomb, Benzene, Between C & D, Red Tape* and *Top Stories* all featured fiction and were responsible for the emergence of a very distinctive literary style. Joel Rose and Catherine Texier, the editors of *Between C & D*, said that the magazine catered for writers who "didn't feel any affinity for the school of 'dirty realism' or weren't writing 'sensitive' narration teeming with believable characters." They saw their contributors as having "a common inheritance". "They owe," they claimed, "more to Burroughs, Miller, Genet or Céline, or even to Barthes and Foucault or J.G. Ballard than they do to Updike or Cheever." These new Lower East Side or "Downtown" writers wrote a flat affectless prose which dealt with all aspects of contemporary urban life: crime, drugs, sexual excess, media overload, consumer madness, inner-city decay and fashion-crazed nightlife. It was an instantly recognizable style with an obvious appeal to a young metropolitan readership and the group soon widened to include writers from all over America. Of the three original "brat-pack" writers to be published in Britain, Tama Janowitz had strong links to the Lower East Side arts scene; Jay McInerney and Bret Easton Ellis were younger and somewhat distanced from the original "Downtown" group although thematically and stylistically they are very close relatives.

At this time British critics were uncharacteristically busy extolling the virtues of another group of American writers, the "Dirty Realism" authors with their evocations of blue-collar *angst*. They seemed not to notice the development of a parallel literary movement in the cities and, in that the New York writers were the inheritors of this other, subterranean tradition of modern fiction with its debt to the European avant-garde, a tradition routinely ignored in Britain, this was not surprising. In addition to the influences Rose and Texier describe one would have to add Hubert Selby whose descriptions of New York life in *Last Exit to Brooklyn* and *Requiem for a Dream* paved the way for the new generation. Group names are always problematical and only useful as a critical shorthand. The New York group have been given a number of tentative titles including "Downtown", "Post-Punk", "New Narrative" and even, in a ludicrous piece of literary recycling, the "Lost Generation". We finally accepted the name "Blank Generation". It establishes, through Richard Hell's anthem of the same name, the necessary link with punk and conveys something of the flat, stunned quality of much of the writing.

A group of writers that can include Kathy Acker, Tama Janowitz and Patrick McGrath is of necessity large and diverse. Our intention was to provide an in-depth reading of writers such as Bret Easton Ellis and Jay McInerney who, despite much media attention, have never really been closely examined. At the same time we wished to introduce some of the other writers of urban fiction who might be less well known to British readers. We also wanted to include a number of women writers and gay writers. We hope that our final selection is representative of this extraordinary period of literary creativity in New York.

In recent years many people have commented on the widening gap between academic literary criticism and the everyday coverage of books in the media. Unfortunately, literary studies in the wake of post-structuralism have become so abstruse that the general reader is very unlikely to read criticism for pleasure. This seems a real loss, particularly as criticism of film, art and popular music has seemed able to retain this general readership without losing the capacity for sophisticated and informed analysis. As we wrote, we found that there were those who urged us to dismiss deconstruction and postmodernist theory; having been through it all and come out the other side they were now bored with these discussions. On the other hand, there were those—the majority—who had never felt at ease with all the writings on postmodernism and critical theory and who wanted them explained. We wanted to write in a way that would alienate neither group. We wished to be of use to scholars of American literature and at the same time to appeal to the general reader who might have read and enjoyed some of these novels and be interested in discussing them. It was impossible to ignore the debates surrounding postmodernism because most of the novels we looked at centred on these issues: consumer capitalism, media saturation, societal breakdown—the whole contemporary technocracy. We have tried to combine cultural analysis and literary criticism in such a way as to show how these novels, far from endorsing the worst aspects of a greedy and corrupt consumer society, together constitute a revealing critique of this society and illuminate all its darkest, weirdest corners.

Dazed consumers, urban deviants, middle-class bohemians, sexual outcasts and other disconsolate riff-raff drift through these metropolitan jungles. From Soho to SoHo, from the Left Bank to the East Village, the city is the same. These are novels much concerned with the eternal verities of urban life: popular culture, fashion, music and style—and we have tried to find a way of writing about them that remains true to their intentions. Critical theory has superseded fiction and poetry to an alarming degree; students carry books by Lacan or Baudrillard where once they read Camus or Olsen. Whilst not denying the insight and interest of much theoretical writing we wanted to put the focus back where it belongs: on the creative artist. Novels provide us with clues: they are mirrors that reflect visions of our own lives and it sometimes seems miraculous that they are still being written, and still being read. No one should feel excluded from a passionate engagement with modern fiction; it does not belong to academia. Literature is for us all a still, small voice of calm and sanity in a clamorous ocean of hyperbole, frenzied advertising and ecstatic misinformation. Ironically, fiction is now the closest we're likely to come to truth and as such it should be loved and cherished.

E.Y.
G.C.

Children of the revolution

Fiction takes to the streets

"Now is the time of departure. The last
streamer that ties us to what is known, parts.
We drift into a sea of storms."
            Derek Jarman, from the film *Jubilee*

There used to be a very small, xeroxed, one-man magazine which appeared at irregular intervals in New York during the late seventies and early eighties. It was called *Sleazoid Express*. It devoted itself to appalling grind-house movies, urban street-life, interviews with dossers, winos and junkies and long rants by the editor and sole contributor, Bill Landis. At the beginning of the 1980s he wrote: "Money and strange diseases . . . [are] the sexual signposts for the present decade."[1] Bill Landis was a man of some prescience. It took considerable foresight to perceive that during the ensuing decade the erotic and the financial would become inextricably intertwined and the mindless sexual libertarianism of the past twenty years would gradually assume the shrouded lineaments of the medieval Death or plague figure, skull, scythe and all. In retrospect, the eighties have much of the maddened frenzy of a millenarianist decade as if the Four Horsemen themselves had rounded Ludgate Hill and were thundering into the City.

Our images of the 1980s have already become fixed, homogenized. Looking back, a grotesque memorial tapestry streams past: the baying packs of yuppies and estate agents, an army of entrepreneurs in red braces and jelly-coloured spectacles. They are roaring right-wing platitudes, they are rigid with cocaine. Multitudes of blondes in black lycra jerk and steam in a million tiny clubs. No one sleeps, greed is good, the aristocrats have left the tumbrils, brushed off their voluminous satins and are throwing balls grander and madder than ever before. There are orgies of gross eating, a million pounds is nothing, the sky bristles with aeroplanes, giant glittering buildings spring up above the cityscapes, only to lie dark and tenantless. A constant confetti of dirty contracts, laundered money and drug profits falls like soiled snow, there is the stink of corruption and sickly blasts of insanely-priced couture fragrances. Above it all the gerontophilic courts of Thatcher and the Reagans kick up their legs in glee as buildings, trains and planes explode and endless showers of Aids babies, homeless lunatics, murderers, beggars, homeboys and hookers, tearing at lesions and bullet wounds, tumble slowly past. This is the world we have already, mercifully lost. It was one wherein it was harder to have a social conscience than to pull up cosily around the roaring VCR and sink dully into the warm sensurround of total consumer dream.

The publishing industry was as little immune from the money madness as everything else during this period. Somnolent gentlemanly English firms were sucked into American food conglomerates. There was the constant mighty crash of mergers, like icebergs in the night. Vast advances—a quarter of a million, half a million, a million yen, pounds, pesetas, rands—were paid out for mountains of disposable airport rubbish. Forests were felled to produce door-stop paperbacks embossed with gold and stuffed with cotton-candy verbiage. *The Bonfire of the Vanities* was considered a serious book. Agents, once a fairly lowly form of life, became stars and were seen grinning like hyenas and clutching Andy Warhol's tweed jacket. No one knew—or cared —what art was any more. Feminist houses published accounts of menopausal distress from Denmark and Russia. Serious readers turned towards the Third World and started reading endless strange books about Islam and South American sorcerers.

It was against this background of publishing turmoil, of an

industry divided between hysterical promotion of trash and obsequious worship of old-timers like Saul Bellow and John Updike that Bret Easton Ellis was to achieve such a notable success with his first book, *Less Than Zero*. It was successful, as were similar books by Jay McInerney and Tama Janowitz, for a very simple reason. It appealed straightforwardly to younger readers; it concerned a world they knew, one of drugs and clubs and MTV.

Publishing houses had rather lost sight of the college-age readership and for complex and long-standing reasons. Since the sixties—and not for want of trying—there had been very little in mainstream publishing that appealed to that particular audience. The original Baby-Boom generation were known to have inexplicable and deviant reading tastes. They liked Hermann Hesse and J. R. R. Tolkien. They liked political theory. They liked genre of all kinds—SF, horror, erotica, crime. (This was the generation that produced Stephen King and for whom he wrote. Interminably.) They read mountains of appallingly explicit comics. Serious readers from this period tended to swim towards the wilder shores of the *nouveau roman*, Pynchon, Burroughs, Black Mountain College and a lifetime of squinting at incomprehensible small press magazines. One trend from the late sixties was definitely towards this, the fringes of literature, the experimental, the avant-garde and increasingly towards postmodern theory. The other trend was probably more important. During the post-war period, the music industry has assumed a virtual total hegemony over the lives of adolescents, providing all that they need in terms of stimulus, nourishment and romance. The disaffected young intellectual of earlier generations would be likely to turn to bohemianism, art, politics and literature, or a combination thereof. After the early 1960s when Bob Dylan demonstrated that a persuasive way with metaphor paid off, and with *credibility*, the same disaffected youth would almost certainly turn to the music business. And, as talented writers from Leonard Cohen to Morrissey have found, mass worship plus the fulfilment of whatever dreams of narcotic and sexual excess one might have is infinitely preferable to giving readings in deserted arts centres and grubbing along on miserly advances.

Throughout the Punk period young writers continued to hurl themselves at the microphone. The Clash song-writing team and a girl known as Poly Styrene were particularly effective lyricists, chronicling the whole day-glo urban nightmare in ways that novelists seemed quite unable to do. Poets such as John Cooper Clarke, Attila the Stockbroker and, in America, Patti Smith and Richard Hell decided that they were heirs to the oral tradition and promptly took to the stage as well.

Of course not all writers can sing, although they nearly all tried. If tone-deaf, however, they weren't going to be kept out of this vast playground of exotic delights. Many extremely good writers, particularly during the 1970s, became well-known as music journalists. This was an astonishingly vague job description. Being a music critic enabled them to write about whatever they wanted, about whatever random enthusiasms might possess them, be it American automobiles, crime novels, occult history or semiotics; under the benign umbrella of "music" papers such as *Rolling Stone* in America or *New Musical Express* in Britain, the young writer had an intoxicating amount of space and freedom to hold forth on any aspect of contemporary culture or politics. Furthermore, one could stay in *the life*.[2] The playground widened year by year and a competent writer, if not felled by drugs, could carry on till retirement. One could specialize in something obscure, like jazz. If one was good enough, and willing to compromise, one could cross over to the straight press and become a real journalist. Or one could write for the many style magazines—*The Face* or *GQ*—which sprang up in the wake of the music press. One could become an editor, or write books about music or biographies of pop stars. "Music publishing" became a growth area. As long as the good times kept rolling the possibilities were endless. Stay close to *the life* and you could retain the comforting illusion of credibility and integrity, however much money was pouring in. Thus, for two decades, by this strange route, the music business stole writers and readers. There were drawbacks, of course. It was a boys' barrio which did not extend much of a welcome to women in either role. And few people who sprang from the sixties counter-culture were writing serious fiction.

The youth culture of 1960-80 proved astonishingly resistant to the serious novelist. Tom Wolfe, an astute social commentator if indifferent novelist, remarks on this with wry bemusement in his introduction to *The New Journalism*. He describes: "waiting for the novels I was sure would come pouring out the psychedelic experience . . . but they never came forth . . . I learned later that publishers had been waiting too. They had been practically crying for novels by the new writers who must be out there somewhere, the new writers who would do the big novels of the hippie life or campus life or radical movements or the war in Vietnam or dope or sex or black militancy or encounter groups or the whole whirlpool at once. They waited . . ."[3] Who did they get? Ken Kesey. Twenty years later Thomas Pynchon finally produced his great acid flash-back *Vineland*, the only novel to deal seriously with the rococo extravaganzas of the newly mediatized sixties. It was greeted with confusion and derision on account of its subject matter being uneasily poised between being an excruciatingly embarrassing memory and a newly fashionable phenomenon in the form of New Age neo-hippiedom. In any event Tom Wolfe had been correct when he wrote: "This whole side of American life that gushed forth when post-war American affluence finally blew the lid off—all this novelists simply turned away from, gave up by default." One book, twenty years on was no answer. Wolfe suggests that the problem lay in the fact of novelists seeming "to shy away from the life of the great cities altogether. The thought of tackling such a subject seemed to terrify them, confuse them, make them doubt their own powers."[4]

In the early years of the sixties the culture shock was immense and no one, it seemed, could establish a language or tone to encompass the confluence of bohemianism, squalor, excess and black humour that comprised the counter-cultural world. Martin Amis, hampered by his own distance from that world and by his total ignorance of street talk, succeeded to some extent in *Dead Babies* by setting it in the future. Culturally it was a world dominated by fashion and a writer, even if linguistically adept, could not hope to present a fictional portrait that would not have dated by the time the ink was dry. The entire confluence was dependent upon continual, tiny shifts in style nuance, cults, status and music. Furthermore, it seemed that if one took a serious, adult look at the whole status-crazy, drug-addled nexus, the cyber-spatial, nerve-shrivelling intensity of the urban megalopolis, one responded with horror. Hubert Selby for example wrote the best book ever about youthful drug-addiction, *Requiem for a Dream*—but, deeply pessimistic, it is not a book that is ever introduced to young readers in school or college. Novelists, by and large, took a very long time to assimilate the profound societal shifts of the post-war world. They had to learn to handle a word-hoard, a Pandora's Box which once opened, threatened to bury them alive in a shrieking ticker-tape of muzak, print-out, sound-tracks, speeches, lyrics, talk-shows, and rap. It took twenty years before they could hope to produce anything other than a blast of brand-names, twenty years for Pynchon to write *Vineland*, for Paul Auster to produce his cityscapes and Seth Morgan the street-talking jive of *Homeboy*[5]—or for a young author to write *American Psycho*. Happily there are indications that we are only now at the beginning of a fictional renaissance, with writers who can handle the contemporary city. There was also in general, during that period, an actual shortage of creative writers. The ambitious money-hungry ones were in advertising, the neurotic boy poets were riding the swings and roundabouts of the music business, and the women were almost certainly grappling with feminism in one form or another. And so, Hunter S. Thompson, Tom Wolfe, and the other "New Journalists" with Zola-esque pretensions had "the whole crazed obscene uproarious Mammon-faced drug-soaked mau-mau lust-oozing modern world all to themselves."[6] For a while.

During the 1980s the younger readers and writers who concern us here and those others who had remained largely alienated from mainstream publishing were to be involved in considerable changes. The readers from the original Baby-Boom generation had by now become middle-aged and they remained largely responsible for supporting a plethora of small, independent publishing houses including the feminist, gay and left-wing presses. The literary underground of experimentation and small presses had never quite gone away, even in Britain. (As Paul Valéry had put it, "Everything changes but the avant-garde.") After William Burroughs, Kathy Acker was the only real inheritor of this bohemian tradition to cross over fully into the big-time publishing world. Acker, who lived for a long time in London, has commented on the lack of a literary "underground" in Britain: "I came out of a poetry tradition—the Black Mountain poets, the Language Poets. No such traditions exist over here. The underground just isn't known here. I mean, a huge network that's been there for years and years . . . there's no such thing here."[7] This is, of course one of the reasons why English critics are so ill-equipped to deal with much of contemporary fiction, why English writing remains so mired in a parochial backwater. Acker suffered from a degree of misunderstanding from the British press that, she said, amounted to "slander"[8] and that similarly stemmed from the lack of a strong British counter-culture in writing. During the eighties the enormously diverse elements that comprised the American counter-culture seemed to gather strength and show some indications of producing new writers. This American underground which, as Acker points out, had never gone away over there could be glimpsed by English readers in books and magazines like the Re/Search publications and Amok's Fourth Despatch catalogue. This latter offered all the books traditionally venerated by the "underground" from de Sade and William Burroughs to Bakunin and Chomsky. The obsessions ranged through Mind-control, Occult Theory, Exotica, Psychedelia, Genetics, Cyberpunk, drugs, film and performance art. Fourth Despatch's books, they said, "offer unflinching looks at mayhem, virus and decay: dissections of the current global power structure; sexual impulses spinning out of control; psychiatric tyranny and schizophrenia; tribal rituals and ethnographic documents; psychedelic reality-maps; the tactics of individual subversion and autonomy; and other stark visions of our times."[9] The stuff of fiction?—not in England. Despite a seemingly irreconcilable diversity of interests—from neo-Nazi, sado-masochistic body-fascism to New Age euphoria and smart drugs—the American art underground was—and is—an enormously eclectic and diverse community. Its sources reach far back into our century, into Modernism, Dada, Surrealism and the Beat generation. It has maintained the bohemian traditions of experimentation and artistic excess and has nourished generations of disaffected young artists. Britain has always maintained its philistine distance from the European avant-garde and its American off-shoots, which has guaranteed that the English novel has become increasingly limp and etiolated during this century. The American literary/artistic underground provides a sort of on-going, slow-burning cultural revolution which has no parallel here.

Independent publishers, however, have tried to represent this. Semiotext(e) is one such. Hanuman Books in New York, which publish volumes looking like small pastel cakes of soap, have a list which is a roll-call of the international avant-garde from Jean Genet and Max Beckmann through Taylor Mead to John Ashbery, Gary Indiana and Cookie Mueller. A seminal New York fiction magazine, founded by Joel Rose and Catherine Texier in 1983, *Between C and D*, was published as a computer print-out with the words "Sex, Drugs, Violence, Danger, Computers" on its covers. They nurtured a range of writers who included Texier and Rose themselves, Tama Janowitz, Patrick McGrath and Dennis Cooper. Some of their contributors were eventually identified as "brat-pack" writers although this derisive term has little meaning beyond being a convenient media label. Most of the writers covered in these essays can be located, at least at the start of their careers, within the American art-underground, at a particular intersection of the artistic, literary and social worlds of New York. Ellis, McInerney and Janowitz might seem to English critics to have sprung from nowhere, writing incomprehensible froth, but although they may not hail from the deepest, maddest recesses of the underground as detailed above, they most certainly have links with a comprehensible literary and artistic culture closely associated with the fashionable New York art world of the eighties.

In literary terms Britain did not remain completely static throughout the eighties, although there were those who would have it so. It had become fashionable to despair of young people as readers, to assume that they never read, that they were passive consumers of exclusively aural and visual entertainment. There was certainly little enough encouragement for them to read. They were neither inclined to the neo-fogey quibbling of the *Spectator* nor the hearty literary cliques of the Sunday press. English critic John Williams writes this of being a young reader of the time: "Meanwhile I fancied myself something of a reader; this meant I would consume, at a rate of approximately one every three months, a book by the vogue serious novelist of the moment, Salman Rushie, Milan Kundera . . . global Booker prize types. These books I would read about, faithfully buy and faithfully get about half way through, admiring the wit and elegance and being too embarrassed to admit boredom."[10]

Williams at this time was representative of a youthful readership who found these, the rather academic texts of high postmodernism more or less inaccessible, and indeed some of them were so devoid of life that they could be considered large-scale bluff or fraud. I happened to teach English to college students at this time. What did they read? They read of course, the music press, the style magazines, the listings magazines. They stowed away great quantities of genre and pulp fiction: horror—Stephen King was first favourite—crime, fantasy, sword and sorcery. They had invariably been given *To Kill a Mockingbird* and *The Catcher in the Rye*, at school, just as I had been. Although they had no particular objection to these books they certainly found them very quaint. A deep Southern childhood where adults were addressed as "Ma'am"? Twitchy fifties New York preppies drinking highballs (highballs?). What was this shit? To multi-cultural urban students these books were worlds away. There were few serious novels published at this time that held much appeal for young readers. Many of those that might have done (Truman Capote, Tennessee Williams's fiction, James Baldwin) were usually out of print. Colin MacInnes's *Absolute Beginners* was always an acquired taste, the element of authorial fantasy precluding that sureness of tone that can seduce the unsophisticated reader. Anyway, after the embarrassing failure of the film, the book became taboo. When *Less Than Zero* and *Bright Lights, Big City* were published, young people read them. Despite the high-handed tone of the critics and their sneering put-downs, they read these books. They were a relief. They described the known world.

They were also happy to read some of the books published by young London authors during this period. These—which included Michael Bracewell's *The Crypto-Amnesia Club*, Martin Millar's *Milk, Sulphate and Alby Starvation*, Robert Elms's *In Search of the Crack*, Oliver Simmon's touching *Delirium*, Geoff Dyer's *The Colour of Money* and Kate Pullinger's *Tiny Lies*[11] —were at least recognizable. They dealt with young people in London, trying to survive, going to clubs and colleges, brooding a lot. These books may be extremely variable in quality but they were representative of a desire on the part of young British writers to deal with urban reality, commodity fetishism, status, love, sex and, in general, all the acne and the ecstasy of urban late adolescence. And to be fair, they were given a good deal of attention by the press. It is with this group that *Less Than Zero* properly belongs, although it is by comparison—apart from the work of Michael Bracewell—frighteningly sophisticated.

In his book *Suburban Ambush: Downtown Writing and the Fiction of Insurgency*, Robert Siegle surveys the work of many of the American writers covered in these essays. Although he mentions Bret Easton Ellis, Jay McInerney and Tama Janowitz, Siegle prefers to focus on those he sees as most representative of a particularly East Village, grittily authentic postrealism: artists such as Lynne Tillman, Joel Rose and Catherine Texier. Despite their differences however, he does see *all* these writers as being part of the same group, involved, he says, in "the reinvention of

American fiction."[12] Siegle locates the mid-seventies—the very important Punk period, when, as Dennis Cooper describes it in his novel *Closer*, "Punk's bluntness had edited tons of pretentious shit out of America"—as being the point when some of these writers first embarked upon "a fiction of insurgency", a "guerrilla campaign against the imminent transformation of American consciousness into a shopping-mall."[13] He goes on to describe them as follows: "This is the generation of writers about which the Right had been worrying. They schooled in the Velvet Underground, left their naivety on the streets . . . They scattered, reassembled, wrote for small presses and even smaller magazines, balanced jobs copy-editing or programming or typing and filing against their commitment to an art that did not comply with the gallery system's need for collectors' editions or the writing workshops' ideal of the 'well-made story'."[14]

There are obvious parallels here with the Beat Generation group of the fifties. This hand-to-mouth creative striving that Siegle describes is admirably depicted in the work of Mary Gaitskill (see chapter 8). Siegle feels that the works of these novelists "corrode rather than conform to the commodity formulae toward which latter-day modernist fiction tends, just as the writers who create them have chosen *not* to live in the more comfortable academic and professional worlds in which late-modernist fiction still prevails."[15] The anti-academicism is correct; most of the writers we look at have an obvious distaste for the tired experimental strategies and resulting stasis of late, high postmodernist writing. They even have little patience with the writing that would seem to oppose all this, the "Dirty Realism" newly beloved of Establishment critics who find hope in its drab, white-male "writerly" qualities, so redolent of the Creative Writing Workshop. Siegle goes on to suggest that the post-punk urban writers that concern us here are working in direct opposition to "the great culture machine"—which includes academia, the literary establishment and the media—and that their writing has "*utopian*" features, to the point where the authors are not trying to get rich "unless they do it on their own terms".[16] Their work, Siegle says, "opens space mentally, psychologically, semiotically—where simulation, repression and convention have converged to predetermine our Being."[17] The writing also, he says, "shakes up reified relations—roles, genders, social structures." Much of this is true, as any reading of the work of, say, Lynne Tillman or Dennis Cooper will confirm, but Siegle is writing about an extremely diverse group which, by his definition, would include writers as ill-assorted as Kathy Acker and Patrick McGrath, Jay McInerney and David Wojnarowicz. Some are hollow-eyed sixties survivors. Others are very young: Bret Easton Ellis was only twenty when he wrote *Less Than Zero*. Some are more obviously "insurgent" than others. Some would appear to have less disdain for money and the commercial qualities of their work than Siegle might like. However, any attempts to define a literary "group" or art movement are precarious and unstable and this applies as much to, say, surrealism or modernism as it does to these "Downtown" writers. There are always mavericks, defectors, confusions about who participated and who didn't. Siegle is certainly able to locate common strands within the work of the urban postrealists. Ronald Suckenick wrote that, "the form of the traditional novel is a metaphor for a society that no longer exists,"[18] and Siegle is right to suggest that the artists in question are providing metaphors for the society that *does* exist now. Their work is what Raymond Federman hoped for when he envisaged: "a kind of writing, a kind of discourse whose shape will be an interrogation, an endless interrogation of what it is doing while it is doing it, an endless denunciation of its fraudulence, of what *it* really is: an illusion (a fiction)."[19] Federman's words can be applied to many of the books discussed in this volume. He is describing a form of writing which is sometimes called, as noted, "postrealist". Fictional realism, its bare bones now exposed to reveal its wholly "unreal" and illogic strategies, cannot hope to impose its conventions upon what Jean Baudrillard describes as the "hyperreality", the heightened Disneyfied illusions of the modern city, so in literature a self-aware "postrealism" has evolved which makes few concessions to the deceptions of classic realism. Siegle is also very illuminating in his account of the literary influences upon the Downtown authors. Although these can sometimes be hard to detect in the work itself they most certainly include, as he suggests, William Burroughs, Donald Barthelme, Robert Coover and Harry Mathews as well as, in Europe, Jean Genet and much post-structural theory including Michel Foucault, Jean Baudrillard and Roland Barthes. Last but not least, Siegle affirms the extent to which every single one of these writers has been influenced by *mass culture*.

Nonetheless, even within Siegle's uncontentious list of influences and interests there are qualifications to be made.

It is now generally accepted that postmodern fiction is, as Linda Hutcheon has suggested, "a preferential forum for *discussion* of the postmodern,"[20] in that it reflects on what Fredric Jameson has described as "the emergence of a new type of social life and a new economic order."[21] When writing of postmodernism both Hutcheon and Jameson are referring to life under consumer capitalism; the fun-house of desire ruled by spectacle, simulation and media. The postmodern form in literature has come to challenge truths about fiction and about reality in response to the flow of images from this capitalist spectacle and at the same time to self-reflexively examine the ways in which fiction itself is constructed. This is now so well-established that postmodernist fiction has already achieved a form of metafictional classicism known as "high postmodernism". Many of these writers, who include Umberto Eco, John Barth, Donald Bartheleme, Robert Coover, D. M. Thomas, E. L. Doctorow are, as Siegle points out, highly esteemed and very influential but they are all very theoretical writers, heavily dependent on what Eco has called "the game of irony". This kind of writing gradually tends towards a point where it has only the most minimal and self-conscious relation to anything that might be called "reality". It is so deeply involved in irony, pastiche, plays on fictional traditions and author games that, ultimately, it becomes mired in what has been termed "postmodern paralysis". At this point texts can often become extremely dull, or near-unreadable, as if the reader has been trapped by some hopelessly self-obsessed pub bore intent on relating the details of all his dreams. The writers whose work is analysed in this book—Post-punk, Downtown or Blank Generation authors—have a very different engagement with postmodernism. Their fiction arises directly out of their own observations and experiences of postmodern culture, from out of the streets with no name; they are reporting from within a lived reality, not dissecting its constituents from the academic perimeters. In addition, their writing tends to close the gap between "high" and "low" art forms far more successfully than is ever possible in more theoretical metafiction, mainly because many of the younger urban writers genuinely cannot see such a gap. Their entire lives have been lived out within a milieu wherein art and pop music, advertising, films and fiction have always been inextricably intertwined, inseparable one from the other. This does not deny them critical insight but rather denotes an exceptionally sophisticated apprehension of these multifarious semiotic codes.

In much postmodern fiction the use of irony is commonly understood to be the way in which the distance between high art and contemporary mass culture is demolished. Irony however is a much more problematical discourse within the work of the young New York writers. This is because many such artists genuinely love aspects of the Disneyfied consumer culture. They do not secretly despise it, or feel alienated from it in the manner of older novelists or critical theorists. This may account for the blanded-out quality of some of the writing. An analogy can be drawn with the work of Pop and post-Pop visual artists. Although Andy Warhol was personally more or less unequivocally loving about consumer culture his art-works were understood by the critical establishment to be seriously ironic and indeed they had that cutting edge to them. Some of the writing we are considering is closer in attitude to the work of Jeff Koons, whose detailed large-scale simulations of kitsch *objects* and totemic entertainment figures are both iconic and laudatory. Koons entirely lacks the "distancing" effect of Warhol's work, that cool space where a range of quasi-ironic reaction is expected. He has frequently been accused of having himself been blandly "consumed" by the consumer artefacts he portrays. It really is a question of distance. When one exists completely within a culture, as do the younger writers we are studying who have no memory of the certainties and judgements of the pre-sixties world, even though that culture may be a self-conscious and "ironic" one itself in many ways (look at advertising), it is impossible to sustain ironic comment about that culture as if one were writing from without it. In this book we will see a spectrum of relationships towards the dominant culture. Some authors are more obviously confrontational, damning and "insurgent" than others but even those writers actively engaged in the politics of gender, race and sex now find it hard to maintain, from deep within such a notably comfortable and privileged culture, any of the enraged revolutionary poses possible twenty years ago. In *Less Than Zero* the narrator says to a friend, Rip: "But you don't need anything. You have everything." There is a pause and then Rip goes for it: "I don't have anything to lose."[22] Whether this response is heartfelt, smart-ass or both doesn't really matter. The statement hangs there, inexorably. The American dream— "You have everything."

Younger Blank Generation writers Douglas Coupland and Mark Leyner have commented on these issues. Coupland, author of *Generation X: Tales For An Accelerated Culture*, describes his own generation as being over-educated, under-employed and unimpressed with the world they have inherited from previous generations "like so much skid-marked underwear". He understands though that, "A lot of the world would kill to have the problems this group has."[23] Mark Leyner, author of *My Cousin, My Gastroenterologist* and *Steroids Made My Friend Jorge Kill His Speech Therapist* is more than articulate on his literary heritage: "I never had to go through all that shit that postmodernists like Ron Suckenick and Steve Katz and Ray Federman had to go through back in the sixties. I came from the fictional womb like I am. The postmodern battles had already been fought and won." He continues: "I took off from the assumption that plot, character and setting were conventions to be manipulated and played with. Or abandoned. Or humiliated.

Anarchy was my starting point . . . I vandalized the grave of narrative fiction. I've exhumed the corpse and eaten it. You know?" Talking of popular culture, Leyner says: "That's as much a part of me as the colour of my eyes . . . I'm literally made of it. It is me," and notes "I think everybody in my literary generation feels this way . . . Most writing doesn't hold a candle to the exhilaration of being alive and media conscious."[24] Hearing these young writers confirm what has become clear in studying the authors covered in these essays is odd in a way. They know that, already, they are the *successors* to Bret Easton Ellis and Jay McInerney, that these writers are becoming settled and accepted. The entire consumer culture to which they are so happy to belong is proceeding at its usual furious overdrive pace, manically gobbling up new authors on the way. They too in their turn will be discarded.

There is no denying the precocity of *Less Than Zero*, written when the author was a twenty-year-old college student. Ellis was able to pare the book of all portentous adolescent fretting about identity and philosophical truths which, unless handled with J. D. Salinger's knowing assurance, dooms such efforts as unpublishable juvenilia. Bret Easton Ellis, Jay McInerney and Tama Janowitz were the original "brat-pack" writers. In fact they were the *only* "brat-pack" writers. All subsequent, similar books tended to be compared favourably to their work. They had become media stars far too quickly and as such, fell swiftly into disfavour. Initially however it was their technical skill that attracted the favourable critical notices as well as the fact that their work provided a heaven-sent opportunity for literary journalists to comment on such perennially inviting issues as youth, drugs and sex. There was an understandable urge to see in Ellis and his youthful confrères a new generation of scribes such as had not been seen since the emergence of the Beat writers. The fuss and froth was reminiscent of the music press's rapturous discovery of Punk in 1975. No matter that Ellis was apparently assisted in the writing of *Less Than Zero* by his mentor Joe McGinniss, known in Britain as the author of the true-crime bestseller *Fatal Vision*.[25] No matter that these writers had ambitious agents and powerful friends within the publishing industry, no matter that their success was somewhat orchestrated. The press always need an angle and these bright young things with their dead-pan tales of life in the urban fast-lane seemed perfect, regardless of the fact that literary movements do not happen like that but come about piece-meal, slowly, over many years. No matter. These were postmodern writers for a post-modern media, quick, easy, disposable—one-hit wonders. But writers are just not like rock singers and in the end, although they certainly couldn't quarrel with the money, these three were far more wounded and hurt than helped by the build 'em up, tear 'em down tactics of the press. In Britain of course, the blizzard of hype that accompanied them ensured that no one gave them any serious critical attention at all. The name of Bret Easton Ellis is now, at the time of writing, virtually synonymous with hype. There is a vague feeling that his entire career has been artificially foisted upon us, against our will and it is hard to regain sight of the initial enthusiasm that greeted the arrival of his first book in America.

If Bret Easton Ellis and Jay McInerney had a literary forerunner, it is surely F. Scott Fitzgerald. Fitzgerald is a more complex, a more lyrical writer than either but he too was successful very young and became the literary pin-up for the Jazz Babies of his generation. His early work was also understood to have a quasi-autobiographical element and he too felt impelled to chart the behaviour of the young people around him. In Fitzgerald's elegiac paeon to his youth, "Echoes of the Jazz Age" in *The Crack Up*, he recalls the nervous, syncopated pleasures of the twenties and the maddened roller-coaster joy-ride of the Bright Young Things, the first significant Teen generation. "An age of miracles . . . an age of excess . . . and an age of satire . . . This was the generation that corrupted its elders and eventually overreached itself less through lack of morals than lack of taste. A whole race going hedonistic, deciding on pleasure . . . and it seemed only a question of a few years before the older people would step aside and let the world be run by those who saw things as they were."[26] He could be writing of the sixties, if not the eighties. Fitzgerald and his wife, the pouting, gin-crazed Zelda, were media darlings. They were idolized by glamour-hungry wannabees. They lived fast and died young, sad and worn-out. Fitzgerald is particularly interesting in the context of this book; he is probably closer to the ambitious young New York writers of the eighties such as Ellis than any of the other writers—Kerouac, Salinger—associated with youth culture in the intervening years. The twenties were, like the eighties, a decade of extemely conspicuous consumption for moneyed, status-conscious pleasure-seekers and there was an enormous gulf between them and the underprivileged masses in American society. The bums, beggars and hobos that return to haunt the pages of the eighties novel were just outside the periphery of Fitzgerald's world. While desperate to represent the flaming youth of his time, Fitzgerald was also sufficiently astute and puritanical to write critically of that same moneyed high society which so drew him. Eventually, like Gatsby, he was wrecked. The snobbish, luxury-loving, night-clubbing aspects of his persona took over to the point where the serious artist was awash in drink and self-loathing. There are unmistakable parallels with the "brat-pack" writers' own experience of literary stardom in the 1980s, which helps to account for the very slight traces of Fitzgerald discernible in their books.

Bret Easton Ellis was similarly catapulted, virtually overnight, into the full glare of the American publicity machine and, indeed, appeared to relish his position. He could be seen, peering out, sullen and slightly petulant from countless photographs in the company of fatuous celebrities at chic locations and indeed was shortly to be castigated for having so swiftly adopted such a highly visible and notoriously empty public life. The stresses of literary fame in America must be very great—Fitzgerald, Truman Capote and Norman Mailer all had to be soothed by high society as well. However there are still significant differences between Ellis's success as a representative voice of the younger generation and the careers of previous youth chroniclers. Writers who had previously captured a youthful readership, Fitzgerald to some extent but certainly Salinger and

Kerouac, all had years of serious literary endeavour and disappointment behind them, as well as other adult rites of passage, whereas Ellis seemed to exist solely in the light entertainment industry, as if his early career were indeed that of a rock star. It has become a truism to observe that the gap between endeavour and success for talented rock stars—and by extension today, writers—is now so brief as to allow them no time for development, meaning that they run down quickly and are soon stranded, rich, hungry for further adulation and lacking the material with which to achieve it. This is in itself merely an aspect of the post-war consumer spectacle and the furious pace at which it must transform experience into financially viable entertainment. Young artists such as Ellis or the late Jean-Michel Basquiat are grist to fine-grinding mills. Furthermore, whether it is the sheer speed of the dream machine that produces a somewhat listless response outside of the obsessive rock-music arena, or whether serious writing is now just too negligible a part of the cultural carnival, it is certain that Ellis did not command the devotion and loyalty of his youthful readers in the way that Fitzgerald, Salinger and Kerouac most certainly did. It was as if the more present he was in the media the more insubstantial he became as a writer; a ghost in the machine—the same de-invigoration that has caused Mailer to roar like a bull at his own increasing, perplexing insubstantiality.

There has been an inevitable erosion of the "real" in terms of authentic connections and relationships between artist, audience and work. Ellis, in particular, may have suffered from that eighties *Zeitgeist* which produced a mean-minded and resentful response to success, which meant that the emotions between the fan and the star were, basically, comprised of hatred and aggression rather than love and affection. But ultimately, and most importantly in the literary sense, the reason why Ellis had no hope of inspiring his audience was inextricably involved with the nature of his writing. He would not, could not, could never create a Jay Gatsby, a Holden Caulfield or a Dean Moriarty. The characters in his books, by very dint of their lack of individuality in a homogenized society, cannot be "created", cannot be born as personalities in the old sense, because as Ellis suggests, personality in the manner of individuals can no longer exist. Ellis is describing a world where even the most extreme attempts at individuality are doomed because personality itself has become commodity. For Ellis's characters, and for ourselves, the shadow always falls between the person and the personality. Even to be "natural" is to decode and assume the elements of a consumer crux. Additionally it is impossible in fictional terms nowadays to unselfconsciously create "character" as it existed in the traditional novel or what Jean-François Lyotard called "Grand Narrative". The world in which Dickens could "write" a Fagin is gone. We are in another country where the author is dead and "character" comes to us in wraiths, projections, pastiche, mutating entities, archetypes, comic cut-outs and intertextual refugees from history, film, fiction and myth.

And so, against this background of consumer frenzy and a fragmented fictional landscape, Ellis and his literary peers took to the streets of America. They hoped, as authors always do, to tell the truth as they saw it, although it had become increasingly difficult to "see" anything, let alone render it in text through the blizzard of fall-out from an uncertain, nervously apocalyptic world which seemed constantly poised, like a psychotic at bay with no hostages, on the brink of shooting itself in the head.

E.Y.

Vacant possession

Less Than Zero—
a Hollywood Hell

"It is very prevalent in modern culture, the way in which things become more and more archetypal or stereotypical; even human beings become more that way, through films, so you tend to locate your friends in terms of characters in movies. It's been the case that, more and more, images take the place of reality. Maybe you find out too late that you've participated in something that's pretty damaging to the human species: when things become very collective, you lose the feeling of individuality, of uniqueness."

Claes Oldenberg*

"Our becoming is done. We are what we are. Now it is just a question of rocking along with things as they are until we are dead."

Donald Barthelme, *Snow White*

Less Than Zero is a deceptively simple book. Its Californian setting in no way inhibited the response of young British readers for whom it had an obvious appeal. Just as decades earlier, the blue-dream ice-cream melodies of the Beach Boys and the Mamas and the Papas could be heard winding through the blackened streets and sleet-sheared stone of northern industrial towns, so *Less Than Zero* offered up its seductive California Dreamin' to a new generation.

The book strikes its initial chord by taking its title from a song by Irish punk rocker Elvis Costello, a clever boy who joined the cultural circus by appropriating the name of its most notorious icon. Thus both the book's title and its singer are second-hand, and revealing of the way in which Ellis's teenagers feel themselves to be at the *end* of things. Excess, experience—the previous generations have run through it all and everything is now worn thin, second-hand. The entire line from Costello goes "Everything means less than zero" and remains self-explanatory in the context of the novel. The "people" in Ellis's book would be entirely accessible to British readers in terms of their tastes, styles and general attitude. The interplay between English and American youth cultures is complex and well-documented. For example, Ellis's adolescents in the book read *The Face*, desperately, urgently. "'I bet you don't even read *The Face*. You've got to . . . You've got to.' 'Why do you have to?' I ask . . . 'Otherwise you'll get bored.'"[1] Throughout the eighties *The Face* was the *sine qua non* of high-style youth culture and has itself been most thoroughly analysed by keen British sociologists. *The Face* both invented and reported style to the point where the intersections became invisible. Frequently this was black American street fashion which was de-contextualized, spun around on British pavements and re-exported to the white-bread American readership. Ellis's Los Angeles is a white city and the children in the book share a broad nexus of stylistic signifiers with their counterparts in British cities.

Ellis's three novels—*Less Than Zero, The Rules of Attraction* and *American Psycho*— are extraordinarily distinct in regard to place. Long ago, in 1959, a now sadly-neglected novelist called James Leo Herlihy wrote of a character in his story "The Jazz of Angels": "She is an object to stare at and think about. This is why: she wears on the outside what most people wear on the inside."[2] I never forgot the line and now it seems to have an eerie application to many contemporary novels. They are objects to think about; they wear on the outside what books used to wear on the inside. All that is elusive and allusive, all that used to be implicit is now explicit. The bare bones of the novel, its skeleton and construction are on display whilst the once dominant themes such as love, ethics or power have become indistinct. The aggressive territoriality of Ellis's books suggests that geography and place, once a fictional hinterland for critics to interpret as they might, have gradually come to dictate the themes and structure of the novel, leaving emotional issues to become amorphous, to function as background. This reversal of background and foreground, now common in fiction, can be seen very clearly in Ellis's work. What is uncertain now is the human element, the moral and emotional imperatives. The novel has to be grounded somewhere and place, as one of our last realities, has started to function as character. The Parisian Situationists of the fifties were the first to see this and they developed the idea of the psycho-geographical *derive*, a drifting in which the observer hoped to subvert the organization of the capitalist environment by wandering randomly through the urban landscape. By not conforming to the planners' intentions and using the environment in the ways it was intended to be used—to make people more organized and economically productive—they hoped to free the unconscious within it and to restore vitality and imagination to soulless landscapes. The Situationists, sensing the increasing centrality of the urban landscape in discourse, constantly tried to re-define and reanimate the city. Don DeLillo's *Libra* is another novel which clearly illuminates this process. In *Libra* character and motivation become obscure and ambiguous beyond the point at which fiction can hope to entrap them and location starts to assume a mytho-geographical personality.[3] So in *Less Than Zero*, it is the messages of the city that dictate plot development and it is ultimately the city, in a final monstrous image, that owns and spawns the people and against whose implacable background all attempts at understanding can be no more than frail rags blown on the Santa Ana winds.

The "story" of *Less Than Zero* is suitably slight. Clay—whose very name denotes adolescent malleability—is our narrator. A college student in the East, he returns to Los Angeles for a Christmas vacation with family and friends. He spends his holiday drifting blankly from party to party, scoring drugs and observing the moral and spiritual disintegration of his friends.

They are all at the mercy of consumer capitalism, stunned by the storm of signs, codes and simulations emanating from advertising and television and all hopelessly alienated from any understanding of their predicament. The book would seem to have some of the classic elements of the modern *Bildungsroman* in *The Catcher in the Rye* mode, although Ellis seems to toy at times cynically with this concept. Certainly Clay is aware of the loss of some childhood "innocence", and disillusion generally pervades the book but as the thrust of the novel is away from the personal towards the city and the *Zeitgeist* so Clay has little chance of maturation as a character. Ellis is dealing with forces which, both in life and in fiction, render Clay barely discernible as a character at all. This is made explicit in the succeeding novel, *The Rules of Attraction*, in which Clay appears as a comical no-account person, a joke, incapable of any sort of personal growth and the concept of the "hero" striving towards maturity is finally, in his case, deconstructed and negated.

Clay's circle in Los Angeles is comprised of rich, jaded teenagers like himself although his Eastern education and apparently superior intelligence allow him to function as commentator and conduit for the authorial voice. These privileged children of the city are, like all Ellis's "characters" near indistinguishable one from the other. "They all look the same: thin, tan bodies, short blonde hair, blank look in the blue eyes, same empty toneless voices."[4] Blonde, bland, materially indulged by much-married, movie-industry parents, they are heirs to the ultimate post-war teen heaven. Their story can be traced in autobiographical accounts of rich-kid California life such as Eve Babitz's *Eve's Hollywood*, or Danny Sugerman's *Wonderland Avenue*. Babitz lightly suggests that during the Depression and War years the intellectuals gravitated to New York and the beautiful people to Hollywood where they went on having beautiful children. When the cornucopia of the sixties made freedom, material comfort and bohemian excess available to everyone for the first time in history, the West Coast children were among the first to define a life-style that, taking its cues from the beatniks of San Francisco and Venice Beach, was to revolve around indolence, surf, sand, and music. It was a way of life which, disseminated through rock lyrics, became familiar to every teenager in the Western world. Everyone wanted to be a rock star and, as Babitz puts it, "[they] either went to Hawaii and took drugs or went to Topanga Canyon and took drugs."[5] One of the central issues in Ellis's novel is how the self-indulgent paradise of California teen-hood is simultaneously the Gothic hell that Clay observes. Trapped within the interminable contradictions of a mediatized consumer society Ellis's characters have no theoretical understanding of the forces that propel them and can only drift further into pain and alienation. In *Less Than Zero* these issues are uniquely foregrounded against the excesses of the Californian back-drop. They are, after all in Hollywood, the heartland of the dream factory.

Mike Davis in his book *City of Quartz* defined Los Angeles as a futuristic megalopolis. The gross political inequalities in the city make for a continually destabilized community and the vast wealth from a confluence of corrupt and neo-corrupt elements (narco-terrorism, labour organization, film) produces countless varieties of self-interest. The town itself is the sort of micro-technocracy towards which all Western consumer societies are inexorably tending and as such it is emblematic of all capitalist societies wherein "everything is possible, nothing is safe and durable enough to believe in, where constant synchronicity prevails and the automatic ingenuity of capital ceaselessly throws up new forms and spectacles."[6] And all this within California itself which, Jean Baudrillard decided, is: "the world centre of the simulacrum and the inauthentic."[7] Everything is exaggerated here; the privileged are more privileged, the rich richer. In *Less Than Zero* Clay criticizes a friend's morally repellent behaviour on the grounds that he shouldn't act like that because "you have everything".[8] This is a crucial moment, a deep fissure in the book; Ellis is raising a fundamental question about human needs in the post-war world. Why, here in consumer heaven, in the ultimate high-tech playpen, are these people so wretched, so twisted? Ellis's own response to their behaviour, and this remains constant throughout his work, is essentially one of puritan disgust. He, apparently, can perceive the possibility of a better, more "authentic" morality lurking beyond the Disneyfication of daily life.

Within the confines of teen heaven itself there is another, a purely stylistic response, Danny Sugerman in *Wonderland Avenue* documents the beginnings of punk rock culture in Los Angeles and describes the ways in which a studied decadence became increasingly fashionable. It is the chocolates-for-breakfast, sunglasses-after-dark poser's paradise. "Gin out of the bottle, dark sunglasses, a filterless cigarette with a very long ash and a complexion pale, better if verging on translucent. Sunlight was out. Nightlife was in."[9] This was the ideal although the inescapable sun, surf and sand tended to make everyone look healthier than they might like. The high-style, gross-out punk that eventually became such a feature of Californian teen-hood was a curious cultural artefact in that it was entirely without substance. It was pure influence, the teenagers were acted *upon* rather than initiating action and thus California punk remained curiously frozen in its own death-rot, shock-horror, narcotized pose. The violent negativity and jittery nihilism of English punk was originally born of energetic revolt on the part of kids who hated the drab realities of dole-queue London life in the seventies. Some of the British punk kids including John Lydon of the Sex Pistols made enough to escape, to get out. They went to California of course. They were what Joan Didion called "Dreamers of the Golden Dream",[10] pilgrims to the lure and promise of Los Angeles. To them rich, druggy kids in torn black plastic embracing a sort of suburban satanism seemed a bit of a joke.

Thus to readers, English or American, acquainted with thirty years of youth culture, the characters in *Less Than Zero* are instantly recognizable. They are the children of the rock stars and film producers of the sixties and as such have known unparalleled laxity and luxury. Drugs and casual sex are part of their heritage and they speak a universal teenage esperanto overlain with a peculiarly Californian vacuity. Furthermore they are of particular interest in two ways: they are the first generation of pure techno-brats, blissfully, apolitically free of pre-sixties memory. Around them swirls a decade of middle-class fretting. Are they zomboid from television, psychotic from additives, functionally illiterate and with the attention span of humming-birds? Secondly, Ellis depicts them, we now see with hindsight, at a revealing interstice in the early eighties. They are still living the aimless, lightly decadent life of the post-punk teenager. There is, as yet, no mention of the rampant ambition, teeth-grinding greed, remorseless self-improvement and much else that was to eventually characterize the next decade.

Less Than Zero is punctuated throughout by a series of sentences which seem to sneak randomly into the text from the outside world, become imprisoned there and are used by Clay as unifying codas for the book. The first of these is the opening sentence: "People are afraid to merge on freeways in Los Angeles." Spoken by Clay's girlfriend Blair and truncated to "People are afraid to merge" it becomes for Clay an oft-repeated mantra, a rogue thought with the stress falling rhythmically on the word "afraid". Fear is one of the key-notes of the book, a formless, amorphous fear fed by ominous portents and rumours —dead animals, screams in the night, newspaper clippings of atrocities. This latter device is much favoured by contemporary novelists who regularly incorporate such newspaper collages into their books. Joan Didion, California's own Cassandra, haunted by the story of an infant abandoned by her parents in the middle of the freeway[11] was perhaps the first writer to do this. The impact of course lies in the availability of the information, not the nature of the acts which have innumerable historical precedents.

The chapters in *Less Than Zero* are brief and work like sound-bites or Polaroids, a form which echoes the flash-card, low attention span and presumed illiteracy of the Californian culture. From the first page of the book, in addition to the note of fear, a tension, a *difference*, is established between the East and West coasts of America. The East signifies Education—Clay's college is implicitly superior to Blair's attendance at U.S.C.— "the University of Spoiled Children". The East is pallid, intellectual and sloppy; Clay contrasts his pale skin and wrinkled clothing with Blair's "clean, tight jeans". As Clay approaches his parents' house, the tropicality of the landscape with its hot winds and palm trees is emphasized, which seems to make a nonsense of Christmas. Our image of Christmas is almost entirely artificial, a product of consumer concerns, and it is not uncommon for those in tropical climates to go to ludicrous extremes in approximating the twee details of the Victorian greeting card, somewhere between the pounding surf and the satellite dish. It is now, in consumer society, a festival so riddled with paradox that it is not surprising to find Ellis utilizing it in a book devoted to paradox. One of Clay's Christmas party invitations says "Let's Fuck Christmas Together" echoed later in the book by another greeting, "Happy New Year, cunt." The rituals of adult celebration cannot be evoked without dismissive obscenity.

The flip, throwaway tone of Californian cool is already all-pervasive and this adds intriguing depths to the East/West dichotomy. Here, in California, in the decadent sub-tropical heat the social tone is enforcedly one of rigid cool. It is in the cold East, we infer, that there is the heat of intellectual debate, of passionate engagement. This careful handling of tonal paradox is sustained; the surface of the text is as cool and flat as one of David Hockney's Californian pools but there is an insistent sub-textual dialogue between depth and depthlessness. Almost immediately, for example, we find that although Clay's friends may half-enviously criticize his pallor, some of their perfect sun-tans are artificially induced. Trent attends a tanning salon and, as a male model, is concerned lest people learn of this deception. First the shimmering, warm landscape, then the cool perfect people and constantly, beneath it all, the itch of worry and fear—the book, like a film constantly dissolves to reveal turmoil, paradox and panic. And, throughout the novel, transposed against the action, is a vast absence; Clay's Eastern experiences about which we know nothing but with which his Californian life constantly has to struggle. It is as if his former lovers and friends are thrown into fighting with ghosts, with shadows from a world they can never know. In this sense, speaking for another and, we can infer from the sarcastic and judgemental tone of Clay's narration, a better culture, he, as narrator is omniscient. And so Clay comes home, to an empty house. His parents, conspicuously, are absent. "Nobody's home", apart from the dog and of course the maid—that is, "nobody".

So Clay drifts through his vacation with his deepening sense of horror and outrage outlined in that flat, expressionless prose. He is surrounded by people yet only those with a specific narrative function are permitted to approach a condition of "personality". The rest—Trent, Lee, Rip, Alana, are ciphers, flickers on a screen, so indistinguishable that no one can remember who they've slept with or not. "I realize for an instant that I might have slept with Didi Hellman. I also realize that I might have slept with Warren also."[12] Clay really can't remember and what's more, it really doesn't matter. Clay's disquiet, the very faint sense that perhaps it should matter is only one part of his vast depression and sense of pointlessness, which pervade the book. Otherwise it is merely an accurate social observation: few, in those pre-Aids days could recall all their lovers.

The ephemerality of Ellis's characters is more than just a postmodern self-consciousness about the fictional device of "creating" character. It is one of the bleakest and most ominous aspects of his vision, one which reaches its tragi-comic apogee in *American Psycho*. It is part of the sense of synaptic overload integral to our society. Patrick Bateman's terrible, despairing cry in the video store— *"There are too many fucking movies to choose from"*[13]—in *American Psycho* is the frantic, universal response of the consumer maddened by dizzying excess. There are too many people, there are too many things and they have both become interchangeable. There is no space, no time for humanitarian behaviour or emotional connections. "If you're not busy being born you're busy buying."[14] Other novelists, notably Thomas Pynchon and Don DeLillo, have tried to deal with the labyrinthine ways of information overload in contemporary society but only Ellis really suggests the awful emptiness of human disposability and meaninglessness, the misanthropia that licks daily at our consciousness. Hubert Selby, some of whose work anticipated Ellis in intriguing ways, also had the habit of naming characters with a seeming carelessness and indifference— "Harry" or "Mary" but this was balanced by a humble sense of their archetypal qualities. Ellis's characters do not even exist as archetypes—we are sometimes given the sense that they do *have* individual qualities but that these are so spurious, negligible and second-hand as to be not worth mentioning. This is in itself ironic as contemporary America promises personality and personal liberation to individuals as part of the cornucopia of consumer choice. They are encouraged to spend their lives lovingly dissecting and nurturing their precious psyches in a ferment of personal growth, therapy, self-help, counselling, hypnotism, channelling, re-birth and a million other expensive forms of charlatanism, until they emerge, shrink-wrapped, into exactly the sort of worthless, uniform mediocrity that Ellis is citing. All in all, Ellis's disinclination to invest character with meaning is a reflection of a society overloaded with the endlessly circulating signs and signifiers of consumerism which are themselves devoid of meaning and doomed to revolve forever without substance or hope of signification in an "orgy of indifference, disconnection, exhibition and circulation."[15] The only roles available to people are those of audience, consumer and star. Individual character, encouraged towards a sense of dramatic projective participation within the simulations (Everybody wants to be a star, everybody wants to be on MTV, everybody will be "famous for fifteen minutes") has also come to function as pure signifier without identity, without soul.

This question of "soullessness" should be addressed. The characters in Ellis's novels are invariably described by critics as being "disaffected" or "affectless". These are criticisms which have also been levelled at every generation of post-war youth. This notion of the moral zombie whose soul has somehow been sucked away by televisual violence is a true contemporary bogeyman, a constant fret to the chattering classes. This horror is supposed to exist in its purest form in the rise of the serial killer or "psychopath". It was inevitable that Ellis, whose dominant theme is affectlessness should eventually choose to explore such a powerful and popular myth. The "psychopath" was first defined by Harvey Cleckley in 1941 in an eccentric publication called *The Mask of Sanity* which is, curiously, still consulted today. Generations of psychiatrists seized gladly upon Cleckley's creation: a human automata, without conscience, incapable of remorse, blindly obeying the dictates of the id. American journalist Janet Malcolm has pointed out that this is in no way a new addition to the human pantheon.[16] The notion of the body without a soul, that which impersonates the human, from the Golem to various occult stereotypes has long been enshrined in history and myth. Cleckley's apparently handy little definition illuminates nothing, tells us nothing new. "Affectlessness" or "Psycho/sociopathy" is a recent term for a very old, very profound fear and the way the accusation has been levelled at each successive generation of post-war teenagers reveals how very deeply the old order was threatened by the impenetrable codes and rigid cool of its children, the vast distance they seemed to have travelled away from their parents and the known world, the old world. This *Clockwork Orange* scenario, this fear that the Manson family will come round to visit and *never go home*— which provided the scenario for Wes Craven's classic horror film *Last House on the Left*—is beginning to slacken off and lose its resonance as the world becomes increasingly rinsed of the old moral imperatives and re-peopled by those who, in Baudrillard's phrase, are "born modern".[17] In focusing on the issues of affectlessness and de-individualization—heavily underscored by the appearance of another of Clay's credos, "Disappear Here", taken from a traffic sign—Ellis goes to the heart of all that we mean by postmodernism in society. Although the "conscienceless" character has always been with us, the defining of teenage rebels as "affectless" has diminishing resonance as *everyone* in society is increasingly reduced to that state of immaturity requiring instant gratification that used to be the hallmark of angry adolescence. As more and more people are "born modern", are born into the spectacle, their "affectlessness"

—still so puzzling to the moralist—is an inevitable aspect of their alienation and their attempts to numb this pain with an orgy of consumption.

Ellis's novels are remarkable in that they depict postmodernism—life under consumer capitalism—with great clarity and accuracy. The Parisian Situationists, a revolutionary political group founded in 1957 whose analyses were close to those of Herbert Marcuse and the Frankfurt School, were the first to define the "spectacle". Drawing on Marxist theory they argued that in the post-war consumer boom people had become alienated not only from labour but from their own lives, from their own desires and pleasures. These were re-packaged and sold back to them as part of the "leisure" industry. Commodity relations had come to permeate every aspect of life; social life, erotic life, knowledge and culture, and this process inevitably alienated us from our own lives.[18] The capitalist "spectacle"—all the codes, messages, images and representations emanating from a superfluity of communications, information, technologies and virtual realities —was immensely seductive. It promised to satisfy all desires, relieve all burdens, fulfil every dream—but one could only achieve this nirvana through consumption. ("How can you live in a world in which you pay for everything?" wrote Situationist Raoul Vaneigem.[19]) Leisure, culture, art, information, entertainment and knowledge were all being reproduced as commodity and sold back to the consumer. Everything became "life-styles" to be consumed so that our entire reality, as it is for the characters in *Less Than Zero* became a second-hand one. The Situationists hoped to subvert the "spectacle" but post-structuralist and postmodern theorists started to point out that "revolution" was as much part of the spectacle as everything else. Ironically it was Situationist sympathizers such as Jean-François Lyotard and Jean Baudrillard who helped to freeze any hope of political response. Postmodern theory collapsed the Situationist distinction between the "real" and "authentic" and the spectacle. After the failure of May '68 theorists increasingly argued that there was no existence or "reality" beyond that in discourse and that the idea of the individual having "authentic" desires and experiences was fraudulent in that subjectivity or individuality itself is *produced* by the network of discourses in which we live. Nevertheless the ideas about the "spectacle" remained central to postmodern theory. The "spectacle" grew bloated and monstrous over the years; no area of life remained untouched by commodity relations. "Authenticity", "meaning" and "reality" were subsumed by it. Everything became compromised by its role in this dominant spectacular culture. Baudrillard began to argue that within the "spectacle", or what he called the "hyperreal", all sense of real value and meaning was lost. Forever. In the ever-accelerating process of simulation and reproduction, the Disneyfication of the world, reality could exist only in its reproduced and represented "second-hand" forms. "America is neither dream nor reality," he wrote. "It is a hyperreality."[20] The "hyperreal" was a free-floating chaos of signs, images, simulations and appearances. It became impossible to distinguish between the "real" and the "apparent", between truth and falsehood. And so it stands at present. There are those who, seduced by language games and the glittering totality of the spectacle, can see nothing beyond it and those like Ellis who appear to have a nostalgia for "truth" and "meaning", who judge and reject the hyperreal. Ellis manages to present in a very pure form the homogeneity of the modern world and its tendency to reduce people to characterless ciphers, to passive consumers. His characters are consumed by boredom, by apathetic dissatisfaction. They are frustrated and powerless. They are unable to see that their desires can never be fulfilled because these are artificially created in response to commodity relations. Consumption merely reproduces alienation and isolation; that which they consume is part of a cynical process of production designed to generate capital. Commodities are intrinsically dissatisfying in that they mirror alienated social relations. Ellis's characters are driven to extremes in their efforts to experience *something*. To feel. "I wanted to see the worst," says Clay.[21] When every aspect of life is mediated by commodity form it is impossible to experience anything without the mediation of commodities. People are seen in terms of their commodity value—youth, beauty and so on. The characters in all Ellis's novels are the ultimate consumers, victims of the hyperreal, doomed to life-long cycles of unappeasable desires. Ravished by the spectacle, they are largely alienated from educational processes that could illuminate this alienation. They embody all the depthlessness, centrelessness and cultural schizophrenia of the postmodern world. What is ironic is that whereas the novels themselves embody affectlessness, their very existence denotes, vast, outraged affect. Within them lies a furious subterranean humanism fully cognizant of the threat posed by all varieties of lack of affect.

Fred Pfeil in his essay "Makin' Flippy-Floppy: Postmodernism and the Baby Boom PMC" has argued that postmodernism "is preeminently the 'expressive form' of the 'social and material life-experience' " of his own generation and class, that is, the Baby-Boomers of the Professional/Managerial class.[22] This, by implication, includes their children, who people Ellis's books and who may, as I have already suggested, epitomize the postmodern sensibility in its purest form, unsullied by divisive memories of the unitary pre-fragmented society of the past. Although Ellis's fictional children similarly spring from the white, well-to-do middle classes of America, being so young, they have not experienced the vast cultural and politico-economic upheavals of the late 1960s and early seventies. The postmodern is the only world they know. They have inherited its treacherous freedoms without dialectics.

Pfeil goes on to distinguish what he sees as the salient characteristics of the postmodern sensibility. Pfeil too, after Baudrillard, points to television and its invasion of the private domain as being the single most important medium in contributing to the destruction of the old, autonomous, unified ego. It has been replaced, he says, with the "consumerized self" whose identity must constantly fragment and dissolve in the face of relentlessly invasive marketing. The private sphere has been offered up to the dominance of the market-place. "Public and private space are lost," writes Baudrillard. "The one is no longer a spectacle; the other no longer a secret." In tandem with the mediatized dissolution of public and private selves Pfeil notes a decisive breakdown in the hitherto antagonistic yet mutually dependent categories of high culture on the one hand, "mass" or "popular" culture on the other. Ellis's teenagers, awash in a blizzard of ceaselessly circulating codes, clichés and slogans live by the light of MTV and some long to appear on the screen—the prospect of becoming pure image, painless light is quite possibly the nearest many of them—and us—have to a concept of satisfaction. They live in a deluge of pop songs, magazines and televisual trivia. At one point someone borrows a copy of the Cliff notes on *As I Lay Dying*; the substitution of the ubiquitous study aid for the actual high cultural Faulkner text hits nicely at both the intellectual limitations of the characters and at a society which can subsume and represent anything, just as the choice of that particular title further defines Ellis's sub-text.

Pfeil also comments on the deindividualization which he too sees as an inevitable feature of the consumerized self's endless construction, fragmentation and dissolution at the hands of the invasive, all-pervasive, media. I have tried to make clear how essential it is for any reader of Ellis's novels to confront—to feel—his progressive representation of deindividualization and to consider the implications. One may protest the inviolability, the importance of the autonomous ego—but it may now only function as a unified entity in conditions of primitive threat. Otherwise the sheer confusion of contemporary consciousness, our identification with different aspects of a fictive media, the odiously intimate constant consumption and recycling of mass fears and fantasies which comprises the media process leads to a blurring of what we regard as the self and the loss of our capacity for authentic, autonomous action without the shadow of self-consciousness. Most importantly, this endless strip-mining of the collective self leads to one end. When, as it were, the tide is out and we can see the naked palings, what is exposed is hunger and desire, in the deepest, most atavistic sense. Ellis refers to these avid, demonic appetites in the last section of *Less Than Zero*, the most striking lines in the book: "The images I had were of people being driven mad by living in the city. Images of parents who were so hungry and unfulfilled that they ate their own children."[23] "Hungry . . . unfulfilled . . ." This is the centre. This is now the only certainty.

Deep, appealing desires—for romance, adventure, excitement, style, risk—are whipped up to the point of frenzy. By their nature, being fictive, they are unappeasable. One can pour every variety of experience and product, usually expensive, onto the flames, but everything is the same, nothing will suffice, nothing will satisfy. This is the Faustian pact between capitalism and the consumer. Ellis makes very clear, particularly in his portrayal of Clay's two younger sisters, barely into their teens, how quickly even pre-pubescent children will become jaded. Any quest for "real" experience, something that will end the cycle of craving and desire is almost always equally doomed because our approach will still contain the same measure of fictionality and our object—religion, marriage, whatever—be encased in the same discourse as that from which we flee. Only something which is entirely itself, entirely predictable and entirely immune to being drenched with words and images can hope to satisfy, which is why the use of hard drugs is so omnipresent in advanced consumer societies despite all the rhetoric, so hypnotic in other fields, directed against them.

Such characters in *Less Than Zero* as are allowed to sharpen into individuality all illustrate aspects of this postmodern condition of jaded disatisfaction. Daniel, who attends Camden College with Clay in the East, decides at the end of the vacation not to return East for the next term. He first appears in the novel with a deep flesh wound to his hand, a fatal flaw, as it were, a crack in the armature through which flows all the mindless blandishments of Californian teendom seducing him from college and all that it implies.

Blair, Clay's girlfriend in Los Angeles, is a girl with some force and integrity—"some sort of confidence or some sort of courage," says Clay.[24] She is marginally less vacuous than her girlfriends. Her presence indicates Clay's emotional impoverishment, the difficulty he has in feeling anything at all other than self-pity and vague moral distress. Clay is indifferent as to the sex of his lovers, so attenuated are his physical impulses, and he goes to bed with a boy named Griffin early in the book. Clay's relationship with Blair has deteriorated since he went away to college but he recalls a week they spent in Monterey before then which is presented as a miniature of their involvement and contemporary teen romance in general. At first their holiday in Monterey is an idyll: they make love, walk on the beach, light candles and discover a crate of champagne. However by the end of the week they were both drinking heavily and "all we did was watch television" and they leave.[25] This reveals very clearly the bleakness, the unappeasable hunger at the heart of the book; the continual sense of agonizing famine in the midst of plenty. Blair and Clay are young, rich, attractive and "in love" yet the conventional accoutrements of a happy romance—sun, sea, sex—bore them quickly. It is all used up within a few days and the bone-deep restlessness causes them to turn away from each other, to re-focus on the ever-present television which will be selling them dreams of exactly the kind they are engaged in. They consume their own happiness, bolting it down as though something in their awareness of themselves as this lucky, privileged couple were sickening them even as they glut. It is as though the advertisement-like, hyperreal qualities of their situation render it tenuous and unreal. What is there to say? What is there to do? What is there to be interested in? Nothing. They are trapped in an "endless present" which is intolerable to them and this is common to the other characters in Ellis's books who are continually moving on, leaving the party, the restaurant, the relationship in search of something bigger, something better, something more rapturous; a "reality" that does not exist. They, and their world, is always potentiated, never realized. Potentiation would involve actualization—a "being" in the present, a confrontation of the self in stasis, a condition that would be literally painful; that is, psychically intolerable. Ellis is again describing a general aspect of the postmodern condition—lured by promises of being able to consume the better car, the better relationship, the better self, we have substituted the future for the present. We have to consume and discard the present and our selves in the present in exactly the sort of gorging, careless way that Blair and Clay consume their romance. Their love is, by definition, worthless as soon as it is achieved.

The failure of Clay's relationship with Blair also suggests two further readings. Pfeil comments on what he calls "the decline of oedipality and the erosion of the autonomous male ego".[26] Again he attributes this to the deep structural changes in post-war society. Certainly the role of white middle-class male is one that has sustained more shocks in previous decades than at any time in history and Clay's ineffectuality is a very common response. The ensuing desperation is evident in the popularity of books like Robert Bly's *Iron John* which attempts to restore some sort of primitive authenticity to the rat-in-a-maze that is the urban male. Lastly, to complete Clay's failure in love, there is the fictive quality that romance now has. Love affairs are fictions, or psychodramas in which the protagonists assume roles culled from the collective conscious, the flickering, fluctuating fictions of fashion and film. Our reach for "authentic" emotion is caricatured and illegitimized by the bathos and sentiment we have come to believe constitutes such feelings and we become monstrously coy in aping instant romantic "traditions" (Mothers Day, Valentines Day). Another Los Angeles novelist, Dennis Cooper, writes: "Dan thought of love as defined by books, cobwebbed and hidden from view by the past. Too bad a love like that didn't actually exist. In the twentieth century one had to fake it."[27] When love was defined in books it remained a possibility. Now that the fictions have, via simulations, cannibalized life, the possibility of love seems lost.

Much contemporary cultural theory aligns with Ellis's bleak vision in depicting a society virtually anorexic in its extremes of emotional and spiritual starvation. Nevertheless it is possible to feel that the judgements about mass behaviour made by postmodern theory, and indeed by Ellis himself, have an inhumane and even snobbish aspect and that people have rather more "authenticity" in their lives and emotions and are less vulnerable to hyperreal blandishments than it might appear.

After Clay, Julian is the most highly defined character in *Less Than Zero*. Once Clay's best friend at school, he has become a high-class rent boy in order to pay for his drug habit. Clay resists this knowledge until the end of the book when he opts to stay and watch Julian copulate with a client. It is in connection with Julian that another of Clay's codas slides into the novel— "Wonder if he's for sale"—along with a stray remark made to Julian—"You're a beautiful boy and that's all that matters."[28] These observations on the commodification of the human body in consumer society require little elucidation. Again it is as though the normal value placed, throughout history, on youth and beauty has become grossly inflated, bequeathing us a distortion, a world in which *only* youth and beauty have value and those who do not conform to a disturbingly eugenic ideal are hounded into self-loathing at every turn, particularly in the case of women. Naomi Wolf's *The Beauty Myth* re-asserted the tyranny that post-war feminists had described. In a world which values only the crude absolutes of money, power and beauty, vast sections of the population, including the aged, are denigrated and left to stew in self-loathing; subtle attributes are also valueless and, as Ellis makes clear, this particular tyranny of the physical is beginning to lick away at the hitherto boundless confidence of the male. The gap between the real and ideal, and the intense distaste felt towards those who do not conform leads towards the exterminatory mind-set which triggers some of the murders in *American Psycho*.

Otherwise in *Less Than Zero*, the main concern is death and in this respect the book uses many of the devices of the classic Gothic. From early in the book there are ominous portents—a wild wind that shakes the palm trees, coyotes howling, dogs barking. Soon there is a claim that there is some kind of "monster" loose in Bel Air. There is talk of a werewolf. Someone has disappeared (literally, rather than metaphorically). An apocalyptic, millenarianist tone enters the book. Old Doors songs, Julian singing "straight into darkness . . ."[29] It's the road to nowhere. A boy at a party is told that he smells like a dead animal. Clay's friend Muriel shoots up heroin and he watches on, fascinated by the quasi-erotic excitement in the room as the syringe fills with blood. Clay gets strange, silent phone-calls. The street lights short-circuit. Clay and Blair run over a coyote in the car and it dies in hideous fashion. They go to see a splatter film—supposedly a true snuff movie, that is, a documentary of disembowelment and castration. Blair leaves but some of Clay's friends are sexually aroused. Clay recalls the happier days of his "youth" (they all feel so old) but Ellis is too astute to make this anything of a golden age. Clay accompanies Julian to see a client because "I want to see if things like this can actually happen . . . I want to see the worst".[30] Death, disappearance, annihilation and despair. Pure horror and psychic extinction underlie all that Clay experiences. When Clay objects to the depravity of a friend, Rip, raping a twelve-year-old girl Rip snaps: "What's right? If you want something you have the right to take it. If you want to do something you have the right to do it."[31] This, Ellis is saying, is the prevailing ethos, the bottom line. This is what people are like now; there is no alternative. Savagely puritanical, Ellis selects his horrors and presents them within a patina of blanded-out indifference. Ellis's text, while lacking some of the more obvious postmodernist tricks—absurdism, fact/fiction combinations or overt authorial intervention—is nevertheless a remarkably pure representation of the experience of post-modernity. The book is almost entirely implicit, entirely "elsewhere". The text is slight, attenuated, a performative version of the frail, depleted lives it depicts. Ironically, although Ellis's central theme is affectlessness, the existence of his books, the fact that he writes them, indicates, as noted, raging extremes of affect.

Ellis's other early book, *The Rules of Attraction* (1987), attracted less attention, partly because it was genuinely less arresting and partly because it was little more than a reworking of the themes of *Less Than Zero*. This time it is set in the East, at Camden College. He has some fun with the lightweight American college courses "Symbolism in Cujo", "Trombone Theory" and so on. There is the same lassitude and indifference: "And I come—spurt, spurt—like bad poetry and then what?", the same post-punk attitudes to horror and drugs, and the same comments about the group of barely differentiated characters being "terminally numb."[32] There is more bisexuality. The book contains interior monologues by three characters, Lauren, Sean and Paul. Paul is in love with Sean and claims to have an affair with him although Sean's sections contradict this—it is left up to the reader. Lauren and Sean eventually go away together; they think of getting married but don't. It is all much more down-beat and autumnal than *Less Than Zero* and lacks the glittering edge of the Californian world although the novel serves to undercut and demystify the "Eastern experience" that shadows the earlier book. It is just the same in the East after all. Ellis obviously intended to go deeper into character here but seems unable to animate any of his three principals. Even in passion they are attenuated and directionless. Although there is a great deal of action and detail, it still seems minimal and one's attention is barely held from wandering. It is as if, having articulated the affectlessness and shallowness that so obsesses him he lacks the imagination with which to create anything other. He can only go deeper and deeper into surfaces and this he does, to shattering effect, in *American Psycho*.

Less Than Zero gave a voice to a certain section of teenage society—rich, white, aimless, American—but the experiences described had sufficient universality to claim a wide readership. Although the lassitude and studied decadence of the book may be beginning to look quaint it seems unlikely to go out of print and its analysis of life under consumer capitalism remains relevant as commodity relations and the hyperreal continue to distort everyday experience. It has already been parodied by Douglas E. Winter in his horror story "Less Than Zombie": "'People are afraid to live on the streets of Los Angeles. This is the last thing I say before I get back into the car. I don't know why I keep saying this thing. It's something I started and now I can't stop.' . . . 'Deal with it,' Skip says and picks up the videotapes . . .(he is) trying to score some meth and . . . slams the telephone back onto the cradle and rolls his eyes at me and looks at the posters and says, 'Strange days and strange ways,' and then he starts to smile and I think I get it . . ."[33] When a book attains the status of parody it's usually here to stay. Deal with it!

E.Y.

Psychodrama:
qu'est-ce que c'est?

Jay McInerney and the family saga

> "Francesca's parents really wanted her to go to a shrink
> just in case there was anything wrong with her, in case
> they screwed up somehow, so they can feel better about
> it in advance of even knowing about it and feeling guilty,
> so she goes twice a week and sometimes when she's real
> bored she'll dish out some really bogus crap about her
> childhood or her dreams and take the shrink for a
> horrible ride into fantasyland . . ."
>
> *Story of My Life*

> "They don't realize we're bringing them the plague."
>
> Freud to Jung on arriving in America

"Our literary canon and current American practice reflect the
legacy of New Critical notions of the self-contained art object,
the well-wrought urn; the exploration of the individual psyche in
a relatively domestic context is the predominant mode of our
fiction. Dos Passos sought to record the history of his times, and
even, to affect it."[1]

It is tempting to see Jay McInerney's comments on John dos
Passos as providing a neat critique of his own work. A tidy
equation between the twenties and the eighties—the social
realist being introduced by his more playfully realist successor;
both writers striving for the voice which defines their generation.
Yet while this is in many ways true—both figures are obviously
about and of their history—such a parallel simplifies the actual

nature of the generation/decade that McInerney addresses. For if anything, Jay McInerney's novels are *about* the difficulties in embarking on such a project—the gaps between life as it is experienced, and the writer's attempt to represent this experience. Whereas dos Passos was the ultimate realist, disguising the art of his fiction by a façade of "the natural" (this is what life is *really* like, I'm just here to transpose it), McInerney is forced to negotiate the slippery surfaces of the postmodern (this is how a *life* may appear, I'm here to create it). Trapped in the post-age, the all-too knowing decade, McInerney does not so much embody his themes, as address the issue of how the writer goes about doing so. Yet it is his reluctance to pose as spokesperson for a generation (and his insistence on the problems of being one) that has provoked much of the hostility towards him. The fashion-music press, ever on the look-out for some authentic voice of youth, slated McInerney and his "brat-pack" contemporaries for *not* being the Kerouacs or Fitzgeralds of their time. *Blitz* magazine waged war on these writers for their refusal to act as our bohemian saviours: "The rest of the brat-pack, though, *love* the nightlife, both as participants and documentarists. Their books are full of references to specific clubs, specific drugs, specific records. It's a technique that the beats and the "Lost Generation" writers of the twenties both utilized. But despite any pretensions to literary tradition which the current crop might have, that's as far as the affinity goes. Scott Fitzgerald and his peers presented an account of life as one long, relentless and destructive party, but possessed far more self-consciousness, far less willingness to wallow in transient glory. Kerouac *et al* might have taken on an exaggerated sense of their own importance, but they also realized an underlying urge for something greater, something more personal, a search for spiritual awareness."[2] (Interestingly, this magazine, along with *The Face* and *I.D.*, were champions of electro-dance music, glam fashions and postmodern culture precisely because of their rejection of the hippy notion of art as "spiritual awareness".) Surely, the "brat-pack's" achievement is to suggest the impossibility of abandoning yourself to the road, being at one with your age, relinquishing your consciousness to experience. Their novels are an attempt to negotiate a youth identity within a context that has already experienced the Fitzgeralds and the Kerouacs—the "brat-pack's" distance and essential difference from their predecessors is what they are about, rather than where they fall short.

It is also ironic in these post-Warholian days that McInerney, Ellis and Janowitz should be attacked for their status as celebrities. It is almost as though the mass media age should not be seen to intrude upon the Writer: everyone else can be made into an icon, read as texts or transformed into the public sphere, but our writers should still starve in garrets, untainted by the media glare. Again, this is an expectation based on Romantic individualism, a hangover from our pasts that McInerney & Co. refuse to accept as being valid for our present. What needs to be thought through about these writers is the critical implications of their relationship to the media, the ways in which their positions as literary socialites has worked as a *para-text* to their fiction. The intersections of the writers' lives and that of their characters has been located in the nightclubs, in their sexuality, speculations about their drug use, and cynical responses to their mutual self-promotion. (The alternative—that of the enigmatic recluse, the Pynchonesque withdrawal—has been just as much of a public concern, but is seen as attractive through the absence of the author.) Rather than dismissing their work because of their public profiles, it is necessary to look at how the conflation of these two elements works as a new and often productive model of literary relations.

In his classic study of post-war American fiction, the critic Tony Tanner spoke of the anxiety that its writers feel about working within prescribed structures, be they inherited or imposed: "It is my contention that many American writers are unusually aware of this quite fundamental and inescapable paradox: that to exist, a book, a vision, a system, like a person, has to have an outline—there can be no identity without contour. But contours signify arrest, they involve restraint and the acceptance of limits . . . For restraint means the risk of rigidity, and rigidity, so the feeling goes, is just about the beginning of *rigor mortis*. Between the non-identity of pure fluidity and the fixity involved in all definitions—in words or in life—the American writer moves, and knows he moves."[3]

It seems to me that the brat-pack writers use their position as celebrities as a way of preventing their novels from seeming either frighteningly fixed or incidentally fluid. If the faceless authorial voice of realism is vulnerable to accusations of false "naturalization" and deceitful power, then McInerney's projection of himself as "celebrity-writer" provides him with a subjective edge and frank engagement with his fiction. We know that he is not just describing reality, he is participating in it—and this knowledge acts as an antidote to his work ever seeming monolithic or confining. Tanner again: "My point is that American writers seem from the first to have felt how tenuous, arbitrary, and even illusory are the verbal constructs which men call descriptions of reality . . . So while there is often an almost sportive sense of how easily language can float free from a given environment, there is sometimes a feeling that it is dangerous to get too involved in the unreal world of words."[4] McInerney's profile, with its emphasis on the creative interaction between the writer and his material, allows him to use himself as the litmus test of his fiction, and to report back without any pretence of objective invisibility. Against the dangerously unreal world of words, McInerney offers us his image—a public profile which acknowledges his own complicity with fiction's seductive deceit. The profiles of McInerney, Ellis and Janowitz exist at the junction where the autobiographical concerns of "intention" and "personality" meet the postmodern world of fiction and representation: where the faceless power of narrative is counterbalanced by the performance of the literary ego.

By marketing their literary image as a social concern, the brat-pack are in effect making themselves their own protagonists. What has been read as the indulgence of youth is in fact an engagement with the realities of literature *as an event*. Their resistance to inherited structures acts as an aesthetic justification for these performing authors; writers who are also characters as opposed to the blank sameness of newspaper editorials, statistics and billboards. In short, these writers have made it their project to strip away disguise, enabling us to read the rhetoric of their fiction over the shoulder of their self-advertisement. The brat-pack have been received as thinly-disguised autobiographers; this needs to be reversed. They are literary performers, allowing the reader to observe the observers, their work continually signifying its own activity. In this light, their strategy could be placed alongside Roland Barthes's idea of theft and fragmentation—disruption from within, or, as Bret Easton Ellis has put it: "This might sound pretentious, but as a writer I guess you're always on the fringe, even when you're in the middle."[5]

The self-ironic projections of the brat-pack allow them to maintain the minority status of the writer whilst they continue to make raids upon the mainstream world of New York society.

If the fact of McInerney's fame acts as a corrective/model to his fiction, his first novel, *Bright Lights, Big City*, investigates the relationship between these two elements. Its anonymous hero is a part-time cocaine freak, depressed about the recent separation from his wife, nominally hanging onto a job verifying facts for a prestigious fashion/arts magazine. True to the spirit of the semi-autobiographical first novel, he also aches to be a writer: "You never stopped thinking of yourself as a writer biding his time in the Department of Factual Verification . . . You went to parties with writers, cultivated a writerly persona. You wanted to be Dylan Thomas without the paunch, F. Scott Fitzgerald without the crack-up. You wanted to skip over the dull grind of actual creation."[6] From this brief précis, it may be easy to see how some critics were able to dismiss the book as a kind of yuppie *Bildungsroman*—full of tortured self-searching and struggling-writer romance. Yet what is missed by this reaction is the context in which McInerney locates the role of writing, and the way in which he dissolves the oppositions between fact and fiction. His early comment that, "In fact, you don't want to be in Fact. You'd much rather be in Fiction,"[7] ironically presents its hero as being suspended between the two. The usual distinction between concrete immutable fact and the less solid, more fanciful area of creative output is here presented as a question of preference, a choice of genres: "The people in the Verification Department tend to look down on fiction, in which words masquerade as flesh without the backbone of fact. There is a general sense that if fiction isn't dead, it is at least beside the point."[8]

What McInerney continually teases out of his novel is the sense that American fiction simply cannot keep up with the reality that surrounds it, and that writing must therefore serve the function of self-preservation rather than description or mere escapism. In effect McInerney builds *into* his novel the misgivings that other writers have expressed *about* the novel. Philip Roth for example: "The American writer in the middle of the twentieth century has his hands full in trying to understand, then describe, and then make *credible* much of the American reality. It stupefies, it sickens, it infuriates, and finally it is even a kind of embarrassment to one's own meagre imagination. The actuality is continually outdoing our talents, and the culture tosses up figures almost daily that are the envy of any novelist."[9] It is the "reality" of *Bright Lights, Big City* that seems "unreal"—its de-contextualised newspaper headlines, its fragmented conversations, its drug-induced uncertainties. The conceit of the "writer within a novel", on the other hand, is not so much about playful intertextuality as it is the only way the hero can find certainty, coherence, stability: "You thought of yourself in the third person: *He arrived for his first interview in a navy-blue blazer. He was interviewed for a position in the department of Factual Verification, a job which must have seemed even then to be singularly unsuited to his flamboyant temperament. But he was not to languish long among the facts.*"[10] Fiction is thus seen as a necessary strategy of survival, yet one which is always parodically removed from the facts that it attempts to grapple with. Fiction may provide comfort, but not without an undercutting irony—one which acknowledges that writing is one of the few ways of negotiating an identity, whilst reminding us that such an identity is perilous and unsatisfactory: "Nothing seems to be what you want to do until you consider writing. Suffering is supposed to be the raw stuff of art. You could write a book. You feel that if you could make yourself sit down at a typewriter you could give shape to what seems merely a chain reaction of pointless disasters. Or you could get revenge, tell your side of the story, cast some version of yourself in the role of wronged hero. Hamlet on the battlements. Maybe get outside autobiography altogether, lose yourself in the purely formal imperative of words in the correct and surprising sequence, or create a fantasy world of small furry and large scaly creatures."[11] McInerney's skilful positioning of this self-reflexivity calls attention to the artifice inherent in writing. He highlights the self-awareness (even the narcissism) necessary for such coverage and in so doing undercuts the pretensions of the novel's own mirror-like qualities. The disparity between McInerney's own writing and its description of his hero's literary pondering erodes the possibility of mimetic appreciation and serves once again to underscore the inescapably fictional nature of our experience. McInerney's style is a kind of post-realism (a real-realism?), his characters exist in a world that is *already spoken*, and his meta-fictional pathos suggests that if writing is what helps to define us, it is also the thing that confines us: "This is dreadful. You tear the sheet into eights and slide them into the wastebasket. You insert another piece of paper; again you type the date. At the left margin you type, 'Dear Amanda,' but when you look at the paper it reads 'Dead Amanda'."[12]

This sense of depending upon narrative yet inevitably being betrayed by it is analogous to McInerney's presentation of his protagonists' relationship to their parents. They seek out meaning through their families as well as through fiction, yet still end up being at one remove from both. The narrator of *Bright Lights, Big City* constantly creates himself in the image of adolescence, and is as uncertain about his writing as the schoolboy is about his homework: "You used to feel this way walking into school Monday mornings. The dread of not having finished your homework—and where were you going to sit at lunch? It didn't help being the new kid every year."[13] Later on the same anxiety is echoed: "At a little after ten you put the proofs on Clara's desk. It would at least be a relief if you could tell yourself that this was your best shot. You feel like a student who is handing in a term paper that is part plagiarism, part nonsense and half-finished."[14] We are a long way here from the quaint confusion of Salinger or Harper Lee: the sense is more one of being suspended between adolescent angst and the painful awareness of just how inappropriate such a state of mind is. The teenage dread is not so much dramatized (as with Caulfield or Sport), but is, to borrow Jacques Derrida's phrase, *sous rature*—as though the very presence of the idea works only to emphasize the extent to which it should be absent. It is this conflict between the narrator's image of himself and his quest to displace this with a new one which lies at the centre of the book's psychological impact. And it is with these concerns in mind that McInerney leads us to the book's most touching denouement— the narrator's recollection of his encounter with his dying mother.

From the mother-tongue to the mother herself, the hero's wrestling with fiction brings him, almost inevitably, back to a confrontation with the ghost of his family. As his mother lies dying of cancer, the narrator remembers their bedside conversation:

> " 'Have you ever tried cocaine,' she asked that last
> night. You didn't know what to say. A strange question
> from a mother. But she was dying. You said you had
> tried it.
>
> 'It's not bad,' she said. 'When I could still swallow
> they were giving me cocaine with morphine. To ease the
> depression.
>
> 'I liked it." '[15]

After discussing the merits of cocaine—one of the novel's constant themes—mother and son progress to discussing the book's other recurring motif:

> "Then she said, 'Do young men need sex? . . .

'. . . Come on. What's to hide? I wish I'd known a
long time ago that I was going to die. We could've
gotten to know each other a lot better. There's so much
we don't know' . . .

You began to forget the way she looked then, and to
see her somehow as young, younger than you had ever
known her. The wasted flesh seemed illusory. You saw
her as a young woman."[16]

This scene provides a dramatic cluster around which the
narrator's pro/regression can be both embodied and explained.
For what McInerney presents is not only an Oedipal confrontation, but also the seeds of how this complex goes awry.
This is not to suggest that McInerney lays the blame for his
hero's anxiety at the mother's door, but rather that he sees the
way in which the familial relationship is constructed as inherently
problematic.

Rather than reading this encounter as the novel's "Eden"—a
haven from the cocaine-induced indifference of New York's
nightclubs—it is possible to view it as an extension, even an
explanation, of the rest of the narrative. The mother's interest
and participation in drug use and sexual behaviour holds a
mirror up to her son's own life-style, reflecting it back to him as
something idealized and "illusory". The son's embarrassment at
her candid questioning signals both his recognition of himself in
her and his alienated difference from her. What McInerney
manages to evoke here is a dramatic re-enactment of a very
specific psycho-analytic drive. The theorist Jacques Lacan has
written of the "mirror stage"—that stage in a child's development when it comes to recognize itself as a unified whole.
Instead of the pre-Oedipal blurring of subject and object, the
child begins to construct for itself an integrated self-image, a
sense of "I" as reflected back to itself by a person or object in the
external world. What the conversation between narrator and
mother brings together is the recognition of this "I" along with
the acknowledgement that this sense of self is constructed
through an "illusory" relationship with another. In Lacan's

terms, the "imaginary" and the "symbolic" interconnect—unity is experienced as division. Before the actual conversation with his mother, the narrator reports on his attempt to explain himself to her: "You tried to tell her, as well as you could, what it was like being you. You described the feeling you'd always had of being misplaced, of always standing to one side of yourself, of watching yourself in the world even as you were being in the world, and wondering if this was how everyone felt."[17]

What is so effective about this passage is that it is addressed to the very source which makes it necessary—the family. The "lost generation" is still lost even—or especially—when it returns home. The narrator's point of identification also brings with it the seeds of his alienation. It is ironic that a writer who has been constantly accused of being *ego*-centred, should most accurately describe the experience of being *de*-centred, of being adrift from *one's self*. What McInerney has dramatized in his prose, Terry Eagleton has described in his criticism; Eagleton's comments on Lacan's "mirror stage" seem extremely pertinent to the passage quoted above: "This object (the mirror) is at once part of ourselves—we *identify* with it—and yet not ourselves, something alien. The image which the small child sees in the mirror is in this sense an 'alienated' one: the child 'misrecognizes' itself in it, finds in the image a pleasing unity which it does not actually experience in its own body. The imaginary for Lacan is precisely this realm of *images* in which we make identifications, but in the very act of doing so are led to misperceive and misrecognize ourselves."[18]

McInerney's hero is thus to the mirror, as well as to the mother, born. In place of the cliché of "the misunderstood youth", he offers us a novel which addresses the misunderstandings *about* youth—the contexts in which it is formed, the dynamics by which it operates, the very nature of its discontent. And it is with these considerations in mind that we should now look at the most ambiguous metaphor of the book—its epiphanic ending.

Having failed to salvage his marriage and succeeded in losing his job, the narrator continues to find solace in "Bolivian marching powder", a self-destructive drug binge which smacks of desperation rather than hedonism. As the novel closes, he leaves a weekend-long party and stumbles upon a scene which appears to offer him salvation: "You see bakery trucks loading in front of a building on the next block . . . As you approach, the smell of bread washes over you like a gentle rain. You inhale deeply, filling your lungs. Tears come to your eyes, and you feel such a rush of tenderness and pity that you stop beside a lamppost and hang on for support."[19] Many critics have read this encounter as the novel's catharsis—the hero finding redemption in moving from chemicals, numbness and decadence to an appreciation of the Natural, the emotional, the spiritual. Yet such an opposition may not be as straightforward as it appears, for the narrator's transition from cocaine-culture to bread's simplicity brings with it the memory of a similar transition which we have already seen to be lingering behind the hero's crisis: "The smell of bread recalls you to another morning. You arrived home from college after driving half the night; you just felt like coming home. When you walked in, the kitchen was steeped in this same aroma. Your mother asked what the occasion was, and you said a whim. You asked if she was baking . . . She said she had to find some way to keep herself busy now that her sons were taking off. You said that you hadn't left, not really."[20]

This is the book's crowning irony—the child has "not really" left the mother, he takes the confusion of her memory with him even at the moment of his apparent salvation.

In setting up what structuralists would call a "binary opposition"—Nature/Culture—McInerney proceeds to demonstrate just how tenuous such oppositions are. In evoking the figure of the mother at the hero's moment of epiphany, he suggests that to reject one's life-style is also to embrace those very things that went into constructing it. The baker who seems to stand outside of the bright lights of the big city is tinged with the memory of the mother who instigated the hero's entry into it. This is not escape, it is transference—the re-enactment of conflict rather than its rejection: "The smell of warm dough envelops you. The first bite sticks in your throat and you almost gag. You will have to go slowly. You will have to learn everything all over again."[21]

What McInerney offers then is not some religious re-birth (bread as transcendental symbol), but the necessity of psycho-analytic re-working (bread as emotional re-call)—a process of working *through* problems rather than any simplistic absolution *from* them. The critic Duncan Webster has drawn parallels between this vision of uncertainty and the malign arbitrariness of America's "Dirty Realists": "The need for journalism to divide and pigeonhole could separate recent fiction into "yuppies" and "hicks". The fast-lane, cocaine novels of the city, like Bret Easton Ellis's *Less Than Zero* or Jay McInerney's *Bright Lights, Big City* versus *Leaving the Land* or *In Country*. But things fall apart in both sets of novels, and the world of Porsches is connected to the world of pickups by the constant threat of the unstable."[22]

In the fictional world of McInerney, the point at which our personal histories (via the family) interconnect with our public selves (within society) is the very point at which this instability is created. The past is not seen as a refuge or retreat, but is rather presented as dictating the ebb and flow of the present. Webster again: "The characters dream and struggle to make sense of their lives on the contemporary frontier that marks the meeting of cable television and community, MTV and home. The anxiety many of them feel rarely crystallizes into politics, but both the tiresome self-analysis of the 'Me generation' and the desire to return to a simpler and mystified past are avoided. Instead, there is the nagging feeling that things have gone wrong . . . The feeling that it shouldn't happen to us, but somehow it has."[23] McInerney's achievement is that he both evokes this mood of discontent, whilst at the same time locating it within the more specific context of our familial and social relations. He takes the adage that the past is a foreign country, and replies that not only is it a familiar country, it is the one that we are forced to live in: "You said that you hadn't left, not really."

By calling into question the connection between what we are

escaping *from* and what we are escaping *into*, McInerney problematizes the very genre that he describes at the beginning of this chapter— "the exploration of the individual psyche in a relatively domestic context." *Bright Lights, Big City*, with its insistence on how the individual self is constructed through the other (be that family or fiction), suggests the impossibility of separating the psyche from its domestic context. Whoever and wherever we *are* can only be negotiated through the people and the places we have come *from*. Hunter S. Thompson has referred to a "Generation of Swine". McInerney replaces this with a generation of orphans—illegitimate, de-centred, irrepressibly nomadic.

This sense of abandoned aimlessness and the subsequent desire for spiritual depth both find themselves confronted in McInerney's second novel, *Ransom*. Its eponymous hero is an expatriate who has turned to the mystical promise of Japan in his flight from rootless, affectless America. There he hopes to find the enlightenment denied him by his native land. In setting up the East as a shelter from the storm—a haven of aesthetic purity and moral decency—McInerney is very consciously working within a peculiarly American grain, one which stretches back from Thoreau and Whitman through to Kerouac and Bob Dylan. So what exactly does Japan offer the spiritually-starved American? The answer is perhaps best summed up by the Californian writer Gary Snyder who, in his book *Turtle Island*, describes "a school for monks of the Rinzai branch of Zen Buddhism, in Japan. The whole aim of this community was personal and universal liberation. In this quest for spiritual freedom every man marched strictly to the same drum in matters of work and meditation. In the teachers' room one was pushed across sticky barriers into vast new spaces. The training was traditional and had been handed down for centuries—but the insights are forever fresh and new. The beauty, refinement and truly civilized quality of that life has no match in modern America."[24] In *Ransom* too, Japan seems to its hero "a sacramental place, an intersection of body and spirit, where power and danger and will were ritualized in such a way that a man could learn to understand them. Ransom had lost his bearings spiritually, and he wanted to reclaim himself."[25] The opposition then would seem to be straightforward. Eastern tradition/ refinement/beauty/civilization versus Western commercialism/ vulgarity/brashness/degeneration.

The critic Edward Said has pointed out the ironies of placing Eastern and Western voices in such rigid opposition, and has unravelled them in such a way as to show that this strategy is a kind of philosophical imperialism—an imposition of Western images *about* the East *onto* the East. America constructs the mysticism that it desires, creates the differences it then wishes it could transcend. Japanese otherness—all full of Eastern promise—thus becomes an identity to be consumed, acquired, an essential accessory for any self-respecting Dharma Bum. What gives McInerney's prose its satiric force, is that he constantly focuses upon the exchange *between* the East and West, placing them in distinction to each other, not to emphasize their essential difference, but in order to parody their mutual reliance. With his use of third person narration, McInerney creates in Ransom a character who may be attempting to transcend his self, but who does so in a context which continually signals the extent to which his desire to do so is bound up with his American identity. In an early passage about karate combat, McInerney conflates the Japanese "reality" with its American perception. He describes a scene which may appear to belong to the exotic other, yet the terms he uses render it as unmistakably cinematic: "He was hoisted to his feet; suddenly the landscape looked as if it was flipped on its side, the surface of the parking lot standing vertical like a wall and the façade of the gym lying flat where the ground should be. Then the scene righted itself, as if on hinges."[26] The flavour here is closer to Carradine's *Kung Fu* than any pretence at authentic representation. This is a snapshot of ethnicity very obviously taken through the lens of America.

Ransom's attempt to escape from his heritage then proceeds through a consciousness which serves only to remind us of it. He learns an un-American way of life in a typically American way, moving to another country only to find himself within the global village. Furthermore, the Japan of *Ransom* is shown to aspire to that very America that its hero is attempting to leave behind. In the bar where Ransom hangs out, "The Japanese patrons (vary from) beatnik to proto-punk," the resident band plays American blues covers, sleazy ex-marines use their martial arts in bar brawls, and crass American game shows dominate the TV screen. It is this two-way traffic, the cross-cultural exchange of imaginary identities, that provides the book's ironic cutting edge. American and Easterner each project their romantic hopes onto the other, pursuing their desire for an "authentic foreignness" in such a way as to inscribe themselves into a kind of cultural schizophrenia—a state where they are neither "simply what they are" nor "completely what they wish to be". The travel writer and journalist Pico Iyer has neatly satirized this condition in his excellent book *Video Night in Kathmandu*: "The Westerner is drawn to the tradition of the Easterner, and almost covets his knowledge of suffering, but what attracts the Easterner to the West is exactly the opposite—his future, and his freedom from all hardship. After a while, each starts to become more like the other, and somewhat less like the person the other seeks. The New Yorker disappoints the locals by turning into a barefoot ascetic dressed in bangles and beads, while the Nepali peasant frustrates his foreign supplicants by turning out to be a travelling salesman in Levi's and Madonna T-Shirt. Soon, neither is quite the person he was, or the one the other wanted."[27] The unifying mood of *Ransom* thus becomes one of inauthenticity, a sense of the impossibility of ever immersing oneself in the essence of otherness. Indeed, McInerney suggests that Japan's essence consists of a series of exchanges with other cultures, most importantly its wistful gaze towards America. Again Iyer's description of this cultural trade-off echoes McInerney's own ironic presentation of personal identity and estranged nostalgia. Iyer quotes Paul Fussell's remark that travel is the quest for anomaly, and then continues: "The most remarkable anomalies in the global village today are surely those created by willy-nilly collisions and collusions between East and West: the local bands in socialist Burma that play note-perfect versions of the Doors'

"L.A. Woman" in Burmese; the American tenpin bowling alley that is the latest nighttime hot spot in Beijing . . . or the bespectacled transvestite in Singapore who, when asked to name the best restaurant in a town justly celebrated for its unique combination of Chinese, Indian and Malaysian delicacies, answers, without a moment's hesitation, 'Denny's.'"[28] Similarly in *Ransom*, the Japanese musicians locate spirituality not in the Buddhist temples or karate rituals, but rather "regarded the blues as a spiritual orientation—for them the spirit born in red delta clay out of the soul of black ex-slaves was universal and redemptive. Their Mecca was Chicago. Mojo Domo hoped someday to make a pilgrimage in veneration of the masters— Muddy Waters, Howlin' Wolf, Willie Dixon, Elmore James."[29] In his exile, Ransom finds himself besieged by his home. As he turns away from America, he is confronted by a Japan busy looking longingly at a heritage that he himself is eager to disown.

Ransom's dilemma throughout the novel is that of the decentred ego, a self divided against itself in unfulfilled desire and in its alienation from the fractured familiarity of Japan. It is with this sense of frustrated disharmony in mind, that he turns to the help of a damsel in distress—a Vietnamese nightclub singer who seems to have become unwittingly involved in a gangland dispute. The woman's status as innocent victim and Ransom's ability to directly affect her predicament, appear to offer him some hope for personal redemption. In the figure of Marilyn, our hero sees the actualization of what Japan promised but failed to deliver; she is a person in whom Ransom's ego and ideals can be re-united by a supreme act of self-sacrifice. In strictly Freudian terms, Marilyn is constructed out of the hero's "ego-ideal"—the point at which *identification* ("what one would like to be") and *object-choice* ("what one would like to have") become confused and surpassed by the narcissistic desire for self consummation. Freud himself described this state as follows: "We have said that it is the heir to the original narcissism in which the childish ego enjoyed self-sufficiency; it gradually gathers up from the environment the demands which that environment makes upon the ego and which the ego cannot always rise to; so that a man, when he cannot be satisfied with his ego itself, may nevertheless be able to find satisfaction in the ego-ideal which has been differentiated out of the ego."[30] In his insistent quest for the reality of otherness, Ransom cuts the cloth of his ego accordingly. His friend Miles parodies their status as reluctant tourists, and in so doing provides an unwitting Freudian framework for Ransom's drive:

> " 'The Way of the Tourist consists in not letting
> yourself sink into the swamp of familiarity. It's not a
> vacation but an arduous way of life, requiring
> constant vigilance. Objects and people will try to
> attach themselves to you and become intimate.
> Rooms in which you take shelter and rest will ask you
> to call them *home*. Habits will try to impose
> themselves. And when that happens, you stop seeing
> and thinking altogether. Am I in error,
> Ransom-sensei?'
> Ransom nodded his approval."[31]

By resisting Japan ever becoming "home", Ransom has attached *himself* to objects and people—first Japan itself, and now the character of Marilyn. Yet such attachments are always doomed to failure; their dynamic is one of narcissism, forever grasping at its own shadow, creating an ideal for the self rather than accepting the unsatisfactory nature of the other:

> " 'You know,' she said, 'I could never understand the
> route you took between my place and yours. It
> seemed roundabout. Then I figured that you were
> avoiding the McDonald's on Kawaramachi-
> Imadegawa. It spoiled your idealized Japanese vista—
> pagodas and misty mountains.'
> Ransom didn't choose to argue the point."[32]

Writing about the history of the American psyche, the critic Sam Girgus echoes just this point, arguing that the American quest for wholeness is always conducted through a state of duality: "In the midst of this search for paradise, the American Ego remains splintered. The process condemns the self to fragmentation and disunity. The ideology of paradise forebodes failure. We can see in the quest for paradise the creation of a whole series of historical figures who function as cultural ideals to affirm and sustain the illusion of wholeness and paradise, only to rise and fall."[33]

Ransom's "rise" may be signalled by his self-effacing heroism in protecting Marilyn, but it is his desire for self-possession *through* this action that blinds him to the fact that he is being set up for the "fall". With extraordinary narrative dexterity, McInerney reveals that Marilyn's need for help has been totally fabricated by Ransom's father—a Hollywood TV executive who has hired her to re-claim his son from the clutches of Japan. What appeared to be his ultimate chance for a purity of action outside all social influence, transpires to be a fictional net that he has been entangled in all along. Commerce has been posing as Karma, the chance for Spiritual Cleansing turns out to be nothing more than the glitter of Tinseltown:

> " 'Did he think I'd marry you? That's crazy.'
> 'I'm not sure. I think that was going to be a last resort. He said if you were convinced I was in danger, you'd go back with me to the States. I was going to throw a nervous breakdown.'
> Ransom stood with his shoulder against the closet. He stepped back and punched the sliding paper door. The laminated layers of paper almost yielded to the impact and the wooden frame bowed and popped out of the tracks; instead of a nice clean hole he produced a crumpled mess."[34]

Ransom has run away from the shallowness of America, only to find himself surrounded by the deceptive depth of a movie set. Once more America's Eden falls victim to America's fiction.

If the apparent epiphany of *Bright Lights* is punctured by the mirroring of the mother, what then are we to make of the ground being pulled from beneath Ransom's feet by his father? Is McInerney's drive one of inevitable pessimism—a move towards the resigned acceptance that we are all doomed to live out the never-ending conflicts of our families? For an answer we could do worse than turn once more to the writings of Jacques Lacan. Talking about the role of the Father (the "third term"), he argued for an understanding of the father *as a referent*, as a signifier of law rather than biology, the normative as opposed to the natural: "To speak of the Name of the Father is by no means the same thing as invoking paternal deficiency (which is often done). We know today that an Oedipus complex can be constituted perfectly well even if the father is not there, while originally it was the excessive presence of the father which was held responsible for all dramas. But it is not in an environmental perspective that the answer to these questions can be found. So as to make the link between the Name of the Father, in so far as he can at times be missing, and the father whose effective presence is not always necessary for him not to be missing, I will introduce the expression *paternal metaphor*."[35]

Ransom's father functions at precisely this level, as a term who signifies everything that Ransom seeks to reject, yet one who ultimately offers him a world that he is forced to embrace. What is truly inspired about McInerney's use of this technique, however, is that he presents the phallocentric power of the father *as a fiction*. His involvement with Hollywood and his use of the actress undercuts the seeming omnipotence of his position—it is *seen* to be seeming, constructing its power in such a way as to expose the very terms of its definition: "Ransom's father took a long sip of his drink and paused. He put the drink down. 'I was counting on two things. First, that keen moral sense of yours, the one you like to exercise on your father. It seemed to me you saw this karate of yours as training for some grand confrontation of good and evil.'

'So you thought you'd give me a fake version, show that everything's relative.'"[36]

What McInerney suggests is the precariousness of an identity based in the Name of the Father. The whole movement of the novel has been to inscribe Ransom into the tenuous patriarchial world that he set out to avoid. By revealing the father's influence as being metaphoric rather than literal, the book further suggests the fictional foundations of patriarchy itself. Ransom's final show-down with the psycho-veteran De Vito, thus comes couched in terms which are very consciously cultural rather than spiritual, speaking to the cinema not the soul: "Showdown at sunrise. Ransom wondered which movie De Vito was living out. All of them, maybe. But this, Ransom thought, was his own movie now."[37] McInerney's obvious linking of Ransom's heroism with the Fiction of the Father provides the novel's ironic glimmer of hope. After all the façade of mystic redemption, it is astonishingly liberating to see Ransom's one act of real heroism lying in his recognition of "the heroic" as a construct— an elusive yet necessary fraud: "As Ransom waited for him to speak, he wondered how he should feel, wondered why he felt fine. He felt free to devote his attention to Kano or to anything that he liked."[38]

The phenomenal impact of *Ransom* is to be found in this mingling of fiction and desire, its process of unending subversion and renewal, a kind of continual divorce and remarriage of the self. In the midst of these forces, McInerney presents a world the key sensibility of which is one post-structuralism has termed "structuration"—the absence, indeed the impossibility of stable meanings and permanent relationships. In *Bright Lights* as well as *Ransom*, the psychological and social processes that are designed to regulate our needs and organize cultural identity leave the individual fractured and unfulfilled. The structures by which we live serve only to disguise the lack of structure of those lives—"normality" is an imposture that is continually under-mined by the chaotic drives of the unconscious. The decentred egos in McInerney's novels *do* continue to grow, but always in fragments and often in contradictory directions. This is why the Lacanian framework seems such an appropriate one to invoke, his opaque and apocalyptic writing is particularly suited to capturing the ego's terminal dis-ease. From the mirror-stage and the mother to the metaphoric Name of the Father, the suggestion from both McInerney and Lacan is that the family saga is one that can never be resolved. Writing of the weaning process between mother and child, Lacan remarked: "However long it is fed at its mother's breast, it will always be left with a conviction after it has weaned that its feeding was too short and too little."[39] In his first two novels, the playfully perceptive Jay McInerney appears to have taken these psychoanalytic impulses and infused them with the drama of the domestic narrative. In the Name of the Father.

Ah, men.

For his third novel. *Story of My Life*, McInerney returns to the lean streets of New York. The book is a kind of extended monologue, a journey through twenty-something aimlessness as filtered through the consciousness of its first person narrator— Alison Poole. Alison is a self-professed "postmodern girl"—the product of MTV disposability and answering machine anomie. She comes from a broken home, aspires to being an actress but succeeds only in being a major fuck-up. She and her friends could be characterized as socially mobile, sexually versatile, intellectually frigid and emotionally dyslexic. Their conversation seems to revolve around nothing except clothes, cocaine and the size of men's cocks. From this précis it is easy to see how critics have managed to read the novel as a symptom of the drug-soaked, sex-crazed, style-obsessed eighties. Yet such readings tend to ignore the actual *appeal* of Alison's story. The affectlessness that is described is undermined by the affects of the description. Her monologue is riddled with running gags, cynical asides and comic caricature, so that the flamboyant dynamic of her language constantly calls into question the very shallowness which it seems to inhabit: "So Francesca, she knows everyone, right? Partly because of her family and also because that's her great passion in life, meeting rich and famous people . . . Granted, it's a little bit *too* much sometimes—like, Francesca, I'd like you to meet Adolf Hitler, and she'd be like—oh, wow, I just loved your last war."[40]

In purely linguistic terms, then, "parole" (the specific

utterance of language) transgresses "langue" (the general structure of language). Or, put another way, the nihilism of Alison's pronouncements is outdone by the energy of their performance.

Much of the tension within *Story of My Life* is to be found in this continual friction between the novel's overall sense of waste and futility and the extraordinarily anarchic power of the language which goes into creating it: "Morning after the last night I slept with him I was really sore and itchy and then I get this weird rash so I finally go to the doctor who gives me this big lecture on Aids—yada yada yada—then says . . . I have to take these antibiotics for two weeks and not sleep with anybody in the meantime. I go, two weeks, who do you think I am, the Virgin Mary?"[41]

It is at this junction of fixed meaning ("spoilt youth") and chaotic language that what Julia Kristeva called "the semiotic" can be seen at play. For Kristeva the semiotic is the surplus desire within language that is left over from Lacan's Imaginary and which works to continually disfigure the stability of the Symbolic. Rather than the monolithic series of signs that would point to a view of youth as "irresponsible", "burnt out" or simply "ephemeral", Alison's verbal gymnastics suggest the plurality, the fluidity, the *bisexuality* of her position, so that her linguistic dexterity ends up by negating those very signs that it seems to be creating. This is why Alison's gender is essential to the novel's operations, for in constructing a heroine, McInerney gains access to the polymorphous power of the semiotic. Eagleton perhaps best sums up the disruptive potential of femininity when he remarks: "One might see the semiotic as a kind of internal limit or borderline of the symbolic order; and in this sense the 'feminine' could equally be seen as existing on such a border. For the feminine is at once constructed within the symbolic order, like any gender, and yet is relegated to its margins, judged inferior to masculine power. The woman is both 'inside' and 'outside' male society, both a romantically idealized member of it and a victimized outcast. She is sometimes what stands between man and chaos, and sometimes the embodiment of chaos itself . . . Woman are represented within male-governed society, fixed by sign, image, meaning, yet because they are also the 'negative' of that social order there is always in them something which is left over, superfluous, unrepresentable, which refuses to be figured there."[42]

McInerney presents the transgressive otherness of Alison as a strategy rather than her destiny, a way of negotiating man-made norms whilst refusing to be de/confined by them:

> "And he goes, I bet you don't go out with just anybody.
> . . . and I say to him, actually I fuck practically anybody.
> But in your case I think I'd make an exception.
> And he's like totally blown away that I'm talking like this."[43]

Alison's ability to talk "like this" threatens not only the social world *of* the novel, but also the reader's position *to* the novel. Its apparent invitation to us to classify it as a generic Lost Youth book, must be weighed against the seductive delight that its language takes in going beyond such classification. Kristeva's notion of the semiotic is precisely the paradigm that McInerney's prose invokes—a diffuse, sensuous, anarchic realm that always resists the male pull towards sharp divisions and fixed truths.

It is with this conflation of discourse and desire in mind that we can now look at a productive encounter between McInerney's "postmodern girl" and someone who in many ways could be her Victorian counterpart—Freud's Dora.

During the course of his analysis of this eighteen-year-old hysteric, Freud stumbled across a specifically Germanic pun which forged enlightening links between sexuality and economics: "An opportunity very soon occurred for interpreting Dora's nervous cough in this way by means of an imagined sexual situation. She had once again been insisting that Frau K. only loved her Father because he was 'ein vermögender Mann' ('a man of means'). Certain details of the way in which she expressed herself led me to believe that behind this phrase its opposite lay concealed, namely, that her father was 'ein unvermögender Mann' ('a man without means'). This could only be meant in a sexual sense—that her father, as a man, was without means, was impotent."[44] Freud then proceeds to speculate on whether or not Dora's cough was rooted in a repressed image of fellatio between her father and his lover, and by inference herself. In equating impotence and economics and synthesizing them into oral sex, Freud actually pre-empts one of the central concerns of *Story of My Life*—the way in which financial and sexual exchange are linked as a measure of emotional dislocation. Any opposition between sex and commerce in the novel is made to collapse in on itself, so that far from presenting the differences between romance and exchange, McInerney suggests their interchangeability—two ways of saying the same thing: "Let me just say that in general my feelings about blow jobs is, I can take them or leave them . . . So, like, I usually figure it's kind of I'll-lick-yours-if-you'll-lick-mine kind of thing."[45] The language of Wall Street thus becomes the language of love, the very term "blow job" testifying to the root of sex as being connected to ethics of work and economics.

To regard the characters' sex lives and emotional states as being either "bankrupt" or "lucrative" is thus explanatory as well as being descriptive, for it is precisely within the terms of reference of commerce that such "natural" feelings are both created and judged. Moreover, the only sex that ever takes place within the "present" of the book is always oral—a fact that not only suggests the literally linguistic drive of their desires, but also means that sex is always removed from the sphere of *reproduction*. McInerney's suggestion then is not that sex has been "reduced" to the status of a commodity, but rather that the power relations of capital are themselves sexually driven: "He'd make deals. Like, for instance, I'd be looking through the new Saks catalogue that just arrived in the mail and I'd point to a sweater or something and say, I love that, and he'd go, I'll get it for you and I'd go, really?

" . . . So I'd get tough and make him fill out the order form with his credit card number and seal the envelope before I'd go down on him. And when I was being really hard-ass I'd make him walk it out to the post office with his hard on. I don't know, I think it turned him on even more. The harder a time I'd give him, the harder he'd be."[46] McInerney effectively reverses the principles of "commodity fetishism" (money's ability to *appropriate* the erotic) and presents us with a world in which human beings are driven to mediate *between* commodities, their sexual urges acting as transient occasions for their mutual exchange. To be "consumed" by desire thus becomes an appropriate motif— abandoned to the economy that we find embodied in each other.

McInerney's interest thus centres around the ways in which social and economic practices are physically encapsulated, what Michel Foucault calls "a politics of the body (which relies) on a multiple channelling into the controlled circuits of the economy."[47]

Alison's story is the *business* of her life—the commerciality of her character, the public investment of her actions. In response to Henry James's fascination with the nineteenth-century "commercial person", McInerney appears to offer us "the commodity kids"—a generation for whom capital and desire are inextricably bound up within language and the body. Yet this is not to suggest that McInerney is putting forth a reductive kind of economic determinism, with capitalism conspiring to predestine our every move. For what needs to be emphasized about *Story of My Life* is precisely that it is a "story", it is *about* our ability to represent our public selves, and the room for manoeuvre which such representation allows us.

In his following comments on Dora, Eric Erikson emphasizes the control afforded to her by her ability to dramatize her neurosis: "Dora needed to act as she did not only in order to vent the childish rage of one victimized but also in order to set straight the historical past so that she could envisage a sexual and social future of her choice, call infidelities by their name before she could commit herself to her own kind of fidelity, and establish the coordinates of her identity as a young woman of her class and time, before she could utilize more insight into her inner realities."[48] Representation thus provides a point of intervention into reality, offering us a chance to present ourselves to the world rather than merely being passively constructed by it.

Similarly, Alison's earlier contractual obligation to fellatio is subverted and re-invented by her choice to represent the encounter in her drama class. Dora's metaphoric "acting out" becomes Alison's literal re-en*act*ment, yet both forms of representation serve to free the women from their inscription within sexual-economic identities. The earlier male exercise in power is transformed by Alison into a dramatic spectacle, a feminine charade, a question of representation: "I had the teacher watching me and pretty soon he told everyone else to knock off what they were doing and watch me. I don't know, I was off in my own world, acting. I'm doing something true, I know I'm not just faking it this time and even though it's acting something I'm not really experiencing it's absolutely honest, my reaction, the sensations I'm feeling and I'm completely in my own reality."[49]

Alison the Actress thus prefers "the copy" over "the original", the representation over the reality. Her identity is formed by her ability to resemble herself, her strategy of appropriating a commercially informed sexuality and *re*-presenting it as some-thing embodied *within* herself. The act of representation thus fractures the monolithic conjunction of commerce and sexuality. It takes it out of the realm of economic determinism and into the sphere of expression, circulation and communication. Like Dora in her analysis, Alison's commitment to dramatizing the seemingly repressive allows her to re-invent that which appeared to be fixed as a question of interpretation. In embracing the fictionality of her experience, Alison transgresses the novel's suggestion of sexual sterility and replaces it with a much more fertile expression of *intercourse* in all its forms.

McInerney's project then is to create a fictional paradigm which suggests the inseparability of commerce and self, of money and emotion, while at the same time investing his heroine with the dramatic power to insist on their ultimate discrepancy. It is this tendency to fracture and rupture any stability of meaning that leaves the novel seeming not only incomplete, but also incompletable. Alison begins her story by posing as pregnant to obtain money from her old boyfriend to pay for her drama tuition; she ends it by using her school fees to pay for her abortion. Yet such a cyclical resolution is not as final as it may sound. Indeed the whole flavour of the novel is rather one of *circularity*—the constant need to fragment, re-establish, move beyond, ebb and flow. Alison's finale is thus couched in terms that suggest McInerney's need to step outside of the terms of reference of the novel in order simply to finish it: "Maybe I dreamed a lot of stuff . . . Wouldn't that be great? I'd love to think that ninety percent of it was just dreaming."[50] Alison would "love to think" so, but the very force of her narrative prevents either her or us from believing it. For the appeal of Alison's story of her life resides in its endless transgressions; the sense that there is no end to the task of revealing and concealing the discrepancies between what is spoken and what is said, between what is intended and what is received, between reality and its various representations. Alison's final dream-state suggests the book's governing drive—an immersion in a fantasy which will forever elude a pure meaning. In its adjustments and disruptions, its disclosures and *resistants*, the *Story of My Life* interweaves its beginning and its middle and suggests that there can be no end in sight—a narrative finale that actively resists any finality.

If Alison's story suggests the impossibility of closure, the narrative of *Brightness Falls* would seem to mark a significant shift in McInerney's canon. Here is a novel that appears to embrace convention, the work of a writer who has finished sowing his wilder oats and eased himself into the more adult world of matrimony and mortgages. Gone is the blissed-out hipspeak of *Story of My Life* or *Bright Lights, Big City*; nowhere do we encounter the bruised cynicism of a Christopher Ransom or the warped dexterity of an Alison Poole. What we get instead is a much wider canvas, one that is constructed with a remarkable narrative flexibility and an impressive display of verbal gymnastics. From such a précis it is easy to see how critics welcomed the book as "a novel of maturity", their "coming of age" praise suggesting a relief on their part that the leader of the "brat-pack" has finally grown up and gone straight. The mainstreaming of McInerney is of course a double-edged process—one which undercuts the impact of his earlier work by championing the importance of the later book, as though his previous attention to youth and popular culture was merely a rehearsal for this, his more "serious novel". Drugs and disillusionment, angst-ridden adolescents and fucked-up families can now be dismissed as just a phase he was going through—an exorcism of rebellious youth that was necessary before his inevitable mellowing and consequent taming.

The irony of such assimilation is that the novel in many ways continues McInerney's earlier concerns, and indeed suggests the impossibility of ever fully escaping the emotional and sexual narratives of our younger selves. Its inscription is taken from Robert Hass and stands as much as a testament to McInerney's own continuity as it does to that of his characters: "All the new thinking is about loss. In this case it resembles all the old thinking." Though set in a different social milieu, *Brightness Falls* could be said to be about the ways in which the "new" McInerney resembles the old.

The novel begins where Alison Poole's story left off—in a de-tox clinic. Like a classic Woody Allen routine, the prologue satirizes the American addiction to the overcoming of addiction: "The last time I saw Russell and Corrine together was the weekend of the final softball game between the addicts and the depressives. The quality of play was erratic, the recovering addicts being depressed from lack of their chosen medications and the depressives heavily dosed with exotic chemical bullets aimed at their elusive despair."[51]

The couple in question—Russell and Corrine Calloway—form the book's central focus, a marital and monogamous pivot around which McInerney balances a whole array of characters from the literary and publishing worlds. We get the wounded genius of Jeff Pierce (the writer-addict of the prologue), the slick criminality of Bernie Melman (a mobster who wants to buy a publishing house), the Californian crassness of Zac Solomon

(Jeff's agent) and the lapsed idealism of Harold Stone (Head of Corbin, Dern Publishers).

The novel traces Russell's attempts to take over the publishing house at which he is employed, and the consequent effects of this on both his marriage to the stock-broking Corrine and on the tenuous connections between the worlds of writing and Wall Street, friendship and finance.

McInerney playfully contrasts his characters' present terms of reference with those that they used to inhabit. People refer to their art dealers with the same conspiratorial secrecy that they at one time reserved for their drug dealers. Constant puns revolve around Bob Dylan—"The times they are a changin'" becomes common currency for stock-market conversation, whilst "Mr. Jones" refers to the DOW index rather than the song. The Calloway's record collection consists of old punk records, a metaphor for the speed with which their youthful rebellion has been transformed into domestic nostalgia: "How can you like the Clash, punk-socialist band, and sell corporate equity at the same time? That was the inexplicable mystery of being Corrine Calloway at the age of thirty-one."[52]

What McInerney achieves then is to cast the realities of pragmatism and compromise within the shadow of under-graduate memories and post-adolescent ambition. The protagonists no longer want to change the world, they are too busy trying to survive in it. Russell's decision to buy out Corbin, Dern appears to provide him with a chance to retrieve his youth whilst achieving success. He imagines publishing accounts of American involvement with Nicaragua, of putting his weight behind the tortured Great Novel rather than its usual output of "S & F" (shopping and fucking). Yet in order to finance his attempt he is forced to seek the help of yuppie philistines and crooked big business. Thus McInerney sets up the Faustian pact between criminality and creativity—his protagonist chancing his arm for the sake of his art.

Though McInerney's novel obviously is a transition into the more mainstream terrain of classic realism—a portrait of the eighties painted on a specific social canvas—it avoids the glib

generalities of, say, *The Bonfire of the Vanities*, by focusing on the
specific emotional narratives of the characters within its world.
On the one hand McInerney opts for the sweeping tide of disgust
at his culture's spiritually-barren hi-tech hostility: "The new
puritanism. Sloth, gluttony, recreational drugs were out.
Narcissism, blind ambition and greed by contrast were free of
side- or after-effects, at least in this life, and who was counting
on the other anymore."[53] Yet on the other, he endows his
characters with a depth, humour and fragility which offsets the
danger of them becoming mere vessels of their age.

Russell's marriage, for example, begins to fall apart as he
channels all his energy into his publishing venture. His takeover
bid takes over him: rendering him devoid of the commitment
that instigated his very actions: "Russell's manner of speaking
had changed in the last month. Resorting to phrases like 'the
reading public', he'd gone pontifical, talking about the rights of
shareholders and the stagnation of American business."[54] Yet far
from this convergence acting as a moralistic warning about
corruption, McInerney suggests that the change in emphasis
from marriage to the market-place is part of our overall sense of
psychic and social estrangement. In his gradual separation from
his wife, Russell represents the absence, lack and foredoomed
nature of desire itself. Their spiralling marriage is a constant
reminder of how the institution comes to work as a substitute for,
rather than a legitimization of, our unfulfilled desires:

> " 'Marriages need a certain amount of slack. A lot of
> fond-making absence,' said Casey, whose husband
> traveled incessantly on business.
> Nancy said, 'All men need just four things. Food,
> shelter, pussy . . . and strange pussy.' "[55]

Desire—always after what it cannot have—thus becomes the
dynamic through which McInerney presents his critique of
American society. It is not so much the case that Russell prizes
his business over his marriage, but more that both are driven by
the quest for the ultimate prize of desire. From the bedroom to

the boardroom, Russell dramatizes our need to fill the void, the absence, the incompleteness of our ever-deferred desires. Accordingly, it is during their break up, with Russell in Hollywood and Corrine at her mother's, that they appear at their most intimate and animated. McInerney's romance is thus a re-union within solitude, one whose "future will eventually school them in the pain of growth and separation . . . and leave them alone in the world, shivering at the dark threshold."[56]

It is in the recognition of their separation—even at the point of "starting over"—that Russell and Corrine begin to credit each other with an autonomous identity. The bitter irony of the novel's denouement is that in order for the characters to begin to "grow up" it is necessary for them to realize that they must always, to some extent, "grow apart". Far from celebrating the maturity of yuppie love, McInerney actually suggests that love itself is a form of instability—a state that is continually prone to the recurring dis-ease of desire.

While the characters of his earlier work could be said to all fall victim to the Lacanian model of the "imaginary" family romance, the protagonists of *Brightness Falls* are testaments to the deceptive security of the "symbolic order"—a realm where signifier and signified never quite coincide, where illusion and fantasy are the components of reality, and bodily appetite is caught up in the discourse of everyday life not as a deviation but as part of its inward fabric.

That the novel has been received as the work of a writer who has "settled down" or "come of age" is a reading that works directly against the dynamics of the text. For if Russell and Corrine *do* become settled, it is only by acknowledging the fictional foundations on which such reconciliation is built. Their "salvation" lies not so much in their coming back together as a seamless whole, but in their recognition that such a whole is constructed through the feverish activity of inflated fantasy and infinite deferral.

Whilst the Anglo-American establishment may have accepted McInerney into its great tradition, celebrating his novel as a work of personal growth and development, it has inevitably been a process shot through with conflict and uncertainty—the reader-friendly profile of the writer being constantly at odds with the fragmented ambiguity of his writing. For, ultimately, the "depth", "sagacity" and "solidity" of *Brightness Falls* reside in its characters' acceptance of the reality of their illusions. The initial impetus of the book may appear to stem from their efforts to restrain their desires and move towards closure. Yet the actual dynamic of the text enacts the intrinsic impossibility of achieving either.

Jay McInerney may well be heralded as the chronicler of how the blank generation achieve maturity, yet the cutting-edge of his fiction resides in its suggestion that such a process is one which cannot help but fail to satisfy. *Brightness Falls* is undoubtedly his most accomplished work to date, but its accomplishment is to be found in its recognition that the novel will always, to some extent, have *to be continued* . . .

G.C.

French kissing in the USA

Michael Chabon

> " 'Is our language so impoverished that we have to use
> acronyms of French phrases to make ourselves
> understood?'
> " 'Yes.' "
>
> From the film *Metropolitan*

When Michael Chabon published his first (and so far only) novel
at the age of twenty-three, responses tended to concentrate on its
youthful decadence and sexual precocity. His fey charm and
classic good looks seemed to merge with the novel's eloquent
unease; writer and text were projected as one, the "brat-pack"
had at last found their dandy. In place of Ellis's sparse
postmodernity or McInerney's apocalyptic quest for selfhood,
Chabon offered a prose rich with promiscuous abandon and
articulate sensitivity. *The Mysteries of Pittsburgh* follows Art
Bechstein through the summer of his graduation year—his
ambiguous detachment from his gangster-father, his entangle-
ment in a web of homo- and heterosexual friendships, and the
eventual collision between these two apparently mutually exclu-
sive worlds. Art's heroic drive is to reject the corrupt acquisition
of money as represented by his father, and embrace instead the
sublimated currency of his contemporaries—the language of
learning, the veneer of social bohemianism, the alternative realm
of righteous possession. As the very pun on his name suggests,
Art opposes the laundered money of his family with the purity of
the aesthete—a projection of himself whose value is measured by
its distance from utility. In short, Art is not for sale.

From this brief synopsis, it is easy to see why Fitzgerald provided the most common reference point for Chabon's readers and reviewers. Indeed, the novel's very first line evokes a conscious echo of the opening to *The Great Gatsby*: "At the beginning of summer I had lunch with my father, the gangster, who was in town for the weekend to transact some of his vague business."[1] "In my younger and more vulnerable years my father gave me some advice that I've been turning over in my mind ever since."[2]

Similarly, the network of relations with which Art becomes involved all playfully invite their Fitzgeraldian equivalents. The hoodlum chic of Cleveland and the corrupt gentility of his girlfriend Jane both offer comparison with Tom and Daisy Buchanan, whilst Carraway's description of Gatsby as having a "heightened sensitivity to the promises of life" could provide an apt summary of Art's homosexal lover, Arthur: " 'I don't see myself as an American: I'm an atom, I bounce all over the place . . . I'm always at the outside orbit of all the other, um, molecules.' "[3]

What seems to be emerging then is an unproblematic inheritance by Chabon of Fitzgerald's oeuvre—both writers standing side by side at the junction of propriety and transgression, the reserved and the renegade, the flavour of Europe and the freshness of America. Certain critics have even gone so far as to translate the last of these oppositions—Europe and America—into a paradigm for Art's bisexuality. America with its new-monied naivety is cast as the id, the passport to sexual licence, whereas Europe with its class-bound traditions serves as the ego, the sexual spoilsport, the instrument of repression. Such an equation is certainly not new. From de Tocqueville to Henry James, from Hitchcock to Wim Wenders, there has long been a relationship between Europe and America based on imaginary identities, cultural investment and mutual exchange. If Europeans invented America as a second chance for fallen man, an Edenic world of natural abundance, then America has in turn invented Europe as a moribund point of contradistinction, a place to define itself against rather than with. Jean Baudrillard perhaps best encapsulates this simplistic model of trans-Atlantic relations in his postmodern-packaged travel guide, *America*:

> "The confrontation between America and Europe
> reveals not so much a *rapprochement* as a distortion, an
> unbridgeable rift. There isn't just a gap between us, but
> a whole chasm of modernity. You are born modern, you
> do not become so. And we have never become so . . .
> America is the original version of modernity. We are the
> dubbed or subtitled version. America ducks the question
> of origins; it cultivates no origin or mythical
> authenticity; it has no past and no founding truth.
> Having known no primitive accumulation of time, it
> lives in a perpetual present."[4]

What lies beneath Baudrillard's epigrammatic mysticism is an almost Lawrentian series of oppositions (primitive/cultural, history/reality, truth/image), all of which serve to inscribe Europe and America into their respective *fictions*, rather than acknowledge any real interplay between the two cultures. What makes Chabon's novel so appealing, on the other hand, is precisely that it dramatizes the collaboration and appropriation of Europe and America, and indeed suggests that their identities are inextricably bound up in the exchange with each other rather than in the strict separation of the two. If Baudrillard's critique insists on the antithesis of Europe and America, then Chabon's fiction replaces it with what Derrida would call an *athesis*—the collapse of such symmetry, the reciprocation of opposites, the dissolution of either/or.

In the figure of Art's sometime girlfriend, Phlox, Chabon creates a character who manages to project herself as a marginalized American by presenting herself as a mainstream European. Her aura of French mystique suggests a detached voyeurism, an aloof appropriation of the trappings of her own identity:

> ". . . she was unquestionably beautiful, and yet there

was something odd, wrong, about her looks, her clothing; something a little *too*, from her too blue eyes in their too direct stare to the too red stockings she wore. It was as though she had studied American notions of beauty from some great distance, and had come all this way only to find she had overdone the details: a debutante from another planet."[5]

Phlox's insistence on exile provides her with the opportunity to explore, discover and expand herself, yet it brings with it the dangers of alienation, the ultimate loss of self. When Art first encounters her in the library, for example, he is struck not only by her mysterious beauty but also by an image of her being imprisoned by it: "She was in a window; there was an aqua ribbon in her hair. The window was a kind of grille, as in a bank, at the far end of the corridor in which I stood waiting."[6] Phlox becomes the Girl Behind Bars, her European reserve acting as her gaoler, her ability to invent herself working simultaneously to imprison that self. That true exile of American fiction, Vladimir Nabokov, once remarked that *Lolita* was inspired by a story about an ape who had produced the first ever drawing by an animal—the bars of its cage. Just as Humbert's story sketches out the desire in which he is en-caged, so Phlox's construction of her European "essence" incarcerates her into a prison of her own making. She transports French aestheticism into her American life, but does so as a kind of armchair tourist—selectively, nostalgically, a way of life that is consumed as liberation but reproduced as confinement. The European trappings with which Phlox decorates herself thus become symptomatic of her Americanness, inscribing her into the very culture from which she wishes to stand apart:

". . . she begins to relish such previously unglamorous elements of her vocabulary as *langeur* and *funeste*, and, speaking English, inverts her adjectives, to let one know that she sometimes even thinks in French. The writers she comes to appreciate—Breton, Baudelaire, Sartre, de

Sade, Cocteau—have an alienating effect . . . and her manner of expressing her emotions becomes difficult and theatrical; while those French writers whose influence might be a healthy one, such as Stendhal or Flaubert, she dislikes and takes to reading in translation, where their effect on her thought and speech is negligible; or she wilfully misreads *Madame Bovary* and *La Chartreuse*, making dark romances of them."[7]

Phlox's difficulty in acquiring a French identity is precisely that—a problem of *acquisition*. Her wistful gaze towards France, her prioritization of its culture, her very belief in a monolithic national identity are all signifiers of just how close she is to the country she appears to reject. Chabon's suggestion is that it is an essential part of what it means to be American to glance towards Europe. An ambiguous relationship with the international scene is an integral part of the American heritage, not an aesthetic refuge from it. In his ironic treatment of the interplay between the two continents, Chabon suggests the fluidity of the American ego, its ability to disrupt preconceived positions and reconstruct itself in its ever-changing image.

Far from the Old and New Worlds being presented as a dichotomy, *The Mysteries of Pittsburgh* constantly points to how the one is informed by its ambiguous awareness of the other. Far from being insular or parochial, the novel's title is an ironic testament to the mysteries to be found outside the city's walls— the enigma to be encountered when we Looka Yonder.

Phlox, then, is true to her name. Attempting to move fluidly between America and France, she is fixed into the images that arise from their exchange. Phlox is forever trapped in a state of *flux*, a victim of the Euro-American convention which appeared to offer her liberation. Threatened with a loss of her individuality to bland Americana, Phlox is apt to lose it to francophile fantasies that equally distort her actual relationship to the world around her.

It is one of the wilfully perverse ironies of the book that the character who comes closest to embodying the enigmatic mobility of Internationalism is Art's father, the charismatic gangster. In their encounter over dinner, it is the criminal, not the student, who most easily engages with the various narratives of Europe: "Over the main course he explained the Diaspora, carbon 14 dating . . . and gave a short history of Swiss banking."[8]

Again when Art is asked at a party: "What does your father do?" he first offers the truth of his internal monologue before replying with comic euphemism: "He manipulates Swiss bank accounts with money from numbers, whores, protection, loan sharks, and cigarette smuggling.

'He's in finance,' I said."[9]

This Jewish gangster, with his London suits, Italian connections, Swiss bank accounts and international investments, brilliantly links the common currency of business and crime with a kind of secretive multi-lingualism. His laconic reticence conceals the more internationally potent language of notes, contracts and numbers. Art's father is the true face/mask of the Euro-American—a character who speaks by putting his mouth where his money is.

If the father's criminality gives him access to a universal language, to what condition does his son's bisexuality speak? The obvious liberal-humanist impulse would be to lay claim to the transcendent nature of sex—its opportunities for cross-cultural communication, its ability to rise above the specifics of language and embrace the universal with its protean physicality. Put simply, are love and sex, rather than business and crime, not the real esperanto—the true and pure codes that speak to us all? The answer, I would suggest, is to be found in Chabon's treatment of Art's homosexual awakening, a richly denaturalizing description which lays bare the social mechanisms of sexual camouflage.

Early on in the book, Art confesses his adolescent uncertainties about his sexual tendencies: "There had been a time in high school, see, when I wrestled with the possibility that I might be gay, a tortuous six-month culmination of years of unpopularity and girllessness. At night I lay in bed and coolly informed myself that I was gay, and that I had better get used to it."[10] What may at first have been read as a homosexual "instinct" thus has its origins in the social rather than the natural. Art's fear that he "might be gay" is placed alongside and in deference to his "unpopularity and girllessness". Sexual inclination thus seems to be less concerned with what you are, and more with what you are not. The most "primitive" human drive is revealed to be a question of intense artifice—a social/sexual theatre with a strictly limited array of roles. With this reversal in mind, it is logical, rather than ironic, that Art's initial homoerotic impulse towards Arthur comes after he has been "accused" of "faggotry":

> "Despite the several girls I had loved and made love to since my last year of high school, my childhood weaknesses and sexual uncertainty, all of my suffering as a 'fag' under the insults and heavy forearms of stronger boys, and what amounted to my infatuation with Arthur, all had made me an easy victim to this surprise attack... I asked myself ... if I felt like having sex with Arthur."[11]

Art's sexual inclinations are not *reflected* by the discourse that surrounds him, they are *constructed* by it. He needs to be named "a fag" before he can contemplate indulging himself as one. Chabon's achievement is to present sexuality as an issue of disclosure and pronouncement, secrecy and articulation, an eternal quarrel between language and libido. Sexual identity is not an already "given" position to be declared, but one which emerges through the very act of declaration. Michel Foucault provides perhaps the best précis of this idea when he writes: "Power acts by laying down the rule: power's hold on sex is maintained through language, or rather through the act of discourse that creates, from the very fact that it is articulated, a rule of law. It speaks, and that is the rule."[12]

The problematic nature of Art's versatile sexuality is precisely one of enunciation: how can he know his love when he dare not speak its name? As he himself puts it: "I did not consider myself to be gay ... The city was new again, and newly dangerous, and I would walk its streets quickly ... like a spy in the employ of lust and happiness, carrying the secret deep within me but always on the tip of my tongue."[13]

On the tip of his tongue is where Art attempts to stutter his sexual identity, retreating finally to the mute world of frustrated silence, the demi-monde of inexpressible desire.

The implication of course is not so much that Art should "come out", but rather that he should "speak out"—should attempt to verbalize for himself the socio-sexual space that he occupies. In continuing to identify himself by what he is not, by fashioning himself in relation to some other, Art falls prey to an almost empty circularity of identities, confusingly ungrounded in any linguistic foundations. After making love to Arthur, he asks, "Didn't he know what he—what I—had just done? What had I just done?"[14] By not daring to speak its name, the love itself gets thrown into a state of uncertainty. There arises a panic-stricken inability to attend to speech or body, a state which is actually born out of Art's reticence in speaking *of* the body. In withdrawing from the discourse around his sexuality. Art effectively denies himself the pleasures of that sexuality and is left with what Arthur astutely describes as "the tattered shreds of [his] heterosexuality". Foucault again points to the affirmative pleasures and possibilities offered by an entrance into language:

> "It is often said that we have been incapable of imagining any new pleasures. We have at least invented a different kind of pleasure: pleasure in the truth of pleasure, the pleasure of knowing that truth, of discovering and exposing it, the fascination of seeing it and telling it, of captivating and capturing others by it, of confiding it in secret, of luring it out in the open—the specific pleasure of true discourse on pleasure."[15]

Art's attempt to remove his sexuality outside language succeeds only in having it disfigured and ultimately destroyed by the more ominous codes of the unutterable. The love that dare not speak its name is doomed to suffer in silence.

It is at the very end of the novel, with Art's retrospective assessment of its events, that all the concerns of Europe, language and desire find their dramatic cluster. He acknowledges that his experiences have taught him to value "my vocabulary, my dress, my love of idle talk". The irony here is gently but effectively understated, for the novel has already demonstrated that talk is never idle, but always, to some extent, performative— the act of self-definition, a meeting of the "perlocutionary" and the "illocutionary", the place where information and affirmation translate as a *social* activity: "My father I will never see again, Cleveland is dead. Arthur is now, I believe, on Majorca. But because I can find them so easily in myself, I no longer—*say it, Bechstein*—I no longer need them," (my italics).[16]

Art's hard-won sagacity is not only expressed through his words, it is actually demonstrated by them. His ability to "say it, Bechstein" is the character's ultimate triumph, a defiant announcement in a world hitherto governed by repressive silence and pseudo tongues.

As for Phlox, Art is left like Coleridge with his "useless dream poem . . . a garbled account of my visit to her planet, uncertain of what transpired there, and of why precisely I couldn't stay."[17] The question here is of course rhetorical. Art could no longer "visit" Phlox as he had no desire to become fluent in tourist*ese*. Living in her European fantasy Phlox spoke neither to the reality of her condition, nor with the holistic ease of her French-informed pose. Torn between the alienated language of hetero-sexuality and the frustrated silence of homosexuality, Art is forced to reject both. The act of vocalizing such rejection, of "saying it, Bechstein", is precisely what allows him to grow between the two, to lust with greater faith, to speak with the (un)certainty of hope: "No doubt all of this is not true remembrance but the ruinous work of nostalgia, which obliterates the past, and no doubt, as usual, I have exaggerated everything."[18]

Relationships through recall, discourse and desire, Chabon's trajectory is towards the histories of mystery, rather than the peculiarities of Pittsburgh. As with his collection of short stories, *A Model World*, the ironies that underpin his prose are implicit in his titles. The Euro-American may regard herself as exemplary, as the perfect model, yet behaves with the static all-consuming commerciality of the fashion model. From paradigm to mannequin, from the Art of speech to the (f)act of silence, Chabon presents us with an America torn between the ideal and the insubstantial. His work testifies to the double-edged demands of appearance, the emotional *double entendres* of utterance. Chabon's achievement is to maintain the pose of the dandy whilst seeking to explode the foundations of that fiction.

In his novel and short stories, Chabon exists at the junction where posture and imposture converge and do battle, where decorum and desire merge into the deceptive world of masquerade. Chabon's world *is* a model one, and therein lies its problem. For behind the model lurks the exposé, the expired, the self-destructive exhibition of never-ending desire.

G.C.

The beast in the jungle,
the figure in the carpet

Bret Easton Ellis's American Psycho

> "What I was really interested in was the language, the structure, the details."
>
> Bret Easton Ellis on *American Psycho**

> "Our society desperately needs monsters to reclaim its own moral virginity."
>
> Sylvère Lotringer

> "No pleasure but meanness."
>
> Flannery O'Connor, *A Good Man Is Hard To Find*

The publication of Bret Easton Ellis's *American Psycho* in 1991 was replete with ironies. It seemed as if the world had decided to add to the book all the old-fashioned fictional qualities that it so conspicuously lacked: melodrama, plot, characterization, irony, hubris. The story *of* the book—its publication history, its author, its controversial aspects, its fashionability—had to stand in for the lack of story *in* the book which no one seemed to bother to read in any detail.

Bret Easton Ellis started making notes for his third novel, which he intended to be the monologue of a serial killer, whilst still working on the proofs of *The Rules of Attraction*. The publishing house Simon and Schuster offer a $300,000 advance for the book only to withdraw from publication in the autumn of 1990 after some exceptionally violent, gory excerpts from what is now known as *American Psycho* appear in *Spy* and *Time* magazines. Sonny Mehta immediately acquires the manuscript for Vintage Books. It is published as a trade paperback in America in February 1991 and in Britain, under the Picador imprint, in April of the same year. Its publication was attended in America by furious psychodrama. Roger Rosenblatt in *The New York Times*, under the heading "Snuff This Book", described it as "the most loathsome offering of the season".[1] *Time* spoke of "the most appalling acts of torture, murder and dismemberment ever described in a book targeted for the Best-Seller lists".[2] Tammy Bruce of NOW said it was "a how-to manual on the torture and dismemberment of women" and called for a national boycott of the book.[3] Gloria Steinem suggested that Ellis would have to take responsibility for any women tortured and killed in the same manner as described in the novel. Ellis made some attempt to respond to all this furore in interviews with *The New York Times* and *Rolling Stone*, pointing out that he didn't expect anything better of critics anyway. ("Do most critics' taste extend beyond the hopelessly middlebrow?") He said what might be expected, that the book was a work of fiction and should speak for itself. He was quite clear about his position: "The acts described in the book are truly, indisputably vile. The book itself is not. Patrick Bateman is a monster. I am not. The outrage that has been expressed is totally disconnected from what the book is about."[4] America even wheeled on Norman Mailer, their iconic emblem of Literature, for one last go-round with art and censorship in *Vanity Fair*. Mailer, whose own book *An American Dream* is, as a straightforwardly "realist" novel, far more offensive towards women than Ellis's comic-strip hyperreality, sounded lost. He noted wearily that: "*American Psycho* is saying that the eighties were spiritually disgusting and the author's presentation is the crystallization of such horror." Mailer went on to strike a blow for that old ghost, the classic realist novel: "Since we are going to have a monstrous book with a monstrous thesis, the author must rise to the occasion by having a murderer with enough inner life for us to apprehend him?"[5] Why? In all this media fall-out, these shrieks of "the literary equivalent of a snuff film" and "pure trash" there is a notable absence of any *literary* criticism; the most recent authors mentioned, apart from Tom Wolfe and his *The Bonfire of the Vanities* are Kafka and Beckett. In *The Village Voice*, Mim Udovitch manages after a great deal of work to decide that "this is a good old-fashioned Beckett-esque anti-novel, with all the attendant no-frills—flat characters, monotonously detailed surface description, no plot to speak of and endless repetitions."[6] It is as if no one had written anything in between.

In Britain critics were able to distinguish themselves by exhibiting a near-total ignorance of Ellis's intentions and of contemporary American fiction in general. Along with their counterparts in America they were obsessed with context rather than text. John Walsh in *The Sunday Times* and Fay Weldon in *The Guardian* were almost the only commentators to even attempt a defence.[7] Some critics reacted as though the novel were virtually autobiographical. It was said that Ellis "chose to sit in his apartment month after month imagining unoriginal ways of torturing women (not to mention dogs, gays and homeless people)"—as if he were some demented Son of Sam and not a novelist at all.[8] Feminist groups again behaved as though this were not fiction but a manifesto, a statement of intent. Ellis was accused of making a killing in more ways than one. It was said that he had chosen repulsive sensationalism as a way of ensuring the commercial success that had eluded his novel *The Rules of Attraction*—a wholly unfounded suggestion in that, as mentioned, he started writing *American Psycho* before his second novel was even published. And what seemed to fuel critical rage more than anything was the $300,000 advance retained by Ellis when Simon and Schuster refused to publish the book. This was the familiar British primal scream of hatred at the artist who was not only doing something that they did not like and could not understand but was actually *being paid a lot of money for it*. The unashamed greed and envy that lay behind many of these accusations was typical of the decade and ironically, one of the principal themes in the novel itself. The mass media, in fact, behaved exactly as Ellis and countless other postmodern theorists had already noted they did, leeching away all the drama into their own arena, re-writing the script and re-presenting it to the consumer hordes. The story of *American Psycho*—as opposed to the book itself—uncannily paralleled the fictive themes it explored; it was treated as a fashion statement—controversial, emotive, urgent, very NOW! Early copies became *the* essential fashion accessory amongst the hip cognoscenti and then, as it was disseminated amongst the uncool masses, it was swiftly dropped. Within months it was media history, yawn time. Don DeLillo has commented on the way in which the media consumes and fictionalizes events so that the media itself becomes the source of our fictions. Where once people turned to fiction for plot and character, drama and action they now turn to the filmic or televisual. The ability to ghost-dance freely between the factual and the imaginary is an essential strategy for contemporary psychic survival, as Andy Warhol understood when he decided to treat his entire life "as a movie".[9] DeLillo has also commented on the role of the novelist in such a psychically cannibalistic culture, saying that the writer was now merely "part of the background noise—part of the buzz of celebrity and consumerism" in a world where: "Everything seeks its own heightened version. Nothing happens till it is consumed."[10]

It soon became impossible for anyone to focus on the novel at all, let alone pay any attention whatsoever to "the language, the structure, the details". Had they done so it would have forestalled many of their criticisms. Not since *The Satanic Verses* had a book been so poorly read. It was dismally revealing of the low quality of cultural commentary in England and America. Ellis himself was perfectly aware of the extravagant inanities of the media tirade. "Most of them haven't read it and those who have, I think, have missed it in a big way."[11]

American Psycho is of course a classic of the 1980s. In a sense it *is* the 1980s. It embodies the decade and all the clichés of the decade in the West—the rampant self-serving greed, relentless aggression and one-upmanship; the manic consumer overdrive, exhaustion, wipe-out and terror. The book arrived in Britain at a time when much of this furious, doomed drive towards success and perfection was still dominant. The media had just started wildly signalling that it was over, that it was time to lower our moral hemlines and become gentle and caring for a bit. However, having been activated, the tread-mill kept spinning. People have lives, not life-styles and they cannot be dismantled at the whim of the Sunday supplement. It was hardly surprising that a novel which unequivocally condemned a way of life to which many people had sacrificed their youth and energy was tepidly received; journalists were as much at the mercy of the status-driven conspicuous consumption of the eighties as anyone else and the froth over the book's alleged violence may have concealed a hideous disquiet that the leotards and Agnès B. leggings, the enormous mortgages and obscene restaurant bills were . . . just . . . not worth it.

Don DeLillo had unwittingly described something of the strange, hushed arena in which the book really functioned when he said: "I think everything we do in the West is so easily absorbed by the culture that it is very difficult for art to become dangerous. There is something in the culture that absorbs danger."[12] The critics tried very hard to defuse *American Psycho* by focusing on one aspect of the book—the violence, which turns out, on close reading, to be something of a chimera—and ignoring the rest or dismissing it as boring. Naomi Wolf's assertion that "It was the single most boring book I have ever had to endure" was typical.[13] It probably does seem boring to the careless reader. This is irrelevant because tedium has never prevented art from having an impact. The films of Andy Warhol, one of the single most important artistic influences of the century, are undoubtedly boring. It did not stop them from being dangerous in that they were incapable of being absorbed by the dominant culture. *American Psycho* was a dangerous book. It was not alone in this—it was not even the most dangerous book published that spring. Dennis Cooper's *Frisk*, discussed later, is infinitely more disturbing. What unites Warhol's work and Ellis's novel is that, despite receiving the concentrated attention of the mediatized culture, their art remained un-assimilated precisely because it was comprised of subversive elements so cleverly interwoven with the cultural attitudes of the time that to have fully recognized them, *at the time*, would have proved destabilizing to the commentators.

For the record, *Frisk* attracted minimal attention upon publication in the USA. It was a homosexual-murder novel and thus unimportant, ghetto-ized. When asked if he could understand the feminist horror at his novel, Ellis commented: "But would it offend you if he [Patrick Bateman, the 'hero'] committed the same actions on young men? If they were mutilated, tortured in the same manner, would you be boycotting the publisher?" (Apparently not.) Women have the stage right now and rightly so but Ellis says that he feels no responsibility to write what they consider a "socially acceptable book": "Buy Alice Walker if it makes you feel better. Buy Amy Tan. I don't care what you read . . ."![14]

The literary establishment retains its hegemony by marginalizing threatening material. There is almost nothing published in Britain that both receives attention and could remotely be considered dangerous. When something struggles through, like the novels of Kathy Acker, it is to widespread abuse and misunderstanding. There are various other strategies for rendering potentially inflammable material impotent. The most usual is just to ignore it. The novels of Dennis Cooper and Juan Goytisolo remain mired in the small press underground, admired by the few, ignored by the many, until time or age has tamed them. The works of, say, Jean Genet or Georges Bataille passed almost seamlessly from being small press rarities to modern classics, without ever spending time in the media spotlight or getting the attention they deserved. William Burroughs was received, albeit reluctantly, by the American Institute of Art and Letters, when his work was de-fanged by age. The most telling example of all is that of Hubert Selby, a serious and influential artist, whose ground-breaking work in confronting contemporary urban reality, media fantasy and even, in *The Demon*, ur-yuppiedom has not escaped any of the younger Manhattan writers. The British establishment was forced into a ludicrous trial over *Last Exit to Brooklyn* which

nearly broke down when the jury found the book unreadable—
and presumably very boring indeed.

The fuss and froth over *American Psycho*, when seen in the
context of other unnerving literature seems ever more pitiful. In
the two years previously translations of de Sade's *120 Days of
Sodom*, Guillaume Apollinaire's *Les Onze Milles Verges* and
Octave Mirbeau's *The Torture Garden* had appeared in Britain to
a resounding chorus of apathy, although de Sade eventually ran
into a bit of trouble. This was largely seen for the nonsense it
was—but only because de Sade and the other French authors
had been neutered by time. Their rantings were not *relevant* to
the present—or not perceived to be. Even so, the Apollinaire text
was trimmed by the publishers, Peter Owen. The most offensive
bits were cut and rendered in po-faced précis at the bottom of the
page. This quiet editorial abbreviation is another little British
publishing strategy; the most improbable American texts arrive
here strangely shorn, from Richard Price's *The Wanderers sans*
its infamous "venereal sandwich" to Pamela Des Barres groupie
memoirs. Literary censorship operates in other covert ways. The
independent London bookshops—radical, gay, horror/fantasy
—will all admit now to a careful buying policy when it comes to
questionable books and comics, following years of persecution
by the police and customs.

When exclusion, censorship or prosecution won't work,
ghettoization probably will. Many of the most subversive writers
working now operate entirely within genre; SF, horror, fantasy,
crime, true crime and comics. That these fields receive so little
attention is indicative of the contempt in which they are held—
for no good reason—by the literary and cultural establishment.
Such writers gain a great deal of freedom and, if they are in the
Stephen King class, money, alongside a lifelong loss of reputation
as serious artists. Occasionally writers of some quality like
Thomas Harris—mega-successful after the film of *The Silence of
the Lambs*—Ruth Rendell or Patricia Highsmith will achieve
something approaching respect as well as popular success but
more usually they are left to scrape along on the lean pickings of
cult appeal. A writer of the calibre of Derek Raymond (a.k.a.

Robin Cook), with his bestial, wrenching vision of modern London is likely to remain relatively ignored on the crime shelves until some media smart-ass films his "Factory" series novels.

In short, what distinguished *American Psycho* was not that it was unusual in depicting scenes of extreme sexual violence. Much, much worse can easily be found in small press publications, in genre or in the past. Not to mention, of course, the success and sycophancy surrounding psychotics and killers in films and television. *The Silence of the Lambs*, Jonathan Demme's film in which Anthony Hopkins played the psychotic psychiatrist Hannibal "The Cannibal" Lecter, was showered with Oscars. Criminal trials in America draw huge television audiences. "When Charles Manson is eventually paroled," wrote John Waters, "will *he* have to stand in line outside some crummy, trendy, New York nightclub? . . . Ha! Are you kidding? Right this way, Mr. Manson. Free drink tickets? . . . Yessir!"[15] When Ellis talks of "How desensitized our culture has become towards violence" and how this necessitated the extremes of his novel, he is stating a fact.[16] But it was the combination of overt sexual violence and Ellis's status as a "serious" novelist—young, relevant, living, mainstream—that determined all the hysteria. What was unusual was that such a provocative book should come from a writer who had already been accepted—indeed, groomed —by the most high-toned, respectable arm of the publishing industry. Some of the depressing reaction to the book may lie in the fact that Ellis had transgressed the unwritten contract, had bitten the hand that fed him, had *gone too far*. If he was going to write such filth why wasn't he dead, or underground, or in the ghetto? This isn't to say that there wasn't a frisson of plain commercial joy and excitement at a writer who was effortlessly garnering so much publicity and presumably was going to sell so very many books. Ellis was there; he had to be reviewed, he had to be taken seriously or at least appear to be taken seriously. However the media played their old trick of substituting the image for the actuality and it remains for the street-cleaners of literature, the academics, to come along now and try and soothe everyone with a spot of textual analysis. Bret Easton Ellis spent three years writing this novel, and it *is* a novel—not a "How-to-manual", nor true-crime, not a manifesto or a tract—and it seems reasonable to give it more than three minutes consideration.

In the context of Ellis's other two novels, *American Psycho* is a natural, even an inevitable development. The all-prevailing *kenosis* of his previous work—the evacuation of content, the numbing-out of feeling and sense—together with his interest in social trends, and his expressed belief that only the most extreme and disruptive images or experiences can penetrate the bland vacuity of his generation seem to make the combination of serial killer and the yuppie meritocracy of eighties New York an obvious choice of subject. However, right from the start there are curious tensions and oppositions within the text.

It is an extraordinarily *fictional* text, an over-fictionalized, overly structuralized book. And yet, simultaneously it actually comes closer to being a manifesto, a rhetorical device, than those who accused it of such qualities seemed to realize. From the first line, "Abandon all hope ye who enter here", to the last, "This is not an exit," we are *signed*, we are entered in to what is really a *circle* of hell. Once we have given ourselves up to the text, made the choice to "abandon hope", we have no way out. It is a closed system. These imprisoning, claustrophobic qualities are deftly manipulated in order, not only to force us to live as close to Patrick as is possible in a fictional sense, but to imprint the reader with such force that we cannot ever get out. This is an act of great aggression and confidence on the part of the author revealing a controlling ego which asserts its rights over both characters and readers. It is a gesture of defiance in the face of all post-Barthesian erosions of the authorial actuality. Furthermore it is successful; the reader does not ever get out in the sense that it is thereafter impossible to apprehend the eighties without some reference to their memories of the book.

Ellis's work seems to be on a search-and-destroy mission. In *Less Than Zero* the otherness of the text, the *hope* of the text, lay on the East Coast, in college education, all of which was systematically destroyed and revealed as depthless and banal in *The Rules of Attraction*. The rules of attraction themselves were at hopeless cross purposes and the characters were, emotionally, on the road to nowhere. The otherness in this book, the hope, was adult life, work and mature relationships. And so, in the first chapter of *American Psycho*, Ellis, very explicitly, very distinctively says goodbye to college life, to bohemian life and moves us deliberately into his previously signalled other, the adult, world.

The opening chapter of *American Psycho* is a tour-de-force during which all the ground rules of the rest of the book—the rules of repulsion—are laid out. Patrick Bateman and his friend Timothy Price, both Young, Urban Professionals, leave work and go to dinner at the house of Patrick's girlfriend, Evelyn. Patrick is the narrator, but the author who titles the chapter "April Fools" is immediately asserting himself as the controlling voice and creating a dissonance between Patrick's words and authorial meaning. The struggle between Patrick and the author continues, more subtly, throughout the book, underlining its fictionality and providing a counter-point in direct opposition to the stated text. The authorial voice—or rather, the authorial language—constantly foregrounds the fictionality and rhetoricity—the artificiality—of the book.

We all once knew the narrator, Patrick Bateman. Looking back we can see that he is wearing a two-button wool gabardine suit with notched lapels by Gian Marco Venturi, a cotton shirt by Ike Behar, a tie by Luciano Berbera and cap-toed leather lace-ups by Ferragamo. His hair is slicked back, he has redwood-framed non-prescription glasses by Oliver Peoples and a Tumi leather attaché case. He works at Pierce & Pierce on Wall Street. He is eating a meal of blackened lobster with strawberry sauce, quail sashimi with grilled brioche and cherimoya sorbet. He is a Yuppie, a Clone. He is also an extremely unreliable narrator.

In this first chapter "April Fools", little happens but we receive a great deal of information. In that it acts as a microcosm of the rest of the book "April Fools" is worth examining in some detail. Even the title can be read in two directly oppositional ways and has this in common with all the major events of the novel.

The first line: "ABANDON ALL HOPE YE WHO ENTER HERE is scrawled in blood red lettering on the side of the Chemical Bank..." neatly conjoins the primary themes of blood, despair and banking as well as sub-textually noting our entrance to the novel, as previously discussed.[17] At this stage in the novel some of Ellis's literary devices are a bit brash, a bit crude. He is painting in broad strokes.

We are in New York, in the 1980s. The city is littered with posters for the hit show of those years, *Les Misérables*, forcing us to contrast Hugo's spirited starvelings with the bloated, spiritually impoverished characters of the text. Simultaneously this signals the contemporary "miserables" strewn like rag-dolls over the city-scape; the bums, the homeless, the mental patients, the dispossessed and the disinherited.

In the cab with Bateman, Tim Price—whose very name denotes value—mentions that he has counted already twenty-six beggars that day. Reading from newspapers they discuss the ways in which the city is falling apart: "the trash, the garbage, the disease", Tim, whipping himself into a savage heartless parody of media overkill chants: "Nazis, gridlock, gridlock, baby-sellers . . . AIDS babies, baby junkies . . . maniac baby, gridlock, bridge collapses", cutting quickly to: "Why aren't you wearing the worsted navy blue blazer with the grey pants?"[18]

On the third page is the first mention of violence and murder. Critics have generally asserted that Bateman does not kill until page 131 but any careful reading will reveal that he claims to have disposed of three, or possibly four people before then. In this opening chapter a newspaper report mentions two people who disappear, leaving bloodstains, at a socialite party on a yacht. Bateman reveals shortly that he has recently been at a yacht party and by the end of the book, the bodies, three in fact, have been recovered and are claimed as victims by Patrick. The discrepancy between the original two who vanish and the three who re-appear is only the first example of the myriad discrepancies in Patrick's account. Or did the newspapers get it wrong, as they so often do? Ellis is right to talk of "details".[19] The text is littered with detailed clues, every single one of which can be plausibly countered by an alternative explanation and all of which underline the trickery of the fictional process.

Returning to "April Fools", Price rants on about disease, claiming, in a particularly fine example of mindless vacuity, that you can get "dyslexia from pussy".[20] Before they arrive at Evelyn's house (a brownstone, bought for her by her father) there are already *two* cases of mistaken identity—guys with slicked-back hair, suspenders and horn-rimmed glasses who look exactly like other people they know. Ellis has no intention of deserting his obsession with deindividualization. It is extended so that it functions as the primary plot device.

Evelyn and her girlfriend Courtney are also wearing absolutely identical clothes: Krizia cream blouse, Krizia rust-tweed skirt and silk-satin d'Orsay pumps from Manolo Blahnik. Evelyn, in an hysterical state of tension—eating in is a sort of penance for her restaurant-crazed peers—is arranging a stunning display of sushi; tuna, yellowtail, mackerel, shrimp, eel and *bonito* with piles of wasabi and ginger.

Evelyn, much to the disapproval of Patrick and Tim Price, has guests from downtown; an artist, Stash and Vanden, his girlfriend. Vanden attends Camden, the fictional equivalent of Ellis's own college, Bennington, and the setting for *The Rules of Attraction*. Vanden has green streaks in her hair, is wearing leather, is watching a heavy-metal video on MTV and—horror of horrors—smoking a cigarette. Stash is pale and lumpy, with a poorly cropped haircut and dressed all in black, ill-fitting clothes. They are unmistakably refugees from the adolescent world of the previous two novels. Patrick notes glumly that Stash looks nothing at all like the other men in the room; he has no muscle tone, he has no suspenders, no horn-rimmed glasses and his hair isn't slicked back. In short he is worthless.

Patrick is further repulsed by Stash's behaviour at dinner. Rather than eating a piece of yellowtail he impales it with a chopstick, which he leaves standing straight up in the fish. He soon points accusingly at it and asserts that, "It moved!" On leaving the house Stash pockets his animated sushi and Patrick is sufficiently distressed by this bizarre, arty behaviour to raise the matter later. "Am I the only one who grasped the fact that Stash assumed his piece of sushi was"—I cough, then resume—"a pet?"[21] The implications of Stash's behaviour (so reminiscent of the moment in *The Rules of Attraction* when "Resin wakes up and starts talking to the ashtray") as far as Patrick *et al* are concerned are clear—it is totally unacceptable. Such artistic weirdness is *demode*, old-fashioned, tasteless and worthless. Ellis further semaphores his intentions by having Vanden read an article in "some East Village rag" entitled THE DEATH OF DOWNTOWN.

Patrick launches into an extraordinary, lengthy speech about American domestic and foreign policy indicating the ludicrous contradictions and oppositions therein. We have, he says, to slow down the nuclear arms race *and* ensure a strong national defense, prevent the spread of communism *and* prevent US military involvement overseas. We have to improve health care, social security and education, clean up environmental damage and at the same time promote economic growth and business expansion. He continues, saying that it is necessary to provide food and shelter for the homeless, to combat racial discrimination and promote civil rights whilst taking care to support women's rights and at the same time changing the abortion laws to protect the right to life whilst somehow maintaining women's freedom of choice. He concludes: "Most importantly we have to promote general social concern and less materialism in young people."[22]

Patrick doesn't seem to notice that his speech is nonsensical. Normally it would be read as being terminally cynical. He and Price have already demonstrated all too vividly their attitude to social problems in their taunting and abuse of the street bums. They are materialists to the bone. However what is deeply chilling about the speech is the implication that it is dead-pan. Patrick is incapable of thinking about these issues and noting their contradictions. It is delivered in a media monotone and denotes an abyss between Patrick's daily life and any apprehension of the political realities behind it. This dissociation between life as it is lived on the city streets, between this and the media avalanche that snows us, soothes us, providing a seamless, self-contained, *meaningless* background commentary, this dissociation *is* the reality—for Patrick and for everyone else.

Stash and Vanden leave to "score" in SoHo. This leaves Tim Price, Evelyn and Patrick. The designer litany continues: "I'm lying on Evelyn's bed holding a tapestry pillow from Jenny B. Goode, nursing a cranberry and Absolut."[23]

Tim moans about Evelyn's "artiste" friends, saying he's sick of being the only one at dinner who hasn't talked to an extra-terrestrial. They sneer at Vanden's stupidity; she thinks that Sri Lanka is "a cool club in the Village" and *High Noon* a film about marijuana farmers.[24] They are so much wiser, so much more adult. Evelyn accuses Tim of gaining weight and losing hair. He retaliates by raising the status stakes and saying that she uses Q.T. Instantan—a very low-rent product. Tim flirts. Patrick tells the reader that Tim is the only interesting person he knows. Evelyn keeps repeating vacuously that Patrick is "the boy next door" and that he, unlike Tim, is no cynic. Patrick whispers to himself, "I'm a fucking evil psychopath," the first of numberless similar statements throughout the book all of which are ignored, misheard, or laughed at.[25]

Finally, Tim leaves and Patrick asks Evelyn why she doesn't have an affair with him, pointing out that he is rich, good-looking and has a great body. She retorts that *everybody* is rich, and good-looking and has a great body.

The central premises have been established: small world exclusivity, status frenzy, high-toned snobbery, conspicuous consumption.

Evelyn states that Stash has tested positive for the HIV virus and she believes he is going to sleep with Vanden that night.

" 'Good', I say."[26]

Evelyn finds this exciting. In this way Stash and Vanden are killed off. They are dead, gone from the text. They never re-appear. It's goodbye to Camden College and the East Village, goodbye to bohemianism, art, poetry, whimsy, creativity and—ostensibly—to drugs.

This is up-town, this is the modern world, the adult world—money, status, pragmatism, skills, market-value.

Thus, in one short chapter, all the major thematic constituents of the book are carefully delineated and intertwined. It's an adult world, an amoral world, a status-driven, food-obsessed world, a world of interchangeable people, a misogynistic world despite its apparent equal opportunities for women and finally a brutal, violent and terrified world.

Ultimately it is Stash, the embodiment of Ellis's earlier fictional *Zeitgeist* who signifies the opposition between Patrick's narrative and authorial intention. His crazy remarks, his affectedly artistic behaviour might just be dumb or they might, all together, provide a sneering, provocative commentary on his up-town night out. Just who, exactly, are the April Fools here?

The text of *American Psycho* also functions as a maze or puzzle. In order for the critical intelligence to breathe within this particular prison-house of language it is essential for the reader to crack the codes of a narrative that is richly littered with clues. In this respect the book works at times as a parodic deconstruction of the thriller, or serial-killer mystery novel. However, in *American Psycho*, the "clues" are all entirely linguistic rather than the unselfconscious plot-based devices of the popular mystery thriller wherein the reader is never required to consider the "artificial" linguistic formations of the text.

While the performative aspects of *American Psycho* directly reflect its content, there is, sub-textually, the counterpoint of authorial condemnation—or so we are forced to assume lest we find ourselves blandly approving of Bateman's actions. In his earlier books, Ellis's critique of character and values was constantly signalled. In *Less Than Zero* such criticisms are very evident and they still exist, to a lesser extent in *The Rules of Attraction*. However in *American Psycho* there is absolutely nothing stated that implies a critique of Bateman's world and his actions, beyond his own jejune philosophical agonizings which, paradoxically serve to render the character less, rather than more, plausible. Critics, noting the lack of overt condemnation in the text, excoriated Ellis for what they assumed was violent misogyny. Of course they could not allow themselves to conclude that the author was condoning acts of mutilation and murder. Here we have again an act of authorial aggression in that the onus is on the reader to interject the moral values so conspicuously lacking in the text. The critic has to decide when to jump ship. For example, many readers would have internalized the aggressive, money-making values of the decade—who is to say that an honest job as a Wall Street broker is such an evil thing? However these same readers might swiftly be revolted by Bateman's attitudes to women, or to the homeless, and at this point would have to dissociate themselves from the narrative and register dissent, assuming that the author shared their disgust or else—and this a trap for the unwary—roundly scold the author for his unsound attitudes, as many critics did. However that still leaves the problem of trying to define when the author himself had decided to distance himself from events. He might, for example, mistrust women but presumably he wasn't in favour of popping out people's eyeballs? This put the critic in the ludicrous position of, firstly, supplying the moral framework to the book and arguing, in effect, for dualism and old-fashioned fictive ambiguity and secondly, of having to tangle with the autobiographical element in fiction—of defining the author's own feelings, intentions and standards. This has the effect of turning the tables on the reader; rather than being presented with a well-ordered fictive universe, secure in its moral delineation, the reader is, forced to engage personally with the text, to fill in the blanks, as it were, if he is not to produce a completely coarse and slip-shod reading. The reader is forced to scrutinize his own values and beliefs, rather than those being provided for him within a Good-Evil fictive universe. The alternative is to reject these misleading binary oppositions that Jacques Derrida has defined as intrinsic to Western thinking and to immerse oneself in the free play of signifiers within the text. Ellis himself does not achieve judgement and closure in the text but an endless circularity and *deferral of meaning*.

This leads us to another of the deepest ironies in the novel, the difference between *apparent* and *actual* writing. The book is written as if to be skimmed. It is written largely in brochure-speak, ad-speak, in the mindless, soporific commentary of the catwalk or the soapy soft-sell of the market-place; the sort of writing that comes up with phrases like "an attractive two-piece with matching accessories", or "As for dining out, the Caribbean island cuisine has mixed well with the European culture."[27] Ellis has said that Bateman is: "A mixture of *GQ* and *Stereo Review* and *Fangoria* . . . and *Vanity Fair*."[28] Yet, ironically, all this demands the very closest of readings. By situating this mall-speak within a serious novel Ellis destabilizes genres and suggests that, in general, a close study of our cultural debris might reveal clues. However, more seriously for the reader of *American Psycho*, the only way out of the all-imprisoning text is a minutely close reading of the book which will definitely establish Patrick Bateman's fallibility. Only by decisively admitting Patrick's unreliability—and the scales are very evenly weighted —can the critical imagination be freed and an approximation of interpretation allowed to begin.

American Psycho continues with its scatter-gun itemization of Patrick's way of life. The chapters are generally short and have blandly factual headings: "Office", "Christmas Party", "Lunch". They function again, as did the chapters in *Less Than Zero* as Polaroids or sound-bites, providing a brief glimpse of what the author wishes to convey. The artificiality of this structure is intrusive. The reader is given no chance to sink back mindlessly into a warm bath of narrative. This is underlined by the fact that the chapters are not, even when they seem to be, sequential. A "Morning" may be followed by an "Afternoon" but close reading—usually of Patrick's wardrobe—will always indicate that we are on a completely different day. Thus the seamless monotone of Patrick's life, which is indeed positively robotic in its round of office, restaurant, gym and bed, is subtly undermined and fragmented by continual narrative jump-cuts.

Ellis continues to describe, in detail, the clothes and accessories of each character as they appear. Again this is a device more complex than it might seem. It irritated many critics because they found it boring, whereas it is of course no more boring than the constant consumer hum emanating from magazines, media and advertising. It is only when this media mantra is foregrounded and heavily concentrated, as it is in the novel, when it is in fact, decontextualized, that it has the ability to annoy, as Ellis was no doubt aware. The novelist is usually expected to rummage among the cornucopia of contemporary information and to extract the telling detail, the revealing style, the right tie, hair-do or sunglasses and to conscientiously apply them to a character in order to accentuate type and motivation, in short, to assemble the outerwear of the character in accordance with the personality and spiritual framework that is simultaneously being assembled in exactly the same way. Ellis absolutely refuses to participate in this process of "constructing" character and in rejecting it makes us overly aware of the "normal" fictional process as encouraged in Creative Writing class. By adorning his characters, as if they were Barbie dolls, in more or less interchangeable haute couture, and, moreover, by duplicating the self-important intonations of the fashion magazine as he does so, he ably deconstructs much of what we mean by "character" in fiction and forces on us an awareness of the surreal qualities of consumer-speak. Douglas Crimp, writing about the use of reproduction and parody in Pop Art says: "The fiction of the creating subject gives way to the frank confiscation, quotation, excerptation, accumulation and repetition of already existing images. Notions of originality, authenticity and presence . . . are undermined."[29] Towards the end of the book, when Patrick's narrative increasingly tends to shiver and shake around the edges, the litany of designer names begins to falter: shoes by "Susan Warren Bennis Edwards" becomes shoes by "Warren Susan Allen Edmonds" and then shoes by "Edward Susan Bennis Allen".[30] For such a tiny detail this is conspicuous in its effects. What ego-madness possesses a designer (and she's certainly not the only one) that she will inflict an insanely complex name on an entire retinue of stockists, advertisers, fashion-journalists and consumers? Why do we meekly accept and repeatedly intone such a vast array of fancy, complex, weirdly spelt (Manolo Blahnik) and obviously self-assumed names? What drives Patrick crazy is driving us all crazy—why don't we all just crack up and start screaming about brand-names and up-town pizza recipes, like he does? Thus, detail by detail, as if bricking up a tomb, Ellis defines Patrick's insanity and our own place within it.

In addition, by his rigid adherence to an adspeak dress-code for his characters, Ellis continues his emphasis upon deindividualization in contemporary society. Finally, and very ironically, Ellis's use of detailed dress-code to obliterate rather than to define character in the traditional sense ends up contributing to the mechanics of the plot in an *entirely* traditional sense—the "plot" such as it is, eventually turns upon the impossibility of anyone distinguishing one character from another.

All the other accoutrements of Patrick's daily life are delineated in the same stun-gun detail as the clothes in the book. Patrick's apartment is a temple to status frenzy and state-of-the-art living. Let us pass briefly over his Toshiba VCR, his Sansui stereo, his Wurlitzer and his Steuben glass animals. From the start Patrick is a cipher, rather than a "character". He is Everyyuppie, indifferent to art, originality or even pleasure except in so far as his possessions are the newest, brightest, best, most expensive and most fashionable. By implication, Patrick's absorption in the minutiae of the moment colludes with the author's intention of negating him as a character. At every step he is being rubbed out because, as the author must be aware, every mention of "real" brand-names and designer clothes dates as quickly as the ink can dry.

Patrick also details for us his *levée* during which he utilises a mind-boggling array of products including: anti-plaque, floss, ice-pack mask, deep-pore cleanser, herb-mint facial mask, spearmint face-scrub, water-activated gel-cleanser, honey-almond body scrub, exfoliating scruffing lotion, shampoo, conditioner, nutrient complex, mousse, moisturiser, alcohol-free anti-bacterial toner, emollient lotion, clarifying lotion, anti-ageing eye-balm, "protective" lotion. All this in a book that Blake

Morrison managed to describe as a work "of Zola-eque naturalism"![31] Beyond the obvious point that no one—not even a girl—could go through this beauty routine every morning and still get to work and the concomitant implication that men have now been herded into the highly lucrative cosmetic market, Ellis's relentless hyperbole here is leading inexorably towards one of the central lines in the novel. A little later in the book, Patrick, in the video store screams: "*There are too many fucking movies to choose from.*"[32] This is a notably unsubtle evocation of the unsubtle sensory overload that effects us all. Daily the cry goes up, the anguished scream from the never-ending moment: "There are too many fucking . . . to choose from." Yams or paw-paws, Clinique or Clarins, am I up-town girl or down-town slob tonight? In this embarrassing plethora of image and reality, we cringe as we gobble and consume, we try to give with one hand and grab with the other (queues in Russia, kwashiorkor in Ethiopia), what shall we buy, take, eat, consume, shit, who are we? This is the boring, mundane heart of postwar consumer capitalism, the hamburger that ate the world, this is it—too much, too soon.

Within consumer capitalism we are offered a surfeit of commodities, an abundance of commodity choices, but this image of plenty is illusory. Our desires are mediated by ideas about roles and lifestyles which are themselves constructed as commodities and our "choices" are propelled by these constructs. In a world in which the only relations are economic we remain alienated from any "authenticity" of choice or desire. Patrick has been so fragmented and divided by his insane consumerism that he cannot "exist" as a person. Literature has been surprisingly coy about tackling the subject of "I shop therefore I am", as one of the girls in the film *Heathers* says. Bateman's full-throated cry is a fact, a dead-end, a full-stop. The beyond—be it apocalyptic, climatic, atomic, political—remains fantastical and although Bateman's world might now, in the nineties, be fraying at the edges, the consumer spectacle continues to accelerate. The same critic, Blake Morrison, went on to complain that a book need not mirror all the faults it portrays in order to represent them accurately; boredom need not be boring, nor crudity crude. This is the old debate: William Carlos Williams, Charles Olsen and "form and content". Text and context. We have come to accept that the intervention of authorial language must *always* renegotiate the experience portrayed. In Paul de Man's words: "A fundamental discrepancy always prevents the observer from coinciding fully with the consciousness he is observing."[33] This is particularly evident in *American Psycho* where language is actually used against itself, to distort the narrative. However, in his lists of consumer products Ellis does no more than utilize simple rhetorical devices to ludicrously exaggerate, cartoon-fashion, the experience of consumerism and bring it more fully to our consciousness. At its most basic level, this reduces Bateman's reliability as a narrator and any "realist" reading of the novel.

The best example of this process is seen in Patrick's description of a TV show to which he is addicted and which airs every morning. *The Patty Winters Show* is presented as a talk show not unlike that of Oprah Winfrey and throughout the novel Patrick laconically records the subject of the latest Winters show, frequently interposing his observation against the most incongruous scenes, be they murder or mergers, just as the show itself with its melodramatic content is inappropriately dumped in a million homes. During the novel Patrick tells us that the show covers such subjects as multiple personalities, autism, nuclear war, Nazis, mastectomy, dwarf-tossing, Teenage Girls who Trade Sex for Crack, how to make your Pet a Movie-Star, Princess Di's beauty tips, and many more. As a simple example of the daily fragmentation of our consciousnesses by tabloid mentality, Ellis's use of the show is competent, if uninspired. However, Patrick also tells us that the show featured an interview with a boy who fell in love with a box of soap and an interview with Bigfoot—"to my surprise I found him surprisingly articulate and charming."[34] Also, Patrick tells us, one day on the show a Cheerio sat in a very small chair and was interviewed for an hour. Now these assertions raise much more interesting issues. First, the reader is again called upon to intervene, to supply, in this case, not the moral framework of the book but the sanity. At which point does Patrick's sanity diverge from the general insanity of the show? Out there in tabloid heaven it is certainly possible that someone might believe themselves in love with a box of Ariel and want to tell the world about it. But surely they couldn't have talked to Bigfoot—this is television, not print. And even the most flexible reader must discount the possibility that a small cereal was interviewed for an hour. So, Patrick is not watching what's on television? At what point did he diverge and start misleading us about the show? Some of the earlier episodes are "authenticated" by Patrick's workmates. But after that—Psycho City. Of such small puzzles is *American Psycho* composed and therein lies much of the humour and pleasure of the book.

Once the tenor of Bateman's days has been established we get some closer glimpses of his social life—drinking sessions with the boys, much jolly racist, sexist bantering coupled with nervous status frenzy as they try to outdo each other in the matter of acquisitions—be they women or engraved business cards. Money remains the bottom line at all times and everyone has difficulty distinguishing their friends. They all look interchangeable and as Ellis has largely refrained from providing any detail of character the "human" element is consistently devalued adding to the impression of an author manipulating robotic puppets. Much energy is expended in securing reservations to fashionable, ludicrously expensive restaurants where food is tortured into iconic artefacts. Food functions as art in the book, paintings themselves being no more than an investment. One of Patrick's first hysterical outbursts occurs in a restaurant where he starts screaming, in a frenzy, about the perfect pizza: "a pizza should be yeasty and slightly bready and have a cheesy crust!"— with all the passion that one might usually reserve for art or politics.[35] This hysteria, besides being funny, defines the miserable limitations of Patrick's world and confirms the fragility of his mental state—anyone who has that much invested in a pizza recipe has to be seriously disturbed.

The first event of importance occurs during a visit the boys make to a nightclub called Tunnel. The gimmick in this club is a set of train tracks which vanish—into a tunnel. After the usual business of scoring poor quality cocaine and trying to pick up girls, with Patrick announcing, as always, unheard: "You are a fucking ugly bitch I want to stab to death and play around with your cunt," Tim Price shouts to Patrick that he is leaving.[36] He stresses it, "I'm getting out . . . leaving." He starts screaming, "I . . . am . . . leaving". Where to, Patrick wants to know, "Morgan Stanley? Rehab?" but Tim "just keeps staring past the railings, trying to find the point where the tracks come to an end, find what lies behind the blackness."[37] And Tim does leave, leaping onto the tracks, running through the flashes of the strobe lights and receding into the tunnel. Tim, who is the "only interesting person" Patrick knows vanishes right into the book, into the text.[38] Tim cannot "leave" the book as his only "existence" is within its pages but he can vanish deeper into the black *tunnel* of the authorial imagination. In cancelling the only character with some pretension to personality, Ellis again emphasizes his artistic control and his decision to people a book with characters whom he resolutely refuses to (con)form into "interesting" representations of human beings. In addition, of course, Tim's vanishing determinedly re-locates Patrick in a joyless, tedious world where panic boredom is never far away.

More than ever now, "everyone looks the same".[39] Patrick's sick sadism is increasingly mentioned. He has rented the *Body Double* video thirty-seven times so that he can masturbate over the scene where a woman is drilled to death by a power drill. He reads endless true crime biographies, Ted Bundy, Son of Sam, Charles Manson. A crack appears in his apartment ceiling. His narrative has its weird slippages—can an "Italian-Thai" restaurant exist? Patrick's narrative is dead-pan and such observations destabilize it further. Mim Udovitch pointed out in *The Village Voice* many of the innumerable mis-attributions of pop songs in the book; "Be my Baby" attributed to the Crystals rather than the Ronettes and so on until the *Voice* critic here is finally able to gasp out: "SLOW. UNRELIABLE NARRATOR WORKING."[40] This was actually an achievement considering how few other critics had even managed to reach this simple decision.

When Patrick next returns to Tunnel he finds it empty; the avalanche of fashion-crazed revellers has swept on to new sensations. Tunnel has swallowed Tim only to be emptied itself. Patrick's progress is marked by the continual "death" or wiping-out of whatever has gone immediately before. There is no continuity either in his "self" or his surroundings. There is just the endless circularity of text and an incessant *re*-creation within text. His narrative continues, at times, to collapse into near-meaningless fragments, a blur of obsessions and possessions: "Glass of J&B in my right hand I am thinking. Hand I am thinking . . . Porsche 911. A sharpei I am thinking."[41] Patrick takes what he claims to be blood-stained clothes to the dry-cleaners. Meeting a friend there he claims that the stains are cranapple juice or Hershey's Syrup and indeed, they could be. This is the first of numerous occasions where one can either accept Patrick's version of events or choose an alternative, and quite ordinary explanation.

One of Patrick's acquaintances mistakes him for a man called Marcus Halberstam; he is constantly mis-recognized. The question begins to arise: Who *is* Patrick? We know of his *fictional* existence. He is the big brother of Sean Bateman in *The Rules of Attraction* and has already made an appearance in that book. He works at Pierce and Pierce which was Sherman McCoy's investment firm in *The Bonfire of the Vanities*. He knows people from other "brat-pack" novels; Stash could be the person of the same name in *Slaves of New York*. Patrick tells of a chilling encounter with Alison Poole, heroine of Jay McInerney's *Story of My Life*. It seems as though Ellis is re-inforcing the fact that Patrick's only "existence" is within fiction. And we know from Roland Barthes just how bizarre is the fictional construct, how illogical, incongruous and contradictory is the contract between writer and reader. We know too how much time postmodern fiction has spent in deconstructing and disentangling the implicit agreements that lie behind fictive "realism". Ellis, in one of his interviews, has challenged the expectation "That novels must have traditional narrative structure . . . You would think that most writers in their twenties would want to fool around a little bit—would want to be a little experimental—would want to write something a little bit subversive."[42] Any reading of *American Psycho* must take these intentions into account.

By the time Patrick describes a murder in detail he has already claimed to have murdered a number of people: guests on the yacht, Evelyn's neighbour whose head, he says, he kept in his refrigerator, and two black kids. He now kills a poor black bum, slowly and sadistically, in a scene whose terrible pathos is inescapable. Ellis may have intended this in order to highlight Patrick's increasing zombiefication as the murders progress and the most repulsive of acts are described in an affectless monotone. The existence of increasing numbers of homeless people throughout the eighties aroused strong, conflicting responses in the more fortunate, responses compounded of hate, dread and pity. Throughout *American Psycho* the spectre of the homeless is constant; they hover, *les misérables*, like ghosts on the edge of consciousness, a reproach, a reproof, a warning.

Ellis has sound reasons for his sensationalism and, moreover, it is inextricably intertwined with the technical sophistication of the book. Unfortunately the violence overpowered critical response to a point where few were able to see the humour of the novel. This is understandable perhaps, but the book is, in parts, extremely funny. Ellis has said: "I used comedy to get at the absolute banality of the violence of a perverse decade."[43] Two of the characters, Luis Carruthers and his girlfriend Courtney Lawrence, seem to evolve, almost against the author's will, into fairly animated personalities and as it is Luis whom Patrick next attempts to murder, it is worth examining the couple in slightly more detail.

Courtney is a ditzy, romantic beauty, strung-out on lithium who shows traces of sensibility and loyalty from within her tranked-out haze. Patrick goes to bed with her while Luis is out of town, a highly comic coupling. While Patrick builds furiously towards his orgasm he realizes there is . . . some sort of problem and, pulling out, goes stumbling around the apartment. He is looking for the medicine cabinet. He needs the . . . water-soluble spermicidal lubricant! He needs it badly—he absolutely cannot have sex unless his obsessive-compulsive need for the correct consumer product is satisfied. He dabs on the lubricant, re-applies his latex sheath and bounces back onto Courtney who gasps, "Luis is a despicable twit."[44] No. Someone has misheard again. Similarly product-dazed, what she moaned was: "Is it a receptacle tip?" It isn't. They have to sit up and discuss the *force of the ejaculate*. They manage to half-heartedly complete a sex act that is completely bedeviled by consumer products, with Courtney wittering on to the end about Norma Kamali bikinis, "antique cutting boards and the sterling silver cheese grater and muffin tin she left at Harry's."[45]

Similarly, any encounter with Luis tends towards the farcical. When he returns from his business trip to Phoenix he describes the dinner he had with his client, a routine-sounding affair of roasted chicken and cheesecake. Patrick gets anxious, confused "by this alien, plain-sounding list". He asks feverishly, "What sauce or fruits were on the roasted chicken? What shapes was it cut into?" Luis is confused. "It was . . . roasted," he says. Patrick demands to know what the client's bimbo had. Scallops, apparently. "The scallops were grilled? Were they sashimi scallops? In a ceviche of sorts? . . . Or were they gratinized?" "No, Patrick", Luis says. "They were . . . broiled." Patrick then thinks for a while. "What's broiled, Luis?" "I'm not sure," he says. "I think it involves . . . a pan."[46] There lies the gulf between the yuppies and the rest of the known world.

Even Patrick's attempt to *murder* Luis is farcical. When Patrick decides to kill Luis it is in the vague, unrealistic hope that Courtney who might be a "shallow bitch" but is a "physically superior, near-perfect shallow bitch" might spend more time with him if Luis were dead.[47] Mindlessly he asks himself: "Would I ruin things by strangling Luis?"[48] Deciding that he wouldn't, he follows Luis to the men's room and puts his hands round Luis's neck, hoping to crunch his trachea. However Luis, who is known to be bisexual, totally misreads Patrick's intentions. He kisses Patrick's left wrist and look up at him shyly and awkwardly. " 'God, Patrick', he whispers . . . 'I've noticed your'—he gulps—'hot body.' "[49] He speaks in "a low, faggoty whisper" and begs Patrick not to be shy.

Despite the comic aspects of Patrick's discomfiture, this and later scenes with Luis where Luis expresses his hopeless love have an oddly tender and touching quality.

From when Patrick tries to murder Luis, the book becomes darker and more relentless as the body-count mounts inexorably. Patrick has already announced once, in a restaurant, "My life is a living hell," but no one responds.[50] He has had a sort of breakdown where he staggers around town, "sweating and moaning and pushing people out of the way, foam pouring out of my mouth . . ."[51] He shoplifts a ham, eats it, throws it up and meets some friend from Wall Street who greets him as "Kinsley". "I belch into his face, my eyes rolling back into my head, greenish bile dripping in strings from my bared fangs."[52] The man is unfazed which suggests that either, once again, Patrick's narrative is seriously askew, or that the legendary tolerance of New Yorkers for terminal weirdness is well deserved.

Patrick kills a sharpei, he kills an old gay man, he hires whores and tortures them. He endures a nightmare Christmas, describing shops crammed with "bookends and lightweight luggage, electric shoepolishers and heated towel-stands and silver-plated carafes" and so on and on in passages reminiscent of Nicole Diver's celebrated consumer binge in *Tender Is the Night*.[53] Evelyn's Christmas party involves guests wearing antlers on their heads and bar-tender elves singing "O Tannenbaum". The pressure mounts.

The following summer he kills a broker he envies, Paul Owen, dining with him first under the name Marcus Halberstam, which is who Owen thinks he is anyway. Imitating the victim's voice he leaves a message on the answering machine saying that Owen has gone to London. After a revoltingly explicit ax murder he puts Paul's body in a sleeping-bag, drags it past the night doorman and down the block. He runs into two friends, one of whom asks him what the general rules for wearing a white dinner jacket are. Is any reader still taking him seriously? He next kills an ex-girlfriend from college, Bethany, in a fit of furious jealousy. He nails her to the floor with a nail-gun. We learn a little of Patrick's background from Bethany: the fact that he is independently wealthy and doesn't have to work, only doing so because "I want to fit in".[54] Patrick's psychological profile is in general, so slight and muddled as to deliberately reject the pleas of all the Norman Mailers of fiction for an "inner life".

After each of the major killings—those of the black bum Al, Bethany and the several in the chapter "Chase, Manhattan"—there follows, either immediately or very shortly afterwards, an extremely strange, bland analysis of pop music. Al's murder is followed by a chapter on Genesis, Bethany's by a chapter on Whitney Houston and the mass murders in "Chase, Manhattan" by one on Huey Lewis and the News.[55] The change in tone is so marked, so extreme that at first it seems impossible that "Patrick", not known for organized thinking has "written" them. Written in the style of middlebrow AOR rock journalism they use the first person so any straightforward reading of the text would assume that they were indeed intended to have been "written" by Patrick. However their entire presence is so at odds with Patrick's narrative performance that one is tempted to read them as further evidence for the non-reality, the not-thereness of Patrick, as they seem to indicate, through the narrative voice, an entirely different personality. The language is sophisticated and emotional—"It's an epic meditation on intangibility, at the same time it deepens and enriches the meaning of the preceeding three albums . . ."—and much concerned with feeling and maturity.[56] Each of the chapters, but particularly the one on Huey Lewis, concerns the maturation of a creative artist and in this there might be a clue as to what comprises the "absence" in *American Psycho*. As previously noted, *Less Than Zero* was postulated against an absent "other", in its case education and the East. *The Rules of Attraction* moved on to deal with and destroy that particular illusion and in this second novel the "absent presence" was adult life. *American Psycho* moves us into that life, into the grown-up world but what is now absent is maturity, growth, successful relationships, marriage and parenthood. Ellis, in these rock-critic chapters, suggests firstly that there is another "personality" in the book, not Patrick, not, except by default, the author, and secondly that this personality defines, particularly in his analysis of the career of Huey Lewis, the absence of personal growth and maturity in the novel as a whole. Towards the climax of *American Psycho* a sort of salvation is offered to Patrick in the form of the love of his devoted secretary, Jean, and although this is an utterly mawkish, clichéd device and intended to be seen as such, nevertheless, it is to Jean that Patrick makes remarks such as, "I just want to have a meaningful relationship with someone special."[57] Some part of his personality is striving towards maturity.

Eventually Paul Owen's fiancée hires a private detective, Donald Kimball, to investigate Owen's disappearance. Patrick is able to offer useful insights along the lines of: "He . . . ate a balanced diet."[58] Paul's diary of course states that he was having dinner with Marcus Halberstam but Marcus has been interviewed and found to be telling the truth when he said he spent the evening at a club with a group of friends, all named and . . . including Patrick Bateman.

Patrick spends the summer with Evelyn in Tim Price's house in East Hampton. It is the classic romantic idyll which swiftly degenerates—all too soon Patrick is microwaving jellyfish—and as such closely reminiscent of Clay's doomed holiday with Blair in *Less Than Zero*. The hopeless and rather sad black comedy of Patrick's relationship with Evelyn is epitomized by his presenting her with a gift-wrapped, chocolate frosted urinal-cake in a restaurant which she gamely, innocently tries to eat, gasping at intervals, "It's just . . . so minty."[59] Patrick then claims to have terminated the relationship (without killing her).

Patrick continues to kill girls and to desecrate their bodies. It is these torture murders and the killing of a child at a zoo that, naturally, attracted most critical attention, but in fact Patrick is a thoroughly democratic killer and by the end of the book the body-count, by my reckoning stands at thirty-three and covers the entire cross-section of race, class, age and gender in New

York society. At one point he takes two prostitutes to Paul Owen's "ridiculous-looking condo", tortures and kills them there. In blood he scrawls the words "I AM BACK" on the wall above the faux-cowhide panelling and follows them with a "scary drawing" which he says "looks that this"[60]. A blank space follows.

The novel now rapidly approaches its climax. The sex murders become more extreme and Patrick claims to torture a girl to death with a starving rat. These killings are robotically described: "I'm wearing a Joseph Abboud suit, a tie by Paul Stuart, shoes by J. Crew, a vest by someone Italian and I'm kneeling on the floor beside a corpse, eating the girl's brain, gobbling it down, spreading Grey Poupon over hunks of the pink, fleshy meat."[61] Real murderers *have* been known to behave in such ways towards their victims but the way this is presented is such an extreme manifestation of blanket blank that it can only be read as a parodically hyperbolic comment on affectlessness and a further destabilizing of Patrick's competence as a narrator. Boundaries are being eroded. Even if we believe it to be remotely possible that someone might try to grind a woman into meat patties and cook her, sobbing all the while, "I just want to be loved," we can only respond, in this context, with sick hilarity.[62] "I guess you walk a very thin line when you try and write about a serial killer in a very satirical way," says Ellis. "There's this new sensitivity. You cannot risk offending anyone."[63]

In the seminal "Chase, Manhattan" chapter Patrick goes completely berserk. He rages through Manhattan killing first a busker, then an Iranian cab-driver and then, just after the narrative goes into the third person, he kills some cops. At this point the novel seems to enter into a parodic version of a cop-killer thriller: "he returns their gunfire from his belly, getting a glimpse of both cops behind the open door of the squad car" and so on.[64] Patrick flees towards Wall Street, shooting a night watchman and then, as the narrative reverts to the first person, he is "safe in the anonymity of my office".[65] A helicopter appears, a SWAT team leaps out, a half-dozen armed men make towards the entrance on the roof, flares are lined up everywhere and Patrick has phoned a friend, Harold Carnes, who predictably, isn't in. Patrick leaves a message confessing to "thirty, forty, a hundred murders".[66] The cops are all approaching, police cars and ambulances surround the base of the building and "night turns into day so fast it's like some kind of optical illusion . . ."[67] It *is* some kind of optical illusion. The next chapter opens with the sane, sensible account of Huey Lewis and the News and the one after that finds Patrick back in bed with Courtney.

This chapter must be the final nail in the coffin of Patrick's credibility. Ellis has already created a most unusual creature, a serial sex-killer who is also, at the same time, prepared to kill absolutely anyone. (In his *Rolling Stone* interview Ellis claims, weirdly: "I thought maybe serial killers would protest the book.") Killers have their *modus operandi* and in "Chase, Manhattan", Ellis compounds the absurdity by making Patrick both a serial-killer and a mass murderer, two quite distinct types who have never been known to co-exist in one person. Mass murderers (Charles Whitman, James Huberty) blow up suddenly, kill as many people as possible in a single incident and are invariably shot by police. Serial killers (Ted Bundy, John Wayne Gacy, the Yorkshire Ripper) are usually sexually motivated, careful and cunning and can remain in action for many years. However, lest anyone actually believes that Patrick Bateman could have continued with his everyday life after this rampage, we are given several more quite distinct opportunities to make up our minds.

One hundred and sixty-one days after he left the two escort girls dead in Paul Owen's apartment, Patrick returns to find the apartment, which is extremely valuable, up for sale. A real-estate agent, "distressingly *real*-looking"[68] and a yuppie couple are present. There is no trace of "the torrents of blood and gore that washed over the apartment". The place stinks of roses. There are dozens of bouquets. After Patrick has asked about Paul Owen, the estate agent warns him to leave, saying, "Don't make any trouble." Can it be possible that a dreadful double murder was concealed for the sake of a grasping real-estate sale?

Patrick runs into Harold Carnes, the person to whom he made his confession on an answering machine. During the conversation Carnes manages to address Patrick as "Davies" and as "Donaldson" and apparently believes that the message about "Bateman" was a joke. "But come on, man, you had one fatal flaw: Bateman's such a bloody ass-kisser, such a brown-nosing goody-goody, that I couldn't fully appreciate it."[69] Carnes also mentions that Evelyn dumped Bateman. Patrick starts to shout, insisting, "I killed Paul Owen. I did it, Carnes. I chopped Owen's fucking head off. I tortured dozens of girls," although, interestingly, he doesn't mention what might have seemed necessary which is that he *is* Bateman. Carnes brushes him off saying that his assertions are simply not possible he—had *dinner* with Paul Owen—*twice*—in London just ten days ago.

This might *finally* seem conclusive but we must still remember the constant confusion of identity throughout the novel.

Lastly a cab-driver attacks Patrick saying that he killed his friend Solly, another cab-driver and that Patrick's picture is on a WANTED poster downtown. Patrick recalls killing a foreign cab-driver, an Armenian he thinks now, not an Iranian, during the chase sequence, but certainly not a Solly. The driver steals Patrick's Rolex and Wayfarers, which is probably all he wanted to do anyway.

Thus we are given three distinct opportunities to weigh up Patrick's narrative, with evidence assembled both for and against its authenticity, as in a court of law. That so many critics accepted Patrick as a "real" killer in the face of all this is a massive testimony to careless reading. However, and this is the most important question raised by Patrick's narrative, what difference does it make whether we believe Patrick committed some, any or all of the murders, or not? We have still had to read all the detailed descriptions of the killings and the effect on us is exactly the same. Whether Patrick's murders are fantasies or not, within fiction, they are all fictional. Thus we are forced by the author to confront the definition and function of fictionality itself.

This leads on to an even more basic question about Patrick's role. At around the time that all this comes to a head, Patrick is being offered pure, untainted love by his secretary, Jean. In a chapter entitled "End of the 1980s" he indulges in some heavy-duty musing about the tragic nature of contemporary reality: "Individuality no longer an issue . . . Fear, recrimination, innocence, sympathy, guilt, waste, failure, grief, were things, emotions that no one really felt anymore. Reflection is useless, the world is senseless. Evil is its only permanence. God is not alive. Love cannot be trusted. Surface, surface, surface was all that anyone found meaning in . . ."[70] This sophomoric philosophizing appears to be delivered seriously, although it is nonsensical placed against the enormity of the crimes Patrick has claimed to have committed. As he talks to Jean about her feelings for him he continues to think, this time about himself: "My personality is sketchy and unformed, my pain is constant and sharp . . . This confession has meant nothing." He also states to himself: "*I simply am not there*",[71] and it is tempting take him at his word. Perhaps the Patrick we know simply does not exist and the person talking to Jean, tentatively accepting her love and experiencing an "epiphany" is another Patrick, the real Patrick, the one who Carnes sees as a "goody-goody", whom Evelyn rejects, who is given to thoughtful, if somewhat cloying considerations of popular music and who kills no one? He and Jean see a baby. "I feel I'm moving towards as well as away from something and anything is possible."[72]

Anything *is* possible. Around this time Patrick, although he seems to have stopped saying he kills people after his conversation with Jean, appears to be going madder and madder. He has started drinking his own urine, laughing at nothing, sleeping under his futon and flossing his teeth constantly. His automated bank teller has started speaking to him and "I was freaked out by the park bench that followed me for six blocks last Monday evening."[73]

Ellis also writes: "And, for the sake of form, Tim Price resurfaces, or at least I'm pretty sure he does."[74] *For the sake of form? I'm pretty sure he does?* With the authenticity of Patrick's narrative in shreds, with Patrick operating as at least two and possibly three personalities and with statements like this one we are forced to ask who is Patrick, really? The "Bateman" known to the guys and to Carnes is seemingly not the person who tells the story of the book. Who *is* Patrick? *I simply am not there.* Is he perhaps Tim Price who vanishes so deeply into the book, whose East Hampton house Patrick stays in and who now re-appears, strangely elusive on the subject of his absence. ("It was . . . surprising" "It was . . . depressing".[75] Where has he been? Inside the book, in Patrick's brain?) Is Patrick one of the *other* guys in the book, fleetingly mentioned, always around? Might Patrick be Paul Owen whose apartment he appropriates? Could he possibly even be . . . Marcus Halberstam?! Who knows? The person who tells the story, who fantasizes about impossible murders does not "exist" in any traditional fictional sense. We might as well consider him a spirit; the *Zeitgeist*, all-yuppie, all-corrupt. Or we could regard him as the sense of humour so notably lacking in his circles, created in Patrick's voice to render black comedy from the intolerable. Patrick is device. He is never the author and at the same time, like all fictional devices, he is always the author.

Much of the frustration felt by critics as they tried to grapple with the book's apparent context stemmed from a vague sense of Patrick's *insubstantiality* as a "character". It was impossible to get to grips with him—because he wasn't really there. Ellis talks of "becoming" Patrick for hours at a time while he was writing and it seems as if while in this state of possession Bateman started to "write" Ellis. Patrick is annihilated in language and it is impossible to tell when the rigid authorial control may have ceded "meaning" to the involuntary forces of language itself. Patrick is "wiped-out" between the two spheres of life, the public and the private. His agony consists of the way his interior life keeps leaking into the public arena only to be inauthenticated, so that he has to reinforce his "self", his "identity", in ever more extreme and violent ways. It is a basic tenet of postmodernism that the public and private spaces of life are being eroded, are blending—blanding—into one hyperreal theatre. It could be that Patrick is annihilated at precisely this juncture, is unable to realize his "self" without a collision of the public and private which then destroys any autonomous "ego". Of course the interplay between the public and private spheres mimics the fictional process itself; an author always extrudes the interior into the public arena. However, in Bateman's case, within the text the juxtaposition and erosion of the public and private worlds seems exceptionally central to his story and accounts for much of Bateman's confusion and incomprehension in relation to the world. He does not understand the boundaries of the appropriate and inappropriate, the acceptable and the unacceptable; his "personality" debouches haphazardly along a spectrum from the most secret and interior desires to the mannered conventions of a highly-sophisticated society. This is post-modernity in process, knowing no limits, uniting desire and entertainment within spectacle. An individual "personality" cannot sustain these contradictions; an individual "personality" in which Id, Ego and Super-Ego go into melt-down is doomed. It is doomed to psychosis, schizophrenia, gibberish non-language—and we see this happening to Patrick before he implodes completely within the text. Patrick *is* a cipher; a sign in language and it is in language that he disintegrates, slips out of our grasp. Patrick is Void. He is the Abyss. He is a textual impossibility, written out, elided until there is no "Patrick" other than the sign or signifier that sets in motion the process that must destroy him and thus at the end the book must go back to its beginnings and start again. This process reveals his invisibility and re-signs him to a circle of hell where he can never find resolution or autonomy in that he "exists" only to disintegrate. Patrick becomes in effect, feminized, excluded from "existing" in language; he is the void, the mystery, the threat of dreadful desires, the uncontrolled libido, the unconscious, the dark side of the moon. As "nothing" Patrick is dangerous. As a person, as a consumer, he cannot exist; he is an impossibility.

American Psycho is what Roland Barthes called a "writerly" text. It invites the reader in to play amongst its games and inconsistencies. Unusually however, unlike most "writerly" texts it is not deeply subversive or dislocating. It has nothing in it of what Barthes termed rapture, "bliss" or *jouissance*. For all the fuss it lacks the "shock, disturbance, even loss, which are proper to ecstasy, to bliss".[76] Texts of bliss are extreme, threatening, they bring us towards death or annihilation; Barthes mentions Georges Bataille. *American Psycho* might seem, superficially, to be such a text but in fact it is not at all. It is far closer to what Barthes termed a "text of pleasure": "the text that comes from culture and does not break with it."[77] Ellis might be very critical of his culture, his text may be an experimentation in many ways but he comes from deep within that culture and cannot be said to pose anything of an anarchic threat towards it. The faults Ellis perceives in contemporary culture come from an old-fashioned, straightforwardly moralistic reading of it. His books present terrible amoral deviations, which, if rectified, would restore to society all the moral values it has lost and would revive a more wholesome dominant culture. Ellis's vision is conformist and conventional. He is skilled at presenting disintegration within postmodernity and his energies are straightforwardly judge-mental and condemnatory. He is denunciatory, a supporter of the status quo and in relation to this it is ironic to what a large extent he has been depicted as some sort of literary tearaway. Insofar as Patrick Bateman is allowed to operate as a unified entity, before his persona is totally shredded, he functions as a rhetorical device, the Devil's Advocate whose consumer manifesto merely highlights what Ellis has referred to as the "spiritual" malaise and ugliness of the eighties. Like David Lynch, Ellis is merely "weird on top" not "wild at heart". Just as in *Twin Peaks* the "identity" or "meaning" of the murderer behaved like language, slipping from signifier to signifier, so Ellis too is inventive, deconstructing within language the existence or "meaning" of *his* fictive murderer. Both Patrick Bateman and "Bob" from *Twin Peaks* through their actions "murder" the order of a moral universe and slide us into postmodern chaos. Behind them lies the conventional nostalgic vision of a lost world where actions were not random, where emotion was authentic and where everything once made sense.

American Psycho should be taken seriously; if it is as blunt and simplistic as its critics claim how have they managed to miss everything of significance within the book? It is an important text. Ellis manages to take his obsession with deindividualization in consumer society to its extreme and demonstrate that Patrick, in his role of ultimate consumer, someone who is composed entirely of inauthentic commodity-related desires *cannot* exist as a person. He is doomed to fragmentation and disintegration.

American Psycho represents all that we mean by Post-Punk or Blank Generation writing in that it is written from deep within consumer culture by an author who has never known anything else and who consequently lacks much of the critical ambivalence and the political disquiet about popular culture evinced by older novelists and theoreticians. At the same time it has its own agenda which is anything but blank. Despite his unease with moral absolutes the author is determined not to flinch from representing that which he undoubtedly condemns. Although Ellis is skilled at representing contemporary society it would seem that, unlike many postmodern theorists, he maintains a belief in a "reality" or morality somewhere beyond the spectacular blandishments of the hyperreal consumer circus. As it seems unlikely that he inclines towards revolutionary politics, it is natural to assume that like David Lynch he might have a vision of some more edenic moral universe, pre-postmodern fragmentation and commodity fetishism. At the same time *American Psycho* is a sophisticated high postmodern text. All the theoretical constituents of postmodern culture are there—the commodity fixation, the focus on image, codes and style, the proliferation of surfaces and the deindividualization of neo-fogey characters who "play" with the past—"I'm pro-family and anti-drug"—and in doing so embody irony and paradox.[78] The text itself participates fully in the "conventions" of postmodern literature: the unreliable narrator, the lack of closure, Eco's "game of irony", double-distancing, a refusal to mirror "reality" and a constant examination of the ways in which fiction is ordered, ever aware of its own status as discourse and construct. Thus *American Psycho* can be seen as a classic text at the end of the high postmodern period and simultaneously as playing its part in the slow emergence of an American renaissance that attempts to transcend these fictional games, and re-establish, from deep within consumer culture, other ways of writing fiction and apprehending American society as it approaches the millennium.

E.Y.

Notes degree zero

Ellis goes west

"Basically I have one feeling . . . the desire to get out of here. And any other feelings I have come from trying to analyse, you know, why I want to go away . . . See, I always feel uncomfortable and I just want to . . . walk out of the room. It's not going to any other place or any other sensation, or anything like that, it's just to get out of 'here' . . ."

Richard Hell

" 'I want to go back,' Daniel says, quietly, with effort. 'Where?' I ask, unsure.
There's a long pause that kind of freaks me out and Daniel finishes his drink and fingers the sunglasses he's still wearing and says, 'I don't know. Just Back.' "

Less Than Zero

Whereas Elizabeth Young's discussion of Bret Easton Ellis in the present volume has centred around the novelist's ability to embody the "postmodern sensibility", here I am interested in placing *Less Than Zero* alongside other versions of Los Angeles—the city of sounds rather than angels. In moving from the art-school neurosis of the East Coast's Talking Heads to the bleached-blond melodies of the Beach Boys, Ellis takes us into the world of California Screamin'—West Coast anxieties that run like fault-lines through images of LA.

From its title and epigrams onwards, *Less Than Zero* comes saturated in music. On MTV and the radio, in clubs and conversations, adorning T-shirts and bedroom walls, pop music acts like the novel's Greek chorus—a running commentary, apparently at random yet always appropriate. The characters' affluence and lifestyle—all Porsches, jacuzzis and cocaine—places them in a context that is closer to that of the musician than that of the usual pop consumer. Instead of presenting us with the standard star-gazing pop fan, Ellis's conflation of audience and artist opens up the novel to a wider discussion of youth culture and Californian affluence.

Los Angeles is a city that is represented in books and in films, but is usually done so as being faceless, identity-less. Apart from some familiar icons—the HOLLYWOOD sign—it is a city that is defined through names, rather than visual images—Sunset Strip, Beverly Hills, Hollywood Boulevard. Writers as diverse as Alison Lurie (*The Nowhere City*), James Ellroy (*The Big Nowhere*) and Mike Davis (*City of Quartz*) have all defined LA through its sense of absence—a place where there is no *there* there.

This goes some way to explaining why the city has perhaps best been captured by Europeans: the English-educated Raymond Chandler, David Hockney, Wim Wenders (*The State of Things*)—artists all who encapsulate the aesthetics of the LA Law—the inalienable right to corruption, comfort and the cinema.

Yet *Less Than Zero* features no Europeans, and only Clay is allowed to present himself with the distance of the outsider. The novel's location is as fragmented as its narrative, set in parties, clubs, sushi bars and cafés. These settings are linked by car journeys rather than any real sense of place; a spatial blankness which, as Elizabeth Young points out, mirrors the characters' ethical emptiness.

Ellis's LA is a void filled with commodities: cars, clothes, chemicals and bootleg cassettes of Spielberg's *Temple of Doom* (price, $400). Characterization is mediated through brand names—BMWs and black 501s—whilst music is reduced again to names—names of bands, names of clubs, names on T-shirts. Yet rather than merely dismissing this technique as Ellis pointing to the "logo-ification" of West Coast culture—a kind of saturation name-dropping—it is possible to see how the book organizes and juxtaposes these logos in such way as to provide an index for LA's displaced identity. This sense of being at one remove does not necessarily entail a distance from pop. Indeed a brief survey of Californian music could suggest that it is its very essence.

Warren Zevon, that self-styled Werewolf of American New Wave, has a song entitled "Desperados Under the Eaves", a truly haunting song that places its narrator in the Hollywood Hawaiian Hotel, listening to the air conditioner hum. The song ends with harmonies from a Who's Who of seventies LA musicians.

This particular piece of music can be seen as encapsulating the distinctive sound of West Coast pop—harmonies that suggest a search *for* harmony, the yearning, longing sound of California dreaming identifying itself as the hum of air conditioning. The innocence of the Beach Boys, the outlaw chic of The Eagles, are relocated as happy hour self-pity. The song's irony introduces another theme pertinent to Ellis's Los Angeles—the proximity of comfort and disaster, the narrator predicting that he will still have to pay his motel bill even if the building slides into the ocean.

The co-existence of ominous portents and plush materialism suggests that the key to the myth of LA is to be found in its fears. Nathaniel West springs instantly to mind—his pseudonym embodying the desire to Go West, his car-crash death warning of the dangers of doing so. His 1930s novel *The Day of the Locusts* seems seminal: his hero's painting is called "The Burning of Los Angeles", the book's climax is the riot of voyeuristic mid-Westerners who find themselves excluded from the pleasure-dome of cinema. Californian comfort is threatened not so much by Marxism as it is by the movies, its fears seem grounded in the frustrated quest for pleasure rather than the specific drives of politics. Neil Young's "Revolution Blues", for example, from *On the Beach* is a black comedy inspired by Charles Manson rather than, say, the Watts uprising or the Berkeley student riots.

The shadows cast over the city are the potential brutality of

West Coast culture as well as those of nature—Manson-style serial killings, AIDS and overdoses. Whilst the deep south's TV preachers re-state the social as the sinful, Hollywood's disasters are either rendered in terms of the financial (Cimino's *Heaven's Gate*) or within a chain of scandals and deaths that stretches from Fatty Arbuckle to John Belushi's overdose in the Château Marmont.

Which is not to suggest that Los Angeles is just Hollywood or California some wealthy vacuum, but that representations of the West Coast seem inevitably to combine dark intimations of disaster with the "sun, sea and tax revolts" image of the city and consumer paradise.

If LA offers a vision of affluent apocalypse, one need look no further for its soundtrack than that most derided of bands, The Eagles. Their "Hotel California" is symptomatic of the state's threatening comforts, the singer wondering to himself if he is in heaven or if he's in hell. Like Ellis himself, The Eagles speak to a condition of imprisoned luxury, a world where you can check out anytime you like, but you can never leave. The very status of the song as a kind of hippy "Our Tune" (and one that is wonderfully parodied in Bill Bryson's *Lost Continent*), seems to underscore its point—it is trapped in our consciousness as much as The Eagles are trapped in their paradise, potentially pleasurable, frighteningly inescapable.

Such portrayals of California are often accused of being overly sympathetic, the chic gloss of West Coast music seeming to hide a subtext in which the dole-queue kids in record stores are being asked to feel sorry for the misunderstood and unhappy rich.

Indeed one thinks of Roland Barthes's comment that, "the most reactionary remark of human history, the alibi of all exploitations, [is] that "money doesn't make happiness". Why should we feel sympathy for the cocaine kids when most of our worries are about phone bills rather than therapy fees? The answer, I would suggest, lies in the specific contradictions of California, an area which might be more fruitfully explored by a comparison of John Lahr and Joan Didion.

John Lahr's essay on John Gregory Dunne and Joan Didion

(in *Automatic Vaudeville*) argues that they could only be considered good writers in a "society indifferent to literature". With the knee-jerk moralism of Leavis, or the essentially English anti-Americanism of Orwell, Lahr condemns California for: "the general absence of community, the moral stupor, the greedy self-aggrandizement, and the emotional impoverishment that characterize and enchant the place." Whilst Lahr's critique might at first seem an appropriate response to the valium-drawled indifference of Clay's narration, it *does* miss the pluralism and diversity of the Californian landscape. The gay community, for example, appears to prefer the relative freedom of San Francisco to Lahr's idyllic Leavisite "community".

Lahr seems so fixated with a cliché of LA that he wilfully misreads Didion's work. His reaction to her "Holy Water" essay mentions "the pampered landscape through which she moves", while her provocative descriptions of Californian swimming pools (not as symbols of affluence but of control over the environment) soon have him reaching for his Brecht.

The point that needs emphasizing here is that Didion's "Holy Water" explicitly rejects this idea of a "pampered landscape". Her childhood recollections of the Sacramento Valley focus on summers of dry wells, winters of floods and dynamited levees. "Even now", she writes, California is not "all that hospitable to extensive settlement". Her work re-introduces the significance of fires, earthquakes and aridity amongst the shimmering West Coast surface: "The apparent ease of Californian life is an illusion, and those who believe the illusion real live here in only the most temporary way." In place of Lahr's "moral stupor", Didion offers us subtropical rain, the Santa Ana wind and the consequent winds: "Los Angeles is the weather of catastrophe, of apocalypse."[1]

Put simply, there is a material basis for the apocalyptic strain in *Less Than Zero*, a geographical reality that constantly informs the novel's moral panic. Like the drought which acts as the protagonist in Polanski's film *Chinatown*, the environment is as much a prime mover of Californian culture as is its affluence. Clay hears songs on the radio about earthquakes, there are fallen palm trees outside his home, winds threaten to break windows, the rains begin and he reads "about the houses falling, slipping down the hills in the middle of the night".[2] There are rattle-snakes out in Palm Springs and coyotes run through the streets and canyons near Clay's house having killed neighbourhood cats. It is this mixture of envy-inducing wealth within a terror-producing environment that prevents *Less Than Zero* and California from seeming populated with rich-kid self-indulgence. There are not many earthquakes in Hammersmith, and brushfires are rare in Headingley.

All of which is to say that it is the difference in material conditions that go some way to explaining the double-edged nature of Californian wealth. The notion of trauma and the idea of risk are more than a Los Angeles pose—they are literally the facts of life, and may explain why California contains both Hollywood *and* the Silicon Valley.

In Ellis's world disaster is transformed into spectacle, his characters possessing a fascination with car-crashes that rivals even that of J.G. Ballard. Richard Hell of the Blank Generation said to Lester Bangs in 1976: "The thing is that people don't have to *try* not to feel anything anymore; they just *can't* . . ."[3] Clay echoes precisely these sentiments: "Nothing makes me happy. I like nothing." His theory is that it is "less painful if I don't care", his only desire "to see the worst". Hence the litany of snuff movies, gang rape, homosexual prostitution and corpse-gazing.

This use of horror can be read as the impossibility of irony, a technique that seems to come easier to the East Coast than to the West. Clay sees the alphabet written on a friend's wall, but notices that "most of the letters aren't in order". The propriety of literacy is secondary to the tortured need for expression. The sarcasm of Randy Newman's "I Love LA" is lost on Ellis's characters, most of whom could well be the target of his song. This refusal to engage with the playful aspects of pop is obviously connected to the West Coast's passion for American hardcore. Its extreme noise terror is seen as the most authentic rejoinder to the image of LA as affluent suburbia. Bands like

Black Flag raise murderers like Manson to cult status—the most authentic director of a Hollywood splatter-film. Hardcore's drive is the furious flight from irony, the search for the sound of LA.

For a novel that is often commented upon for its dead-pan prose, *Less Than Zero* is remarkably fluent in its use of pop culture. Though its characters may be stereotypes, Ellis organizes them in such a way as to disrupt any bland generalizations about the "blank generation". The Valley Girls, the Californian punks, the Eastern preppy, the Yuppies and the brat-pack—all suggest the potential for a fluid-mobility amongst the surfaces of the postmodern world which he defines.

The novel's use of music reflects these cut-up clichés: its title comes from Costello, its epigraphs juxtapose X and Led Zeppelin. Clay's memories of The Eagles, Fleetwood Mac and Tom Petty are mixed in with LA punk and various appropriations of British pop. Whilst English rock writers often snigger at the way in which Americans get styles wrong (the Pistols' reception in LA, the Beatles' imitators in the sixties), or else moralize about the Stateside corruption of musicians (Rod Stewart in the seventies, Lisa Stansfield now), it is important to remember that it is precisely this re-working and re-location of genre that allows pop music the space in which to develop. *Less Than Zero* uses music not only as its soundtrack, but as a form that can produce the contradictory, the unexpected, amongst the scratch-video lives of its protagonists.

California comes steeped in preconceptions and clichés, it exists in our imagination through its names and its narratives. In connecting itself with the very heterogeneity of this culture, *Less Than Zero* paradoxically offers us a fresh insight into it. Within its tired indifference and blasé-faire name-dropping, Clay's voice actually speaks to the Californian *difference*. Precisely nowhere, new and unknowable—California: Über Alles.

G.C.

A city on the kill

Joel Rose's lower east side

> "At any rate, all these features—the strange new feeling
> of an absence of inside and outside, the bewilderment
> and loss of spatial orientation in Portman's hotels, the
> messiness of an environment in which things and people
> no longer find their 'place'—offer useful symptomatic
> approaches to the nature of postmodern hyper-space
> without giving us any model or explanation of the thing
> itself."
>
> Fredric Jameson

> "If there is a New York sound, it's probably the sound
> of people looking for cheap apartments."
>
> Vernon Reid

When a rock band decides to call itself The Dead Kennedys,
their name conjures up a vision that takes the aborted nature of
its ideals as read. JFK's hopeful promise, his speeches and
charisma, are already assumed to be asphyxiated: The Dead
Kennedys were an invitation to the post-mortem of the American
Dream.

In choosing to entitle his novel *Kill the Poor* (after a DK song),
Joel Rose is signalling his distance not only from Kennedy
idealism, but also from post-punk rebellion. He is taking us even
further down the road to nowhere, into the realm of post-
nihilism, a world where referential parody and agit-pop polemic
merge into a form of desperate indifference. Whereas The Dead
Kennedys' song was a battle-cry of frustrated oppression, Rose's

novel is the death-rattle of such chic negativity. If punk's celebrated epigram was that they had No More Heroes, Rose and his writer-wife, Catherine Texier, respond by insisting that now we have No More Anti-Heroes. From New Wave to No Wave, the Sex Pistols prophesied that we would have No Future: Joel Rose's writing shrugs its shoulders in agreement, the difference being that the Pistols' future is Rose's present.

So to the book itself. Is it anything more than a suicide note from a society suffering from a terminal malaise? Or is it a form of liberating misanthropy, its relentless aggression offering us some cathartic release from the grind of postmodern paranoia?

The answer, I would suggest, lies not so much in the writer's attitude to his subject, but in the sites and the cities that he chooses to locate his subject. If *Kill the Poor* smacks of murder and mystery, the question is not so much Whodunnit as Wheredunnit—geography as suspense, the criminality of our surroundings.

The story of the book, such as it is, focuses on one Jo-Jo Peltz, a down-at-heel street news-vendor whose life revolves around his struggle to find stable surroundings for his wife and baby amongst the ravaged tenement blocks of Manhattan's Lower East Side. He projects himself as a soldier on the front line, fighting a constant battle against the muggers, dealers, junkies, winos, pimps, gangs, thieves, whores, arsonists and spooks who populate the Alphabet City where he lives. There runs throughout the constant fear of mobocracy, the threat of the ethnic melting pot boiling over, the menace of anarchy waiting to happen.

Such urban jungle horror is familiar enough terrain. As far back as Walt Whitman, writers have pointed to the "roaring, tumbling, bustling, stormy, turbulent" cityscape of New York. Upton Sinclair's *The Jungle* still finds a contemporary resonance among artists as diverse as Grand Master Flash and Spike Lee, whilst the photographic essays of Geoffrey Biddle's *Alphabet City* still testify to the potency of the image of the city in decay. Waldo Frank's *City Block*, Albert Halper's *Union Square* and Ann Petry's *The Street* have all documented the impact of life in the naked city, employing an uncompromising realism to underscore the harsh brutality of the dense and dislocated metropolis. How this genre works, of course, is to show the city as defining its characters, moulding its inhabitants, giving birth to a person who it then deforms. The protagonists of urban realism are always its victims, slaves to their environment with the plot operating as their struggle for liberation. The city is the place where human depravity is constructed, it is the background against which we read the motivations for the characters' actions.

Though very obviously products of the city, the characters of the urban realist novel of, say, Dreiser and Dos Passos remained just that—characters. Always invested with some implicit nobility, their struggle with their surroundings enables them to rise above those surroundings with stoic heroism. They may be products of the environment, but they are always the performers of the novel.

What is remarkable about Rose's novel is that he places his "characters" in such a relation to the city, that they barely function as characters at all. He conflates a social vision of the city with the formal aesthetics of the novel itself, so that an individual's history, narrative or persona seem to get lost amidst the all-consuming presence of the Lower East Side. Whereas it was commonplace for the 1930s realist to talk about the impersonality of the city, a place of collective solitude, in the 1990s it seems that it is precisely the personality of the city that poses the threat to our individual psyches.

The opening of the novel points to just such a paradigm: "My daughter goes to daycare directly across the street from where I live. Three doors away is the temple where my grandmother married. Six doors away was my grandfather's tailor shop. Across the street is where my mother was born."[1]

Rather than the conventional lamentations about the city eroding family networks, this passage suggests that the city is the only reminder of how the family functions. The city is not so much a backdrop to familial relations, it has effectively taken their place. The daughter, mother and grandparents only exist insofar as they can be allocated a place among the city's network; their very being is *legitimized* by the all-pervasive memory of place, location and space.

The drug addicts too function not so much as rap-style casualties of urban jungle fever, but more as puns for the city's ever-expanding vocabulary. Junkies refer to using cocaine and heroin respectively as going "uptown" or "downtown" whilst "between C & D" (incidentally the name of Rose and Texier's literary magazine) refers both to the alphabetized avenues as well as to the drug-fuelled transition between Coke & Dope. The relationship of junkie to city is not merely that of inhabitant to environment: it is the relationship of addiction itself. The hop-heads' bustle is the city's fix; their mainlining speaks as much to the arteries of freeways and subways as it does to the relation between needle and arm. The relationship between drugs and city is conflated to such an extent that the very language of the book is all to some extent a running gag, a *double entendre* shared between the city and its smack:

> "I looked at little newborn Constance in my arms, and he says, 'It's so small,' and I say, 'Yeah, blessed be, It's amazing that all the parts work.' His eyes narrow. He says, 'What?'
>
> I said, 'You heard me. *Works!*'
>
> 'Works? Two bucks,' he says, and makes a little sign with his thumb and forefinger like a plunger on a syringe.'[2]

Infantile innocence and junkie cynicism are not so much a point of dramatic contrast, as they are the occasion for the city to deliver its punch-line. Junk, in language and in chemicals, feeds the habit of the city; the actual users are as disposable as their syringes, they exist only to satiate the cravings of their surroundings. If the novel refuses to produce any anti-heroes, it *does* insist on supplying us with an endless source of heroin.

Whereas in classic urban realism ethnicity functions as a point of definition, in *Kill the Poor* it operates as yet another focus for disjunction. Rather than signifying a specific cultural heritage, it works to illuminate the absence of such difference, casting its characters as an amorphous mass whose individual racial identities are irrelevant to the homogeneous metropolis:

> "Annabelle is right. Yolanda is black. She helps Velma with the school. And Sequina, she's black. And Vanessa, she's brown, half-and-half. And Milo, he's Italo-American, like canned spaghetti. And Tana, Portuguese and Uruguayan, Mara is Latvian. And Mr Ben and Mr Hans and Tao and Jenny, and on, and on . . . all American."[3]

The inhabitant's race does not furnish them with any sense of self, nor the narrator with any respect for their differences. If in the novels of Richard Wright or James T. Farrell, the city functioned as the informing background to the lives of the protagonists, then Rose effectively reverses this. It is the people who form the backdrop to the city's personality. Their families are merely its memory, their drug abuse nothing more than its diction, their ethnicity no more than the city's local colour:

> "My neighborhood reminds me of South America, not North. The brick tenements are steamy tin shacks. Yesterday I noticed that a shantytown is being constructed on Sixth Street. Where the city knocked down all those abandoned buildings and dope houses, now people come with cardboard and tin and build huts."[4]

The people of the novel are not so much products of the city as they are refugees within it. They exist at the city's discretion, relegated to the wings while the metropolis basks in (vain) glory centre-stage.

Throughout the novel there is constant chatter about a movie being filmed in the neighbourhood, the neighbours themselves all vying to become extras in it. This is a pivotal motif, an acknowledgement that location is more forcefully central than the population. The people of Alphabet City aspire to being superfluous to the cinematic demands of the city, becoming an *extra* would be a legitimization of what they already are. Without the confirmation of cinema they are all "the man in the street"; what the movie offers them is the chance to become "a ghost in the machine", a shadow in the city's shimmering light: "Benny and Segundo are standing on the roof and Steven Spielberg's across the street building his set . . . I recognize it. This is what I been looking for. This is what I want. A neighborhood. Right."[5]

The neighbourhood only exists, is only *experienced* as being real, when it is constructed as one of the fictions of Hollywood. Cinema brings with it the promise of cohesion, the imposition of narrative, the resurrection of history. The very notion of an authentic community is thus itself fictitious, a symptom of our estrangement from our environment rather than its cure. A song such as Tom Waits's *In the Neighborhood* is less an evocation of communal bustle, and more an admission of its absence. What both Rose and Waits explore is a kind of instant nostalgia, a vision of the past that comes packaged in the artefacts of the present. Writing about a visit to Frank Gehry's house, Fredric Jameson expands on the contemporary artist's inability to re-create history without invoking our estrangement from it: "We must proceed on to the most archaic parts of the house itself— the older surviving stairs, bedrooms, bathrooms, and closets—to see not merely what it was that had to be even partially transformed but also whether that traditional syntax and grammar is susceptible to Utopian transformation."[6]

He proceeds to point out that one experiences the remnants of the past not as themselves, but *as an image of themselves*— speaking from the hermetically sealed vacuum of the museum rather than the vibrant recollection of yesteryear: ". . . it is a present reality that has been transformed into a simulacrum by the process of wrapping, or quotation, and has thereby become not historical but historicist—an allusion to a present out of real history which might just as well be a past removed from real history. The quoted room therefore also has affinities with what in film has come to be called *la mode retro*, or nostalgia film: the past as fashion plate and glossy image."[7]

This is precisely the statis that Rose's characters occupy. They neither "exist" in their place nor lament its loss. Indeed the only access that they have to a sense of place are the crumbs that fall from the table of Hollywood. They are all extras, transients and passers-by: the star of the movie-within-the-novel is the city itself. Jo-Jo's apartment is in effect the city's dressingroom, his tenement block's dereliction a cheap make-up job, his yearning nostalgia an already-written script: "Steve's [Spielberg] tenement looks absolutely real, more real than any of the honest-to-goodness tenements around the neighborhood. At one point sixty artists were up on the scaffolding, painting the facade brick by brick. The detail is fantastic. You gotta admire it."[8]

Jo-Jo's admiration is not misplaced, for the magical dissolve of the cinema seems to be the only force of (un)reality to compete with the neither here nor there hyper-space of the city.

If, in the novels of Bret Easton Ellis, place begins to function as character, Rose's writing takes this idea to its ultimate extreme. The city, rich in character, saturated with its own narrative, allows for a far more intimate exchange with the reader than either the marriage of Jo-Jo Peltz or the neighbourly relations that surround it. The city is all-pervasive and irresistible, with not just a name but a gender of its own: "They just reversed what they had. Brook-lyn, Lyn-brook."[9] The people must identify their place yet cannot experience it. The result is that both their geography and their personalities are left impoverished.

When there is a fire in the apartment block, it is the architecture itself that is in possession of the novel's passionate warmth and burning desire: "The firemen have axed everything in sight . . . On the stove there is a pot of beans. Curiously, the pot is not scorched. The beans are warm, cooked in the blaze."[10] The occupiers on the other hand are seen as withdrawn and inanimate, *in*humanely afraid that they may be accused of being the arsonist—the tenement's rapist.

Rose's achievement is to bring about a reversal of "natural" surroundings and cultural inhabitants. The buildings are never represented as being of brick, aluminium or glass (which they might be if considered part of nature), but are cafés, sleaze-bars, brothels, delis and temples. The city itself is thus the desire for God, sex, shelter, work and drugs. It is the people who are "naturalized", emphatically composed of flesh and blood, dismissively prone to frailty and decay. The physicality of the characters—that which should separate them from their artificial dwellings—can only be translated in terms of that artifice:

> "She says she tastes the tenement dust on me, the dirt, the old and acid, the same dust I tasted downstairs. She says she tastes New York."[11]

The problem, the novel suggests, is not so much that man is alone in the city, but that he is *surrounded* by himself—his own desires and aspirations, his histories and ambitions. Unlike the process of consumption, where a person absorbs an object into his or her life, the city absorbs us into the magical life of its presence. For a man inside the city, his self is not inside his body, but around him, outside him, *extra*neous to him. Far from being alienated in the city, the people exist as its aura. Regardless of gender or ethnic identity, the characters in *Kill the Poor* are all "street-walkers". Whilst New York creates an intertextual sketch of its own future, its inhabitants are condemned to the shadowy hinterland of what will someday be real. Their actuality is the city's disposability—"Kill the Poor" is not a call to action, it is merely an acknowledgement of an on-going process: "Now is there any confusion as to what has happened here?"

"I live in a building, actually two buildings (tenement twins, one-hundred-year-old sisters), where the landlord abandoned his property . . . In the dim past, one building, invaded by junkies, had a fire. The top two floors burn up and the last few tenants vacate . . . Live to let die."[12]

Rose's characters do not in this sense even live in the city. Rather they are to be found *in-between* the metropolis and the space it invokes, suspended between the definite and the infinite.

Fredric Jameson once again underscores this idea when he writes:

> "This latest mutation in space—postmodern hyperspace —has finally succeeded in transcending the capacities of the individual human body to locate itself, to organize its immediate surroundings perceptually, and cognitively to map its position in a mappable external world."[13]

This notion of inbetweenness, this socio-spatial breakdown, can be seen to operate around the "newness" of New York. The "New" of the city suggests its reliance upon the moment, the urgent need to re-cycle and abandon. Yet it also brings with it a sense of fresh foundations and the promise of a fixed future. New York thus occupies the schizoid position of having to *preserve* its drive towards *renewal*. The city must both re-invent and conserve, its very fabric being held together by the permanent transformation of itself.

The impossibility of maintaining this imbalance, of accommodating the conflicting demands of spatial turn-over and social roots, goes to the heart of Rose's novel. Whodunnit? Who does kill the poor? The answer, as I have suggested, is not a Who but a Where. If the city is the main character of the book, it must also be the culprit. By teasing its inhabitants into the open spaces of its future, yet refusing them the legitimization of their present, the city constructs both the solitary panic of agoraphobia and the collective overload of claustrophobia.

In his portrayal of the city's slippery presence Rose effectively brings to life a state that has been described by Michel Foucault as "the heterotopia". With his usual punning precision, Foucault's term cleverly suggests how the literal "nowhere" of Utopia is not an absolute, but a diverse function of our heterogeneous present:

> "The space in which we live, which draws us out of ourselves, in which the erosion of our lives, our time and our history occurs, the space that claws and gnaws at us, is also, in itself a heterogeneous space."[14]

In other words, each "nowhere" has its own peculiarities, every space differs significantly from any others. This is why Rose's novel seems to me so significant; for it does not merely suggest the barren neon and fragmented psyches of the city (as in Paul Auster's *New York Trilogy*), but it is also specific as to the characteristics of such absence. In focusing on the amorphous incorporation of gender, race and drugs into Alphabet City, Rose dramatizes their sacrificial exclusion from their location. Rather than treating its characters as either heroes or victims, the novel's decision to minimalize their impact actually mirrors their status. "The heterotopia is capable of juxtaposing in a single real place several spaces, several sites that are in themselves incompatible", writes Foucault. Rose's achievement is to pinpoint New York's several incompatible sites, without either romanticizing the people or universalizing the spatial tyranny of the city. Life and love *do* continue, but they never threaten to transcend: emotions *are* experienced, yet never as catharsis. Not here, not in the unique nowhere of New York's Lower East Side:

> "It doesn't bother Scarlet that Ike and Yves, Mewie and Negrito are all gay. 'Gay people can love each other,' she contends, 'but it's fucking hard living in this suckhole building.' "[15]

Difference is certainly acknowledged, but it is only done so with a note of indifference. Rose's liberals are grudging and impatient, their "heroics" truculent and terminally pre-occupied.

And so Jo-Jo ends his narrative appropriately enough in prison, falsely accused of torching the fire that brought down his block. His innocence is so immaterial to the city's cops as to be not worth "proving" within the novel; to foreground any injustice would be to imply the possibility of justice in the background. It is as though Jo-Jo's fate is so inevitable as to be not worth dignifying with dramatic tension—it is as "natural" as swearing, a throwaway life in the day of the city:

> " 'What you in for, bro?' the E boy asks me.

> I say it doesn't matter. 'Don't ask. I'm innocent.'
> 'Ain't we all, blood,' he says. 'Ain't we motherfuckin'
> all.' "[16]

Jo-Jo's right—it doesn't matter, not in fact nor in fiction. His nonchalant pronouncement of his innocence is no sooner spoken than it is rapidly subsumed by the amorphous population of the prison. The individual "I" is translated into the indistinguishable "all", the very term "blood" signalling our common physicality rather than any real intimacy.

Prison is one more realm of the heterotopia—a space whose function is quite different from that of the city, yet is still experienced as ego dissolution and the triumph of place:

> "Where I come from we got an expression to cover a
> guy in your position, Joe.'
> 'Yeah, what's that, motherfucker?'
> 'Scrotum to the wall!' "[17]

Jo-Jo's character was thin to begin with, in prison we can only assume that it will be stretched to breaking point, as burnt-out as the remnants of his apartment. "The End" of the novel is more of a fading away than a finale, the narrative as exhausted as its protagonist.

What we are left with then is a vast absence, a feeling that characters cannot even be realized, never mind liberated. If the city *is* their personality, and its future their destiny, how are we to negotiate any point of empathy towards them? Rose's strategy it would seem is to match form and content in such a way that his prose acts out the exclusion of people from their environment. This is what things are like, he seems to be saying, why bother dignifying them with a false depth.

Yet this is not the whole story. The novel's rhetoric is so relentless that it is easy to forget the significance of "the poor" in its title. Poverty is so all-pervasive that it becomes the book's norm: Rose's characters are given no point of contrast to remind us of their impoverishment, nor the diction to describe their condition. Poverty is as poverty does, and the book self-consciously toys with just how easy it is to read its economic conditions as natural. Our sense of the characters as insubstantial is precisely their experience of themselves: we approach "the city that never sleeps" with the same insomniacal dread as they do.

This is where Rose's impact is to be found—his ability to evoke the specific conditions of urban poverty by allying himself with the perpetrator rather than its victims. Without recourse to didacticism or polemic, *Kill the Poor* mimes the effects of the cityscape that it inhabits.

In his vision of the heterotopia and its attendant anti-sentimentality, Joel Rose explores the Lower East Side by casting it in the shadow of the New York lights. Consciously myopic, partially *cited*, this is the price you pay for being "a part of it", for being on top of the heap of New York's nowhere.

G.C.

Library of the ultravixens

The Lost Phallus–Where did *I Put It?*—*in the works of Tama Janowitz, Mary Gaitskill and Catherine Texier*

"Slipping through the stitch of virtue,
Into crime"
                    (Djuna Barnes, *The Book of Repulsive Women*)*

i. Bohemians and Bad Girls
It is the 1950s and our heroine is sitting in the kitchen. Outside, a bomb-shelter broods in the backyard. She is watching her mother who, in a flowered pinny and turban is doing a hundred things at once: mixing the Bisto gravy, worming the cat, sudsing the smalls, dashing away with a smoothing iron, all because she's W.O.M.A.N. Her daughter's never going to grow up like that . . . In a trice she's become a pouting, blonde dolly-bird in a crochet mini-dress, bowling down the King's Road in a pink sports car. Next, she's in a kitchen, hopelessly stirring mung beans in some rustic commune, bra-less and unencumbered in trailing cheese-cloth. Another click and she's up at the barricades screaming for abortion on demand, wages for housework and lesbian rights. This year she's wearing dungarees and leather and has a crew-cut. Suddenly she's gone again. She re-appears striding on impossible stilettos through a hushed, open-plan office. Her make-up is discreet, her hair streaked, her suit expensive; she exudes power. She has terrific legs. Then she's back in a kitchen again, as big as a loft. It *is* a loft. She clutches a winsome child dressed in overly interesting jeans and she's doing a hundred

things at once. She looks confused. We've come a long way haven't we, baby? And it's all been so *quick*. All these common, iconic, representations of women with all the pressures they embody, can have flashed past our heroine before she has even reached middle age. They are indicative of the cultural schizophrenia that has engulfed women as they try to appease a contradictory pantheon of contemporary imperatives. The impossibility of internalizing such seismic social change within a short period has led to a cluster of warring responses within literature, feminism and feminist literary theory.

The books discussed in this chapter were all published during the 1980s. To a very large extent, they ignore the feminist movement, at least in any overt way. It became fashionable at this time to, post-haste, proclaim post-feminism, as if troublesome and cataclysmic social change had been assimilated as smoothly as Jello. The success of writers such as Tama Janowitz and Mary Gaitskill, whose fiction certainly avoided any strident feminism, seemed to confirm the emergence of a more sophisticated (more rational? better-tempered?) type of woman whose books would mercifully appeal to all readers, regardless of gender.

Such easy assessments avoided consideration of a number of issues essential to any analysis of the novels, the most obvious being that none of these books could have been written without the experience of feminism and the freedoms, particularly sexual freedoms, that such experience had granted the authors. There was no denying that these new texts resembled not at all the large number of overtly feminist Anglo-American novels whose content was already so predictable as to invite parody. We've all read them: books that pullulate with fluids, books brimming with childbirth and menarche, abortion and menopause. These were books that tried to break the silence and cram centuries of female experience into a few short years of writing, books whose plots frequently celebrated the discovery of lesbian love and lore and that had awful titles like *Women Are Bloody Wonderful*. A few years of this and nobody wanted to pick up a "feminist" novel, let alone write one.

The reasons for so many of these books being vaguely disappointing lay deep within the pragmatic, utilitarian politics of the Anglo-American feminists. England, in particular, with its empirical traditions, had a profound, traditional mistrust of theory and abstract thought which English feminists unwittingly perpetuated without seeing it for what it was—one of the class-ist aspects of the English patriarchy dedicated to impeding thinking and education in society at large. French feminists, versed in the tradition of European thought, were much more open to theory. During the first decade of post-war feminism they were deeply influenced by Jacques Lacan's thinking on psychoanalysis and his belief that the moment of Oedipal crisis and repression of desire for the mother is synonymous with our acquisition of language and entry into the Symbolic Order, our acceptance of the Law of the Father.

Many French feminists became concerned with what they termed *"l'écriture féminine"*. This aligned an attempt to locate within literature the unconscious, repressed desires of the pre-Oedipal period along with the Deconstructionist theories of Jacques Derrida and their emphasis on the instability of meaning in language. French philosopher Julia Kristeva had seen conventional social meaning as encoded in language to be the underlying structure supporting all our social and cultural institutions. She had suggested that the fragmentation of meaning in the pre-modernist work of Lautréamont, Mallarmé and other Symbolists posed a revolutionary challenge to the social order by virtue of its delineation of the immensely powerful and arbitrary rhythms of the unconscious. Kristeva hoped that women writers would be able to dislocate language and patriarchal conventions by a similar use of the "spasmodic force" of the unconscious, further powered by their close gender identification with the powerful, pre-literate pre-Oedipal mother-figure. It was indeed from this area that the most influential and avowedly feminist literature emerged, primarily in the work of Monique Wittig and Hélène Cixous. One could not hope to re-create in textual form what Lacan called the "Imaginary", the infant period when there is no perceived separation from the mother; this being pre-Oedipal, pre-linguistic, any attempt to do so would result in psychotic gibberish. However in *l'écriture féminine*, one could, as Cixous puts it "work on the difference",[1] that is strive to undermine the dominant phallocentric logic of language, oppose the "binary oppositions" between the masculine and the feminine that exist in language and stress an open-ended textuality that would resist "closure" or resolution. Cixous was much influenced by the work of Derrida who maintains that meaning can only be located through the "free play of the signifier", or rather that meaning is always potential, always deferred as we pass from signifier to signifier in language without there being the possibility of a "transcendental signified", an ending or closure. There are few parallels with these writings and theories amongst English feminist novelists apart from in the work of Nicole Ward Jouve, herself French by birth, and Christine Brooke-Rose.

L'écriture féminine resists biologism—that is the Anglo-American feminist emphasis on women as real, biological entities who can only hope to change their status by opposing patriarchy in all its historical and political manifestations. Instead, the French theorists foreground language to the point of gender-fluidity, by stressing the textuality of sex and thus not excluding certain male texts from the "*féminine*". Julia Kristeva asserts that it is not biological difference that determines feminist potential but ourselves as "subject in process": "our identities in life are constantly brought into question, brought to trial, over-ruled."[2] Identity itself is endlessly unstable, endlessly open to change. Kristeva has attempted to align feminism and the avant-garde in an androgynous challenge to the very discourses that make such positions possible. Her project is one of subversion from within, re-defining "*différence*" (which in French denotes both difference and deferral), within the multiplicity and heterogeneity of textuality itself. She feels that the woman and the artist, the feminist and the avant-garde can all converge and dissolve in a deviance that is writing. They would seek to trangress the boundaries of which they speak and in doing so expose those boundaries for what they are—the

145

product of phallocentric discourse and of women's relation to patriarchal culture. Incidentally anarchic, they would ceaselessly deconstruct the discourse they work within and constantly strive to write what cannot be written. Many of these theories are somewhat utopian and often deeply irritating to Anglo-American feminists who cannot see much gender fluidity or polymorphous perversity down the supermarket. Even the French theorists themselves were unable to agree on multiple points of psycho-analysis, class and race privilege, literary representation and the patriarchal implications of theory itself.

The schism between the pragmatic "biologist" politics of Anglo-American feminisms and the language theory of the French groups is further complicated by the "crisis of legitimation", in Jean-François Lyotard's phrase, within post-modernism itself; the erosion of the Symbolic Order and a loss of faith generally, in what Lacan calls the Law of the Father. The various strands within feminism—the theoretical and the fictional, the political and the linguistic—can be seen as mirroring the cultural schizophrenia that has engulfed us. But for the woman writer—imprisoned of necessity within her language—the act of demanding access to discourse still means a submission to the phallocentrist masculine that constitutes the language of the Symbolic Order. On the other hand, to refuse discourse, fictional or otherwise, merely re-inscribes women as the signifiers of mystery, silent, "unspoken". How to work within male discourse while defying it? How to stand outside its voices without assuming the role of female "essence"? For the woman writer there are a multiplicity of problems within these trajectories.

The novels in question, those of Tama Janowitz, Mary Gaitskill and Catherine Texier are neither straightforwardly feminist and celebratory of the women's movement nor do they reflect French literary theory. They do not "work on the difference"; they make little attempt to undermine phallo-centrism, nor do they show any profound commitment towards defusing the bottom-line binary oppositions of male/female within language. They are neither literary experimentations that aim towards an open-ended non-oppositional textuality nor feminisms presented within "ordinary" narrative forms. Are they "post-feminist", post-feminism being the convenient mirage that was foisted upon us during the eighties, along with another chimera, that shy woodland creature, the New Man? Feminism had all been so *worthy*, so *earnest*. Wasn't it a mite *passé*? Human nature doesn't change much, does it? This impulse to turn down the bellowing biologism and re-appear in bustiers and fish-net stockings was more than understandable but reductive in literary terms for women writers. Feminism *did* exist. Language theory *had* developed and a disinclination to engage with either left these American novelists in a curious limbo where most of their work, however sensitive and intelligent, could not really evolve from being entertainments into the disruptive vitalities of art.

The novels in question actually display many of the impulses charted by feminist theory: the urge towards androgyny wherein women reject the dichotomies between masculine and feminine as being, in Kristeva's term, purely "metaphysical"; the desire for union with the Lost Mother of Oedipal theory. Desire is encoded within language and the authoritative act of writing, the "claiming of space" is always expressive of powerful, erotic impulses. If desire and language are synonymous, writing is symptomatic of desire that *doubles back* and *underwrites* or impersonates itself and is then doubly emphasized within the impulsive "ejaculations" of creative text. Women writers incurious about the phallocentrism of the language they assume will tend to re-enact, in unconscious form, the moment of their entry into desire and language at the Oedipal crux, the point at which they locate their phallic lack. In these novels we see, like shadows beyond the text, all the elements of the original drama. ("Doesn't every narrative lead back to Oedipus?" writes Roland Barthes. "Isn't story-telling always a way of searching for one's origin, speaking one's conflicts with the Law, entering into the dialectic of tenderness and hatred?")[3] We see the loss of the phallus, the emergence of desire, the search for the Other, the seductive girl-child, the many Fathers—the Good, the Bad and the Indifferent—and the development of their role as love-object. We note the longing to recreate symbiotic union with the pre-Oedipal Mother, that monstrous, magical figure who contains both Masculine and Feminine; we observe the wounds of the castration complex. Although basic Freudian theory has been spectacularly developed and challenged, notably by Lacan and Luce Irigaray, nevertheless much feminist textual theory is still concerned with the way in which conventional Freudian theory writes out women, condemns them to absence, to being deviations from the male norm, to be forever defined in negative terms as forms of nothingness or no-importance; passive as opposed to the male active, dark as opposed to light, fluidic, emotional, mysterious—emblematic of the unconscious. Thus, in claiming language the woman writer assumes a formidable task and must literally write herself into being.

The chaoticism of women's literature after feminism can be further explained by the urge, the desperate need to "catch up" in a pitifully short time. While much hitherto neglected women's writing from the past was excavated and published, contemporary women novelists had to contend simultaneously with the past and the present. They had to deal with the weight of literary history, they had to re-assess their own, frequently male, literary influences and they had to grapple with all the cultural imperatives of postmodern society. They had to try and form both new identities and new literatures in the teeth of great blasts of feminist theory. It was a formidable task and thus hardly surprising that instant, skimpy "traditions" emerged.

One of these was the American "Bad Girl" writer. These were writers who seemed to have taken every cliché about American womanhood from a century of fiction—they would be fiery, independent, free-spirited, uninhibited—and forced them juicily through the mill of post-war sexual liberation to produce a literary Cosmo girl. The original was probably Erica Jong with *Fear of Flying*, swiftly joined by Lisa Alther and *Kinflicks*.[4] In their work such writers focused on the women who had opened their hearts and legs to the counter-culture in the sixties, and trilled on through feminism and all varieties of sexual experimentation into burgeoning eighties privilege and success. They were bountiful, orgasmic, lip-glossed Amazons. The heroine of a late Jong novel, *Any Woman's Blues*, is the neo-autobiographical figure of Isadora Wing, ragingly concupiscent, complete with chic divorce, goy toy-boy and designer daughter. Jong still wrote like a Hall-mark card. Lisa Alther's heroine in a late book, *Bedrock*, cloyingly confides that, "Hormones had always been her drug of choice."[5] These women gave the impression that nothing would ever stop their fictional heroines; they would soon be picking out low-cut winding sheets and stretching mottled arms from the grave for one last grab of cock. They would presumably, in Joe Orton's phrase, be buried in a "Y-shaped coffin".[6] These writers were selling sex. The books had nothing to do with feminism and were, in fact, positively degrading to women. They promoted a rampant sexual consumerism, set impossible standards of wealth and allure and re-inforced the sexist image of women as hormonal harpies who could never drag their thoughts above the pelvis.

It has to be admitted that the writers under consideration, Tama Janowitz, Mary Gaitskill and Catherine Texier, all belong to this Bad Girl "tradition". They may have weighed in with a chic downtown version and a nihilistic punk allure but the books are still lewd, lustful and explicit, with a genteel veneer of high seriousness and, as such, comprise a publisher's wet dream. If, in addition, the writer presented an attractive package, was young-ish, personable and gave good interview, the marketing machine went into overdrive. This contains a sinister implication for women writers who do not conform to this marketing ideal and may consequently be doomed to media neglect. The writers under consideration here are all attractive women and the considerable material and status awards of their choosing to write almost exclusively about sex has to be taken into considera-tion. Is such writing little more than an astute career move? This is the "Madonna" debate. Can women criticize other women who use their sexuality in an autonomous fashion to become rich and powerful? Surely their rise is a triumph of feminism? Or do they merely perpetuate degrading sexist stereotypes?

Some women now consider that, during the eighties, far from being able to settle permanently into the workplace and consolidate the advances of feminism, women were being subtly undermined by media campaigns that eroded their frail confidence. Susan Faludi, author of *Backlash: The Undeclared War Against Women* considers that neurosis-inducing, glossy chat-show glop about New Men, co-dependency, baby-hunger and Women Who Love Too Much was deliberately intended to destabilize the new-found strength of the single, independent, self-determined woman. But were women really so fragile that they fell into a swoon of anxiety over nonsensical psychobabble? Certainly, during the eighties all types of pre-feminist behaviour from flirting to falsies were once again legitimized and even fashionable. In the eighties, sisterhood was Doubtful, Bitchiness was back. It is interesting to observe however that while the novels in question may avoid straight down-the-line feminism, neither do they tend towards any of the other eighties feminine extremes of power-shopping, ruthless ambition and bitchy back-bite. They all foreground friendship between women and are in general very warm and loving towards their own sex. It seems as though the female character who appears most frequently in these fictions—the bohemian artist and down-town clubber—was totally absent both from the dour-dressing Dworkin dyke set or the power-dressing of the uptown rich bitch. And indeed was it not always so? One of the the most notable absences in literature was precisely that of the bohemian woman artist and the work of Mary Gaitskill in particular went a long way towards re-(ad)dressing this issue.

ii. Tama Janowitz was the first of the "New Wave" women writers to impinge on British consciousness. Here in England we were shielded from the worst of the media circus that surrounded her burgeoning career but we got the message. She was hip, sophisticated. She knew Andy Warhol and Jean-Michel Basquiat! She looked great with her black, tangled, just-risen-from-a love-nest mane of hair, carmine pout and tight-clinched waist. This was no drab, mouthy dyke who was going to go all dismal and angry on talk shows. Janowitz was Lifestyle incarnate—you could be cute and intellectual and celebrated and rich all at once and still have credibility. What more could any woman ever want? In the face of all this the quality of her writing seemed hardly to count. In England, *Slaves of New York* was the first of her books to be published and sold well although critics tended to dismiss it as light-weight trendy New York pap. In fact Janowitz was a serious, thoughtful writer who didn't really deserve much of the image-linked nonsense that surrounded her and precluded her books being read with any real care. However, her first three novels together comprise something of a cautionary tale in terms of postmodern literature.

American Dad, published originally in 1981, was a fairly traditional first novel, although instantly hailed by reviewers as being "new-wave" and "postmodern". It is obviously the work of a careful, considered young writer with a thorough grounding in literature. It is a traditional coming-of-age novel concerning the transformation of character, a *Bildungsroman*, and chiefly remarkable for Janowitz's choice of a male narrator and protagonist. It is relatively rare for a woman writer to adopt the male voice and particularly so at the time this novel was written when there was so much emphasis on the nature of women's experience. In assuming literary discourse at all women become, in theoretical terms, bisexual and it is rare for them to go further and claim the male voice in its entirety. (Kathy Acker is a notable exception.) Janowitz does not use the male persona here to deliver any sarcastic feminist critique of men. Her portrayal of Earl Przepasnick is a gentle and sympathetic one as if she had merely transposed many of her own adolescent memories—as one does in a first novel—into a male body without any particular reflection on the obsession with gender difference that had seized the rest of the Western world. This apparent reluctance to emphasize gender nevertheless comprises a statement of its own. It frees Janowitz from any of the constraints of representing a world newly imbued with feminism which would have been unavoidable with a female narrator. At the same time it allows her to usurp a very male tradition of

American fiction—the sprawling *Look Homeward Angel* summation of youth and adolescence, the small-town look at life in a big country—and by very dint of her, as author, being female, to turn it subtly to her own ends. In a period when, despite all the demands for equality, the two sexes seemed more violently at odds that they had ever been, Janowitz's choice of narrator is brave and seems like a quiet plea for a more humanist, less divisive socio-sexual agenda.

American Dad is a dense and detailed book, written in the safe past tense of childhood. It opens climactically with a murder, a maiming and the memory of a divorce, although these are all swiftly revealed to be incidents which came about arbitrarily, or accidentally. They foreground the thematic thrust of the book which is a description of the lives of children whose parents were caught up in the turbulent cross-currents of the sixties. Such parents, vulnerable and more like children themselves, were unable to bequeath to their offspring the illusions of stability and order that had sustained earlier generations. Earl makes this clear when he says: "He was my father. He should grow up and act like one."[7] The lives of such parents swirled with chaos, divorce, extra-marital partnerships and terrible uncertainties. This enables Janowitz to implicitly deconstruct the traditional coming-of-age novel, which achieves resolution when the hero is able to reach a maturity which makes peace with, and approximates to, the values of the parental generation as in, for example *The Catcher in the Rye* or *To Kill a Mockingbird*. For the children in *American Dad*, however, the question is whether they will be able to survive at all or reach maturity in anything other than a psychologically fragmented state. In this respect they are more akin to Joel in Truman Capote's *Other Voices, Other Rooms*, who had no parents at all and was thus completely at the mercy of random influences. This is the central paradox of *American Dad*; the parents are very much present, very much loved but at the same time they are absent in the sense of being able to pass on coherent values to their offspring. Janowitz proves unable to investigate fully all the implications of this scenario; once Earl reaches adolescence she becomes more interested in detailing the lurid surfaces of contemporary society in the manner typical of her later work and the book loses its original impetus.

The first part of the book describes the childhood of Earl and Bobo Przepasnick after their parents, Robert and Mavis, decide to get a divorce. Robert is a sensual, bearded dope-smoking psychiatrist who occupies a curiously interstitial point in American history; his instincts are those of a backwoodsman, a frontiersman. He learns "to live off the land, fry day-lily bulbs and blossoms, spear frogs, brew tea from sassafras leaves".[8] At the same time these traditional American urges, far from dating him, unite him with the sixties trends towards self-sufficiency and a rejection of overt consumerism. Earl calls him "Paul Bunyan, Abraham Lincoln, Hunter S. Thompson rolled into one", further clarifying the point.[9] In many respects he is a milder version of the demented father in Paul Theroux's *The Mosquito Coast*, who implodes under the contradictions of past and present American realities. Robert similarly claims to be "a man of the future—higher on the evolutionary scale than the rest of society".[10] "It's going to take a while for the rest of mankind to catch up with him," says his son.[11] The mother, Mavis, is eccentric, confused and pitiable. A talented poet, she is constantly defeated by the exigencies of the world. It is clear that both parents have been wrecked on the tides of time; their perception embodies an older world whilst their daily lives are lived amongst the slippages of the new one.

By the time Earl is twelve, the parents are divorced and he has met other young casualties of the divorce wars—sex-crazed six-year-olds, children stoned on LSD or given hash brownies to calm them.[12] As Earl and Bobo get older, Earl comes to understand that the divorce was "the end of Bobo". Before it, Earl says, Bobo was "a fine person, a thoughtful person, but he was a sane person". The divorce "shocked him into a kind of reality that he might not otherwise have experienced. It stopped him completely from suffering an artistic sensibility, it prevented him from being a weirdo of any sort. He was a thoroughly American boy."[13] The inference is that the cataclysmic trauma of divorce or some similar fragmentation of past tradition is now necessary if children are to be "normal" and able to cope with present-day reality—not that this normality, in Earl's view, is to be recommended: it is the opposite of "sane". This establishes a complex interplay of binary oppositions, between the "artistic sensibility" and "normality" in both the old and new worlds. The "All-American" sensibility, once the "natural" product of security and tradition and an edenic past, has always been despised by the aesthetic "artistic" sensibility. Nowadays however, it takes a wrenching "unnatural" event to produce that "All-American", seemingly natural "normality". The divorce, Earl concludes was "probably the best thing that could have happened" to Bobo. He "became normal".[14]

The first part of *American Dad* is a mature work with its reflections on time, schism and the family. What is interesting about the book and, indeed, about Janowitz's work in general is the way in which, as Earl grows up and into the "present" and she concentrates increasingly on this "present" in this and later work, the whole tenor of the writing becomes increasingly "immature" as if traditional maturity, responsibility and understanding were qualities quite useless in apprehending contemporary reality. By the time Janowitz comes face to face with her self and her own milieu in *A Cannibal in Manhattan* her work is positively infantile in its short-sightedness and self-gratification. This, while not, I think, wholly deliberate underlines truisms about the infantilization of the individual in consumer society and the cravings for instant gratification. These lie in such opposition to the very act of writing which by its nature constantly defers meaning as well as deferring reward in a material sense that any attempt to combine the consumer ecstasy of the "endless present" in which we live with fictional form not only implodes "traditional" fiction but requires exceptional control of new forms if the writer is not to slip into a whining mimesis of the immature urges s/he portrays.

After Earl leaves his parental homes he finds it impossible to live up to the heroic image of his father he still retains. The rest of the book chronicles Earl's relationship with various girlfriends in college and abroad, relationships in which he takes a meek, supplicatory role entirely at odds with the images of men prevalent at the time as bullying sexist beasts. Janowitz finally collides with her future subject matter—the observation of strange urban tribes—when Earl meets an American "milky chocolate" model with "raspberry-coloured electrocuted hair" and blue lips.[15] We are nearly in *Slaves of New York* country. Earl finally loses his virginity to this sweet-natured giantess with the room-temperature IQ. The novel rather desperately attempts a traditional ending when Earl achieves manhood by having a baby—called Robert—with another girlfriend, the aristocratic English Elmira. Earl's father is seriously wounded when chopping down trees, trees having been earlier represented in the book as an image of age, history and tradition. The wounding of the "King", the Father, allows Earl to achieve adulthood and to make his peace with the elder Robert. Despite woundings, schisms, the chopping-down of the past, family tradition will struggle on in the form of Earl's new little family, a tradition that has been totally changed and yet, in its essential biological bondings, remains unchanging.

All that remains to be said of *American Dad* is that it performs textually and thematically in a traditional way while seeking out elements of the contemporaneous that co-exist uneasily with the *Bildungsroman* tradition. Janowitz is in transition between the past and the present in fiction as she writes the book. Janowitz also demonstrates a strong interest in anthropology, in cannibal tribes and in adopting anthropology to urban life, Earl speaks of his adventures as "sacred and religious rituals of the highest order . . . food for thought for anthropologists in every land and clime"[16] and this interest in urban "tribes" informs Janowitz's subsequent work. Lastly *American Dad* is an exercise in double consciousness. As a male, Earl can engage in Oedipal struggle with his father and emerge victorious in the traditional way by begetting a son. However this psychic battlefield is subtly informed by Janowitz's understanding of men as being far more vulnerable and "feminine" than they might have appeared had the author been male.

Simultaneously, the act of projecting imaginatively into the male voice is bounded for the reader by the knowledge that the female author has, in life, no such solutions as are available to Earl within the Oedipal crisis. Ironically this triumphant engagement with Oedipality is only accessible to Janowitz through the adoption of a male narrator, a male persona. She is able to use fictional language as illusion to "masquerade" as a man and to cloak gender difference whilst, subliminally, as a woman she re-enacts her own Oedipal struggle by her emergence into "public" written text. The novel is both fluid and uncertain in its combination of traditional "male" and "female" qualities. It is simultaneously dense *and* tentative as the author attempts to resolve the double-consciousness or multiple voicing inherent in its creation.

Janowitz moved decisively into the postmodern with *Slaves of New York*. This was her most successful book and is comprised of a number of brief vignettes of downtown New York life. Many of these had already appeared in magazines including the *New Yorker, Interview* and *Mississippi Review.*

The vignettes in *Slaves of New York* often move into the present, or historic present tense so beloved of postmodern novelists. This has always served several functions. It denotes the "endless present" of consumer culture where linear time and appropriate cause and effect have been blasted away by drug use, chaos theory and media blitz. It mirrors the moral and intellectual flexibility required for survival in a multi-textured, frequently nonsensical and paradoxical environment. It also forces the readers to engage with the novelist's "now", to involve them as closely with events as language will allow. In providing no past-tense "safe distance" it drags the reader into the literary equivalent of co-counselling.

Presentations of urban life at their most flat and affectless approach the imagistic condition of poetry or abstract art and are even more resistant to analysis and theory in that they are not founded in emotion. Janowitz is in general too quirky and critical to achieve this blandness but despite this, and despite considerable literary ingenuity, it becomes increasingly clear that she is not always wholly in control of her material.

For example, the first piece in the book, entitled "Modern Saint 271", describes the experiences of a prostitute. The contemporary call-girl is a figure that appears not only in Janowitz's work but also in that of Gaitskill and Texier and at first their intentions seem clear. As women writing about these all-too familiar male fantasy figures, they demystify and clarify them, banishing forever any connotations of seamy, exotic sleaze and ludicrous tart-with-a-heart/madonna-whore projections and replacing them with human beings. (One cannot but recall Alice Munro's complaint about "the figure of an idiotic, saintly whore": "Men who made books and movies seemed to have a fondness for this figure, though Rose noticed they would clean her up. They cheated, she thought . . ."[17]) Actually, in a different way Janowitz, Gaitskill and Texier "clean her up" too by substituting the nice middle-class girl with intellectual interests, paying her way through college perhaps. Although this incarnation is often far closer to contemporary reality than to the numberless sentimental male imaginings, it is still of course approximate. However streetwise the New York writers are, they all remain nice, educated middle-class kids—I mean, they're not Iceberg Slim, the street-smart black author of the classic memoir *Pimp*. Still Janowitz's portrayal of a prostitute's life does not seek to shield the reader. Her description of the penises encountered by her call-girl is right on the ball, so to speak. "Some blue-veined and reeking of Stilton, some miserly. Some crabbed, enchanted, dusted with pearls . . .'[18] This accentuates the tone of the piece which hovers between a repulsive, squalid factuality and a gentle dreaminess, all qualities which are profoundly welded together in the personality of the prostitute, her life, past and present and her relationship with her pimp. This latter is notably tender and sensitive, banishing all clichés of pimpdom; the intellectual Bob "with his long, graceful hands, his silky mustache, his interesting theories of life and death"[19] is sweetly ineffectual as a pimp although he sensibly comforts her with drugs. "He would softly tie up my arm and inject me with a little heroin."[20] The tender cadences of such sentences which seem to shed soft cloudy halo-lights on the two characters fit admirably with Janowitz's designation of the prostitute as a "modern saint", a phrase which is only barely ironic. This gentleness also foregrounds the girl's own quasi-religious belief that she "was like a social worker for lepers" and that "As in the convent, life is not easy."[21] This holiness, this saintliness, coupled with all the descriptions of the ugly litter that surrounds fiscal sex, raises the whole piece to the level of religious kitsch wherein the sublime must co-exist with mundane sentiment. As a complex evocation of an imaginative modern sexuality the piece destabilizes fixed notions surrounding sexuality, prostitution and religion whilst simultaneously undermining its own assertions with a gentle kitschy gloss. However, there is another more ominous textual reading which lies within the literary evocation of sex for sale. The author, by concentrating so blatantly on sex in the first story of the book, is herself offering sex for sale, in the book. As with the first sentence of Catherine Texier's *Panic Blood* and its insistence on "cunt" these writers are proferring sex, in some form, to the readers, sex which will "sell" the books. Doesn't it always? In this respect, and we must consider that they are using the language of the patriarchy, Texier's book "opens" with, or like, a "cunt" and Janowitz blends authorial voice with the voice of a prostitute, thus immediately "displaying" the text, in invitation, as sexual. This instant sexualization of the text presents the text itself as slut, to be "penetrated" by the reader. The very softness and gentleness of the text itself here, its "female" qualities render it all the more pleasurable as an erotic invitation and there is something questionable here in these authors' insistence on sexual matters. If, in Roland Barthes's analysis, all texts "flirt" with the reader, these precipitately embrace the readers and drag them into bed. No one could ever mistake Kathy Acker's sexual explicitness in language for a seductive invitation but Janowitz, Gaitskill and Texier are offering a very seductive, non-aggressive sexual enjoyment within the "body" of the text of young, beautiful, middle-class intellectuals/authors—or call-girls.

Slaves of New York takes us on a tour of New York City in the eighties, "dust and grit tossed feverishly in the massive canyons between the skyscrapers."[22] Everyone dreams of a better, more creative life. "All the waitresses I knew were really actresses, all the Xeroxers in the Xerox place were really novelists, all the receptionists were artists."[23] Although these vignettes can function as individual stories, many of the characters are linked from one to the other, comprising a sort of novella. There are other, separate pieces too.

In one, "You and the Boss", Janowitz executes a clever pastiche of a style of star-crazed writing sometimes found in fanzines. I have a near identical piece—at least in style—written, in all seriousness, some twenty-odd years ago, by a girl who spent a day with Jim Morrison. Janowitz uses the form to rubbish both the "legend" of a pop star, in this case Bruce Springsteen, and the clone-like qualities of a star's girlfriends. It is very funny. In "real life" of course, Bruce proves to be "larger than life". In fact, "Bruce is the size of a monster . . . his body might take up an entire billboard." Bruce eats "a dozen eggs, meatballs, spaghetti and pizza" for breakfast (all solid blue-collar food) and, worst of all, "He sings while he eats."[24] His home is furnished with the common touch—terminal tack—and so on. In another piece, "Engagements", Janowitz takes a clever swipe at post-structuralist critical discourse. Her heroine attends a Women's Studies Course at Yale but when she re-reads her notes which include the line. "A gendered identity 99% of the time is built onto a person who has a sex", they sound to her "as if they had been written in a foreign language".[25] She gives some more examples, which haven't quite degenerated into such gibberish and decides that this language "gracefully circled a subject without ever landing to make a point",[26] which is fair enough I suppose. As this also makes the point that Janowitz herself is perfectly familiar with these terms one might be tempted to ask why she makes relatively little of them in her writing and to consider the fact that were she more feminist/ more experimental in language she would certainly not have been so successful—or at least not so quickly or so dramatically.

But something about Janowitz seems to convey a genuine sweetness and precludes sinister accusations of calculation.

Some of Janowitz's concerns in *Slaves of New York* are all too familiar from other New York novels; the surreal street-life, the traditional flash of Trash Aesthetic as she describes one heroine's fascination with those tasteless but irresistible offers one finds in junk magazines—"Pegasus pendant with genuine ruby and swirl of faux diamonds"![27]—and inevitably that hideous eighties food obsession. This latter ranges from the parodic, as in Ellis's work ("eggplant-chocolate-chip icecream") to the everyday middle-class New Yorker diet: "Cornish game hen with orange glaze, curried rice, asparagus . . . or fettucine Alfredo with aragula salad . . ."[28] This is probably the worst aspect of New York novels of that period, trapping the English reader in a combination of *Guardian Weekend* and a Foodie convention.

There is also in Janowitz's fiction a subterranean feminist awareness, adroitly twisted to comic effect in the text: "You don't know why you spend half your life trying to scrub your body free from essential oils and the other half smearing stuff onto it".[29] She goes in for a rather endearing faux-naivety too, distancing herself further from her heroines; one of whom, contemplating a vast range of airplane food muses: "It must be difficult to raise the chickens, lettuce and so forth so far off the ground."[30]

Overall the stories that describe a particular circle of art-world characters are probably the least effective; they have an unwitting, inbuilt paradox in that Janowitz cannot decide if these characters are lovable, madcap, zany kooks or thoroughly unpleasant and inadequate human beings. It was this particular indecision that doomed the Ismail Merchant/James Ivory film-of-the-book (although the clothes were good). Eleanor, the central figure, is the one most exempt from this troubling uncertainty. Although she is a loopy jewellery-maker who produces "shellacked sea-horses, plastic James Bond-doll earrings",[31] that kind of thing, she is both innocent, vulnerable and victimized. Janowitz probably means the others to embody a fine literary ambiguity but in this she is unsuccessful and merely returns the reader again and again to the central paradox of their unlikeability. Eleanor's lover, artist Stashua Stosz, is a disagreeable bully and another artist, Marley Mantello, purveyor of neo-classical themes—"The God of Baseball playing a game of billiards with Bacchus"[32], for example—is a self-professed genius, and well-nigh unbearable. Art dealer Victor is not much better. Janowitz undoubtedly intends a satire on the art world and its self-serving lunacies. There is an artist "who paints traumatic situations"—a rape, a car accident—in a medium he "invented himself . . . ground bones and blood acquired from garbage pails outside the meat market." Another "environmental" artist is "moving heaps of mud from one part of Montana to another" and yet another wants "to cover the Golden Gate Bridge in Band-Aids."[33] Janowitz's satiric intentions are severely undercut by her own obvious affection for and interest in contemporary art, a dichotomy that permeates the characters who are simultaneously, and impossibly, supposed to combine crass self-interest and blunted affect with finer feelings and profound sensitivities. Not that the two aspects are inimical in one personality, far from it, merely that Janowitz fails to animate the potential. Although she attempts to raise significant points, as when avid collector Chuck feeds the hungry Marley Mantello a humungous breakfast, a scenario that suggests correspondences between art, creativity, hunger and desire, she fails to develop them. Ultimately we have more shopping-list fiction—fashion, style, quirky sexual detail, consumer jokes— whose most profound statement seems to be that life doesn't live up to advertising. No one is demanding the improbable resolution or the metaphors of her first book but trivia, even if grounded in common emotional conflict, remains trivia.

Janowitz chose to further pursue the role of quasi-anthropologist to the urban nomad in *Slaves of New York*. For example, she writes of men: "When I went out with them it was only to study them further as if they were natural history museum exhibits."[34] In her subsequent book, *A Cannibal in Manhattan*, that particular approach is carried in a cutesy way to its logical extreme. The project must have seemed both ambitious and impeccably postmodern. A noble savage would be transported suddenly to New York City. Unencumbered by Western perceptions and preconceptions he would faithfully record the rites and rituals of this eccentric new culture. From within his innocent voice Janowitz would be able to satirically re-present the entire urban hive in all its cross-pollinated absurdities. Simultaneously she would test the boundaries of the novel itself by providing a photographic "record" of her hero's decline and fall. The reader, aware of the jokey nature of this photographic "documentation" wherein the author's friends impersonate the book's characters, would knowingly collude in the fictionalized artifice and double-bluff. All aspects of the book, from epigraph to index, would self-reflexively participate in this ironic game, questioning and blurring the edges of what actually comprises a book. Furthermore the reader would be excluded as much as included in the joke for the true "story", that of Janowitz's inter-action with her peer-group, would lurk beyond his reach and establish that the reader has no right-of-access nor chance ever to fully decode an author's meaning. It was a bold idea but could only ever have worked through an incredible feat of authorial projection and sustained imagination. The entire concept was initially hobbled by the fact of Janowitz herself possessing a wholly Western set of perceptions and the consequent difficulties of simultaneously referring to and denying this. Although she tries to locate the entire enterprise in the realm of the absurd by using an epigraph from Lewis Carroll's writing, the problem needs a more ingenious solution. Critics and readers also proved intransigent and were puzzled by an enterprise which, for all its subterranean sophistication, struck them as being overtly naive, confused and possibly even racist.

Everything was wrong with the book. Dedicated to Andy Warhol, its inner focus was on Janowitz's private life and friendships. This was less experimental than élitist and readers reacted accordingly. When, in 1928, Djuna Barnes entertained her friends with caricatures and gossip in *The Ladies Almanack*, she had the sense to publish and distribute it privately to interested parties.

Mgungu is an uncivilized savage from, of all places, "New Burnt Norton". (We are forced to note, tiredly, that the author is well read.) He is rescued by one Maria Fishburn, heir to a Great New York family. They are obviously supposed to belong to what used to be called "Our Crowd".[35] This smug expression was used to collectively describe the enormously rich Jewish families in New York (Guggenheim, Seligman, Gimbel, Loeb) who rose to power in the early part of this century. The "Our Crowd" now in the novel is actually Andy Warhol and his art-world henchpersons. For example, the "photographs" of Maria Fishburn are pictures of Paige Powell, Warhol-circus stalwart and *Slaves of New York* film starlet. Mgungu is a knowing modern "savage", a professional "savage" who trades on the commodities exchange with money from the Feed the Infants Federation and knocks up shoddy artefacts for tourists. Maria brings him to New York for a Dance Festival at the Museum of Primitive Cultures, curator Parker Junius (photograph of Andy Warhol). Mgungu goes to a nightclub, meets an improbable Cockney rock star and a lovable delicatessen owner (photograph of Brigid Berlin, old Warhol trouper), Maria marries Mgungu but she is in the clutches of master criminal Reynar Lopato whose main interest lies in Mgungu's ability to concoct a powerful narcotic known as Joy Paul Guilford. Maria now gets the recipe. Lopato fraternizes with a dwarf called Mikhail, plainly modelled on Truman Capote. Capote's ghostly presence further underlines the café society parameters of the novel. Maria is killed and Mgungu, set up by Lopato, unknowingly consumes his murdered bride. Lopato intends to distribute Joy Paul Guilford and appropriate Maria's fortune. As a well-known public "cannibal", Mgungu is an obvious suspect in her death. He goes on the run amongst the homeless on the streets and ends up in prison.

It would be possible, if unprofitable, to pursue the play of intended meanings throughout the book. There is the theme of the innocent abroad, misled by greedy, shifty New Yorkers and their lawyers. There are correspondences between "civilized" and "savage" behaviour and dense multi-textured attempts to locate primal forces in behaviour. The whole book is a turgid satire on modern manners and emits a steady low-grade fog of heavy-handed farce. It is carelessly written and often nonsensical in no very illuminating way—Mgungu's primitive home has patches of "couscous fur"[36] stitched to the walls. Mgungu's language is in simplistic grammatical disarray: "The time did pass"; "the wind was howling very fierce".[37]

Although undoubtedly good-natured the novel does not cohere on any level. The photographs of friends dressed up and credited in the index make an embarrassed voyeur of the reader, excluded from the in-jokes. As a sub-textual commentary on Andy Warhol and his world it might be of interest to the most demented Warholian acolytes—others might as well read his diaries, or a good biography. Like the Ayckroyd/Belushi film *The Blues Brothers*, *A Cannibal in Manhattan* is a private album whose delicate clues to international gossip render it ultimately more inaccessible. As in the case of that particular film, it may amuse those who are heavily drugged—on Joy Paul Guilford perhaps. The final coy references to styling and designers in the acknowledgements make it more than ever a casualty of eighties greed, vanity and the tendency to believe in shallow public myths. It is as much doomed to date as the fashionable world it covertly flashes at us like a stripper granting a swift, pitying peep to a particularly frustrated and under-privileged audience.

Janowitz is not an untalented author but her grip on postmodernist fiction has so far proved shaky and it seems inevitable that she will have to reconsider her intentions. Although many people found *A Cannibal in Manhattan* more or less repellent it may be that, for a time, she was just another Andy Warhol victim (they should have had a Helpline) who succumbed to his whispers of "You're so great! You're a star! You can do anything you want!" ("He always played the evil fairy," claimed an associate.[38])

Janowitz's progression from serious young *littérateur* to high society darling contains an unwitting commentary on such a dizzying social ascent; as in the case of Truman Capote, the higher she rose, the more her writing deteriorated.

E.Y.

iii. Mary Gaitskill

Dancers, models, prostitutes, aspirants; Mary Gaitskill's characters are very similar to those in Tama Janowitz's books and they inhabit a very similar New York. They are on the fringes of the art world, the smart world and they attend the same sorts of openings, launches, loft parties and clubs. They are at different stages of that notorious urban journey from downtown bohemia to uptown success, that pilgrim's progress of contemporary achievement from poverty and artistic ideals to compromise, money and achievement, or, if one wishes to see it that way, from adolescence to maturity.

Deep within the text of novels by Janowitz, or Gaitskill there lies, *sotto voce*, an account of the author's own urban journey and its successful outcome, embedded in the book-as-object. In recording artistic disillusion, heartbreak and failure they tame and subdue those particular demons in themselves. Mary Gaitskill's books in particular, which depend heavily on characterization rather than postmodernist word-play, exude a tremulous quality in their bid for success. The act of writing is a charm against failure—and was "failure" not the most obscene word one could utter in public during the rampantly ambitious eighties? There is something peculiarly heart-breaking in all these stories of pretty New York women and their yearning for artistic careers and in the shadowy figures of the women writers who animate them. The existence of these books is a naked confession of a desperate need. For generations, women have longed to work as writers—however sheltered their lives they were likely to be seduced by the glamours of authorship. In addition, the act of writing itself is a particularly defiant assertion of individuality in a world deeply indifferent to female personality but until relatively recently this longing for artistic expression was almost wholly unrealistic. There was virtually no chance of a woman, unsupported by family money or by an indulgent husband, earning a living in this way within a male literary Establishment. In the post-war years and with the rise of feminism this situation has eased, but not as much as might be supposed. The early years of artistic struggle still require financial support and both Janowitz and Gaitskill describe the clerking, stripping, waitressing and so on that now attempts to provide this.

The desire for artistic validation is as strong as ever—stronger in that women must now prove themselves a "success" in the public arena. The arts have always been a "feminized" aspect of public life despite being an exceptionally demanding discipline requiring "male" qualities of tenacity, strength and ambition if one is to succeed. The arts are no place for inchoate feminine romanticism and Gaitskill is not alone among women writers in having to "murder" such illusions, in having to mock and rub out on the page the "comical" figure of the girl with "artistic" aspirations, lest they stifle her own serious endeavours. The image of women enmeshed in artistic self-delusion—frequently a cruel joke in male fiction—is deeply threatening to the working woman artist who sees therein not only the outline of her own early ambitions but also, unless she can "murder" and escape it, the shape of future failure. The woman artist, whatever her subject, is doomed to record the history of her own struggle with art. Gaitskill's young girls, trying to become writers or painters, embody cruel cultural dilemmas. At the point where art requires solitude, long isolation and concentration they are under all the pressures of sexual display, sexual success, social status and the frenzied search for "love", knowing all too well that their physical "value" is constantly diminishing in a cruelly ageist society. Thus for every novel which records such struggles we see not only the search for a linguistic expression of women's lives within patriarchy but a secret history of the author who has confounded the odds in the story of women in art. For every book we hold in our hand there are thousands unwritten, part-written or set aside with brave self-deprecatory words. Heartbreak indeed.

Mary Gaitskill's first book, *Bad Behaviour*, contained nine stories. It received a great deal of favourable attention on publication. Her work was immediately contrasted with what was by now seen as the emptiness and superficiality of urban fictions by Bret Easton Ellis, Jay McInerney and Tama Janowitz. Reviewers were quick to assert that whereas their books were peopled by "cartoons" or "odd exotics", Gaitskill instead provided the reader with "real people."[1] Leaving aside what we have seen of Ellis's very good reasons for rejecting the creation of "real people" in favour of bland ciphers it is certainly true to say that Gaitskill's primary interest is in characterization. In an entirely traditional manner, plot, action, revelation and denouement all proceed from character in her work. Her technique is not dissimilar to that of Tama Janowitz in *American Dad*, but whereas Gaitskill places her characters uncompromisingly in the New York fast-lane, once there, she does not have the same interest in exploring the wholesale erosion of language and character under the barrage of postmodernity and urban overload as do the other New York writers. This is not to say that Gaitskill can wholly escape the implications of urban fragmentation and uncertainty. Her stories are littered with the usual chic detritus of downtown life, her characters suffer in a "monstrous city"[2] and she tends to avoid closure or resolution in what is by definition an irresolute world. But if these are postcards from hell they have been extensively retouched. The city functions far more as picturesque background here than it does in many other urban fictions. Indeed it approaches the condition of Hollywood romantic backdrop; the picturesque ethnic neighbourhoods, the amusing bohemian squalor, the distressing, but colourful homeless characters . . . Gaitskill's approach has guaranteed her acceptance in its appeal to American sentiment and voyeurism. Her fiction has all the traditional qualities of accessible readability (unlike say, Hubert Selby or Paul Auster). At the same time she gains all the kudos from appearing to report back from a dangerous, perverse,

sexually charged and druggy world. However her traditional—
and very appealing—"literary" qualities necessarily bleed all
this of much of its resonance. It is all something of a masquerade.
As the book moves towards the final story, a long celebration of
middle-class American life entitled "Heaven", it becomes clear
that there is far more innocence than wickedness in her work.
This is no bad girl with missives from hell but a good girl
reporting from the other place. Her feet may be in SoHo but her
heart is with the *New Yorker*.

None of this is meant to detract from Gaitskill's considerable
achievements. Indeed as the tide of obsessive literary postmodernism recedes, her work promises more of a way forward
for fiction than that of many more intransigent writers. Much
Downtown writing, with its origins in autobiography and its
attempts to transcend postmodernist dead-ends, has been
instrumental in trying to define a literature for the future. As the
great tide of theory and paralytic self-consciousness begins to
pass writers are able to re-assess the inherent strengths and
limitations of fictional form and to restore to literature some of
its original potential in terms of the stories that need to be told.
This is not to say that traditional Grand Narrative with all its
divisive didacticism can ever be restored but that as this is
increasingly jettisoned in favour of more diverse representations
there is still much of value left that can be worked with even as
one considers the necessary constraints of the novel form. It is
from such considerations that "New Narrative" writing has
developed.

Let us consider some of Mary Gaitskill's achievements in
marrying conventional literary style to the usual Downtown
concerns of sex, drugs, and deviancy. She succeeds in presenting
a sympathetic, complex portrait of a certain type of woman who
has been astonishingly ill-served by literature; the strong-
minded, intelligent bohemian. Tama Janowitz's portrayals are
extremely lightweight by comparison. Gaitskill's contribution
here is significant. Looking back, briefly, over a century of
literary and artistic history one sees how very common this type
of woman has always been; the "bride of art" in her thankless

role as model, mistress, hostess or muse. And yet where is the free-thinking, free-loving woman successfully represented in literature? The extraordinary community of bohemian women in Paris in the twenties, which included Natalie Barney, Nancy Cunard, Gertrude Stein and Sylvia Beach were usually, when they wrote, more concerned with Joycean innovation than their own supremely fascinating stories. The notable exceptions are of course Colette and Jean Rhys although they were both in their very different ways rather less typical of the bohemian woman than, for example, Djuna Barnes, whose legacy, for all its brilliance, remains elliptical.

Male attempts to describe such women ranged from Ernest Hemingway's crude and clumsy Lady Brett Ashley, through D.H. Lawrence's dogged projections to Aldous Huxley's cruel, derisive caricatures and there was worse to come. The women associated with Surrealism remained so peripheral and, when, like Leonora Carrington they did write, so frustratingly Surrealist that they told us little about themselves. The situation was no better with the Beat writers. Male representation of the women involved was at its most tokenist—sketchy and iconic, as in Jack Kerouac's *Tristessa* or the character of Mardou in *The Subterraneans*. Women writers such as Diane di Prima tended to produce pale Beat myths. It wasn't until Joyce Johnson produced her classic memoir, *Minor Characters*, in 1983 that we received a true impression of the women of the time. Hettie Jones's memoirs of New York bohemia, *How I Became Hettie Jones*, were not published till 1990. In them she writes: "There have always been women like us." Describing their lives she says: "We lived outside, as if. As if we were men? As if we were newer, freer versions of ourselves?"[3] Down all these decades we see a sad story of fervent artistic fellow-travellers almost wholly elided from participation in art by their sex. Out of all this life, complexity and talent it seemed that there were only two, almost equally depressing, types of bohemian women—Anaïs Nin with her cloying vanities or Simone de Beauvoir with *her* brand of self-absorption and self-esteem.

By the time the generation born in the post-war years grew up there were certainly immeasurably more opportunities for women to leave home and participate in experiments of every kind, artistic and sexual. In literature Patti Smith and Kathy Acker are obvious prototypes. It was from the sixties onwards that women's lives tended to go through a series of dizzyingly swift changes. Much art was of necessity preoccupied with the seismic changes wrought by feminism and it is only relatively recently that strong images of urban bohemian women—who cannot easily be dismissed as just "feminists"—have started to emerge in fiction. Were it not for writers like Gaitskill, Ellen Gilchrist or Angela Carter we would still have extremely flawed representations of women artists from male writers.

Clever, moody, neurotic women have certainly appeared in novels by women before—one may think of Mary McCarthy, Margaret Drabble and A.S.Byatt, or Doris Lessing—but they tend, particularly in English fiction, to come from the same sort of straight, limited, upper-middle-class backgrounds as their creators. Their irregularities are very minor and their conformism very deep. The many women who have wholly rejected all this and crossed barriers of race, class and sex to live in bohemian sub-cultures have had no romantic outlaw myths to guide them nor have they written them. Their lives have been wholly transgressive and wholly threatening even to the men, often artists of one sort or another themselves, with whom they lived. There is no *On the Road* or *City of Night* for women. One has to look very hard to find any deep, sympathetic portrayals of deviant women in fiction—in Charles Plymell's *The Last of the Moccasins* perhaps and certainly Mary, the middle-class junkie in Hubert Selby's classic *Requiem for a Dream*. Mary Gaitskill's urban realism may be a touch soft-edged but in creating complex and wholly believable, familiar representations of women living outside conventional boundaries she gives a voice to a type of women whose articulacy in life has continually been choked into inarticulacy in art, either "punished" by male observers or limited by her own feelings of inadequacy and self-denigration. Nowadays certainly the situation is changing: any glance at anthologies of American writing of the sort we are concerned with, *High Risk* or *Disorderly Conduct* for example, will reveal numerous impressions of powerful and deviant women. However, within this, Mary Gaitskill's work is probably some of the most orderly and traditional and the most likely to be accessible to a broad middle-class readership. Thus she has had the opportunity to empower and legitimize, to explain if you like, and create sympathy for a way of life that has been culturally disenfranchised, that has remained "beyond the pale" in the sense of being unwritten. Furthermore she normalizes a kind of life that has become normal for many women—a long period of rootlessness, sexual experimentation and search for self-expression in early adulthood. Remember it is not Gaitskill but her critics who have claimed that "she charts the murky terrain of vice"[4] and so on and so forth. Gaitskill herself entirely lacks that kind of distancing, that view of her subject matter as weird and shocking. It is normal and she treats it as such. It was Gaitskill's publishers who titled the book *Bad Behaviour* and thus aimed it at the prurient and voyeuristic. Her achievement lies in the very disappointing of such sensation seekers, in her ability to blur and destabilize any such conventional notions of female behaviour.

Thus it can be said that while Gaitskill may eschew the more radical, brutal or quirky uses of language in her representations, her complex and detailed portrayals perform a great deal of much needed repair work on women in fiction. The very act of delineating transgressive female behaviour involves, at some level, a struggle with patriarchal attitudes. There is in Janowitz's work the sense of a remote, transcendental male signifier—the Father, the Artist, the Colonizer. Gaitskill's text, in a different way, finds it necessary to display, seduce and act out before a stern (male) gaze and this is indeed what much of her fiction is about.

At the primary level the stories in *Bad Behaviour* are concerned with girls seeking identity through artistic expression —and indeed, one of them is entitled "Trying To Be". Gaitskill's real subject however and the one she goes on to explore in the novel *Two Girls, Fat and Thin* is female masochism, or rather the interplay of domination and submission in women's lives. That the two subjects—artistic striving and female humiliation—are intertwined is indisputable but the links between them are tenuous and obscure and Gaitskill can only intermittently illuminate them. Two of the stories in *Bad Behaviour* explore these matters at coal-face level; "Something Nice" and "Trying to Be" both concern intelligent, ambitious girls who, driven by economic necessity, choose to work for a time as prostitutes. They both meet an attractive, understanding older man as a client in their brothels and he attempts to push their relationship beyond its professional limits. Both girls are aware of the contradictions they embody in their work but neither can prevent themselves from sinking beneath the lies and clichés of their situation, clichés clumsily, helplessly reinforced by the man. Jane in "Something Nice" escapes quickly, although she and the other prostitutes are explicitly identified with the fish that swim endlessly round a tank in the drab, professional bedroom. "Look at those poor dumb things swimming around in there . . . They haven't got any idea of the filth going on in here."[5] In this case the man, Fred, is a veterinarian, which underlines both his status and, implicitly, his attitude towards the girls he frequents. In this story it is the man who suffers loss and pain. A year later, long after she has left the brothel, Fred sees Jane in a café he frequents "because he enjoyed looking at the strangely dressed young people who often went there".[6] She ignores him.

"Trying To Be" is a much more savage story. In order to pay her bills, Stephanie works at times as a prostitute although she conceals this from her friends who are the usual downtown crowd of aspiring artists and writers. Bernard is a lawyer with "kind eyes and an intelligent, inquisitive demeanour". He also has an "almost alarmingly large penis".[7] Like Fred, but to a much more developed extent, Bernard is a sort of parasite, a social voyeur or dilettante; he pursues relationships with the more intelligent and exciting of the girls he meets in the brothel—before Stephanie he was involved with an orange-haired performance artist, although he now can't remember her name. He says he wants "to meet fascinating creatures I'd never

meet in the usual course of my life".[8] Stephanie understands
that, "He loved the idea of kooky, arty girls who led 'bohemian'
lives and broke all the rules."[9] There is a touching aspect to this
certainly—he revels in his Dance Theater Workshop member-
ship which ensures that he gets invited to "fabulous" parties
where the boys wear earrings—but Stephanie is increasingly
aware of his basic contempt for her way of life. Initially she is
flattered by his view of her as "a bohemian, experimenting"[10]
when she knows that she is, in common with nearly all of
Gaitskill's characters, merely "a directionless girl adrift in a
monstrous city".[11] Stephanie leaves the brothel but goes on
seeing Bernard and, after some demurral allows him to continue
paying her. Stephanie tries to have a honest, ordinary relationship
with Bernard; in describing a previous, ruinous affair she says:
"I didn't give a shit about being interesting and mysterious. I
wanted him to love me," and Bernard responds with "fatherly
tenderness".[12] However at some level even this assertion of
Stephanie's is a sort of pose. Everything about the relationship is
artificial as they each project a rigid and unrealistic vision onto
the other. His vicarious, prurient attraction to her supposed
thrilling life-style begins to annoy her. After all, she is just a
"bewildered human" and he "someone who pays me to fuck
him".[13] It becomes increasingly clear that Bernard's interest in
what he considers to be exotic girls like herself is essentially
sexual and that he would feel a kind of disgust in letting them
anywhere near his real life. Despite all the talks about art and
literature they are nowhere near equals. His attention soon starts
to wander towards other sexy girls—"One wants them all,"[14] he
remarks casually and insensitively, not realizing how unbearable
this remark would be to any woman. As a male Bernard holds all
the cards—economic, judgemental, social. He, emphasized by
his alarming member, represents order, society, success in a
wholly male-dominated society, against which Stephanie's little
experiments with living are as nothing. He is the dominant male
against whom, again and again, Gaitskill's fiction has to re-assert
itself. When Bernard leaves finally, without paying, Stephanie at
first breaks down but quickly recovers and starts to piece together

again her flimsy, disorganized life. Gaitskill's commitment to the constituents of such lives, the right of girls to live in this way if they choose, remains unabated.

In another story, "Connection", Gaitskill explores a friendship between two of these girls, Susan an aspiring writer, and Leisha, an actress. Leisha is the archetypal bad girl that the hard-working author has to kill off. She is druggy, selfish, melodramatic and trivial with her "pathetic assertion that she had talent".[15] Although the author makes clear that Susan too went through a period of self-destructive excess and that her ambitions failed as well, nevertheless it is impossible not to contrast her with Leisha. Leisha is every woman author's Other, the bad girl she was or would like to be were all this not truncated by the sober fact of discipline and publication. There is an extraordinarily similar figure in Mary Flanagan's first book of stories: Georgia DeBellis in a wicked story called "A Parma Violet Room (a tale of ruin)". Flanagan's book is titled, inevitably, *Bad Girls*.[16]

Towards the end of the book Gaitskill's stories start to drift away from these concerns, particularly "Heaven", a long golden paeon to the heartbreaking complexity of middle-class family life. However any consideration of the novel *Two Girls, Fat and Thin* must involve a look at the story "A Romantic Weekend", which prefigures the later work.

Beth is waiting anxiously to meet a new lover for the weekend. He remains nameless, a portentous, potential Everysadist. Beth is, on some level, archetypal. She is reminiscent of all the bruised, drifting girls in the book. Beth believes that she is a masochist. In describing a previous relationship she says: "Somebody opened me up in a way that I had no control over. He hurt me. He changed me completely. Now I can't have sex normally."[17] Her new lover, on his part, believes himself to be a sadist. "I won't give you any more pain than you can handle," he announces.[18] But he has doubts about this new romance. It all seems "complicated and potentially exhausting".[19] He also suspects that Beth doesn't really understand what it means when she says she wants to be hurt. From the start the weekend is a disaster. He knows that there is something wrong and senses in Beth "a rigidity that if cracked would yield nothing".[20] He is right. The basic problem is Beth's intelligence. He considers that, "She was in love with the idea of intelligence and she overestimated her own."[21] As she talks on and on about art and aesthetics and intelligence he becomes increasingly weary. He feels she is an "unglamorous creature, who looked as though she bit her nails and read books at night".[22] Walled up in a tacky Washington apartment, their attempts to negotiate a sexual situation are ludicrous. Beth doesn't like being bitten. Or gnawed. Or burned. She doesn't want to be pissed on. She doesn't want to drink piss either. She doesn't want to be beaten. She doesn't appear to *like* pain. As she puts it: "I don't come when I stub my toe either."[23] On the drive home they reach a sort of truce as each of them becomes excited again by their own fantasies and projections as the distance between them is re-established. There may or may not be a future for the relationship. It seems unlikely.

In a few brief pages Gaitskill has touched on a number of common, resonant points. Beth is an intelligent girl, prey to masochistic fantasies who has developed the ever-familiar "Heathcliff" complex. She cannot understand how she could have mistaken this "hostile moron" for "the dark brooding hero who would crush her like an insect and then talk about life and art".[24] This female fantasy of pain and annihilation at the hands of some fiendishly attractive being who is simultaneously and impossibly a soulmate lies at the heart of male/female relationships in our culture and is of course responsible for a million Gothic romances. Gaitskill sees clearly that, in this case, what frustrates Beth's lover is precisely what makes her so exquisitely vulnerable to this fantasy, so that it blends ineluctably with her real life, that is her intelligence and sensitivity. She lacks the "relaxing sense of emptiness",[25] of submission, that he has noted in other women in these circumstances. She contains a "tangible somethingness",[26] which she cannot relinquish and that he cannot demolish. She is not "blank".[27] She is not *stupid* and he lacks the imagination to integrate his attempts at physical humiliation with psychic pain, which is the only sort she can actually respond to. What alienates him is, basically, her masculinity; her autonomous intelligence, her guarding of self. Her "willful, masculine, stupid somethingness"[28] ruins the weekend, he decides. She even looks "more like a boy than a girl".[29] She is serious and desperate but "hatefully self-possessed."[30] She finds him banal. It is not until they recover their social selves in the car and she admits that she often lost her sense of identity so completely on LSD that she couldn't recognize herself in the mirror, that her attractiveness comes back to him in "a terrific rush"[31] in this vision of her "nothingness". They are back where they started. She continues to believe that her masochism could be "the highest form of love",[32] not realizing that this ensures that her relationships will be largely limited to psychic pain and mental torture. It is out of this stalemate where, reflected in the language of their own, personal fantasies, he is the romantic, feminized person and she the tougher "male" identity—as they must be, underneath, to keep the whole sado-masochistic charade in operation—that Gaitskill begins in *Two Girls, Fat and Thin* to investigate what creates these situations and what made Beth like she is.

It can be seen by now that Mary Gaitskill in abjuring all the rhetorical tropes of high postmodernism such as parody, irony, pastiche and intertextuality writes essentially as a romantic. The epigraph to her novel, from Vladimir Nabokov, reads: "All one could do was to glimpse, amid the haze and chimeras, something real ahead . . ." There is no sensitive deconstructive flinching at the prospect of "something real". She stubbornly favours authorial "authenticity", authorial presence, despite all the critical theory which has condemned this as a purely imaginary stance. In this she has much in common with the other writers discussed in this book who, despite some awareness of recent literary theory, are in collective retreat from the more abstruse manifestations of narrative negation.

In *Two Girls, Fat and Thin* Gaitskill tries to trace the roots of power, dominance, masochism and pain in American culture through an in-depth study of two girls growing up in the

American heartland. They are brought together by their shared interest in a cult novelist of the forties and fifties, Anna Granite, a barely fictionalized portrayal of Ayn Rand.

Justine Shade is a refugee from *Bad Behaviour*, a skinny, masochistic, "neurotic, antisocial twenty-eight year old".[33] She wants to be a writer, meanwhile supporting herself by working in a doctor's office. She is researching an article on Anna Granite for "Urban Vision" (*The Village Voice*?). Wishing to talk to "followers" of Anna Granite, she places an advertisement in a launderette where it is seen by a sad, obese girl called Dorothy Never who has known Granite well. Their pasts are evidently about to be thoroughly washed.

Dorothy, who remains unnamed for a long time, sees the notice by chance but has great difficulty in actually contacting Justine. Here we see the process of creative text emerge. Chance can liberate the unconscious. Justine the "writer" is in search of her character. Equally Dorothy as the primary "character" needs to be "written", to be validated, to have her story told. But there is some hesitation, some block in Justine. She eludes her subject who remains, literally "nameless". When they finally meet they both reveal almost immediately that they were sexually abused as children. Dorothy was forced to have an incestuous affair with her father, from age fourteen, and Justine was sexually molested by a friend of her own father when she was five. The power of the "Fathers" is immediately established. They go on to discuss Anna Granite. Dorothy avers that Granite's work and influence rescued her from psychic dis-integration. "It glorifies the freedom of the individual and nowadays that sort of philosophy is labelled fascistic."[34] Justine questions the masochistic element, "the pattern of dominance and submission"[35] in Granite's "very erotic"[36] books, suggesting that the behaviour of the female characters is a denial of themselves as strong, autonomous beings. Dorothy denies that the women are masochistic; they are not "demeaned by . . . subservience to a cruel, dishonest, contemptible man".[37] When they submit, says Dorothy, they do it out of strength and choice, as a gift. She defines this as the difference between masochism and love. Justine goes on to disclose, in an echo from *Bad Behaviour*, that she feels an affinity with Granite's fictional characters. She says that she had a relationship "with someone who sort of . . . in bed, opened me up in a way I had no control over". Dorothy is "intoxicated".[38]

At this first meeting between author and character, a number of oppositions between Justine and Dorothy are presented, the most important of which is that Dorothy is first and foremost body, flesh. She eats. Her physical processes are remarked upon. She is all solidity. Justine, by contrast is nervous, attenuated, coldly intellectual, starved. It would be trite to suggest some sort of body/spirit dichotomy, however, although Justine certainly needs emotional nourishment and Dorothy craves attention and conversation. There is something odder here though, in this insistence on "fat" and "thin", even to the book's title. Justine as a representative of the hip, fashionable world has to be thin. The culture and fashion demand it. (As Eve Babitz once wrote: "Of life in Rockdom, part of the privileged existence and scorn depend on being as slender as a thread. Old people are fat and ugly people are fat but even the children of rock people are gracefully slender."[39]) Mary Gaitskill writes "thin" fiction. Everyone in this book does. The thinness, the grace, the elegance are woven into every poseur's pose in all the dark clubs and fashionable haunts of urban youth. It is an obsession, a decadent heritage. Babitz is right to mention "scorn". Being fat, Dorothy is by definition ugly, the perennial outsider, as the novel swiftly makes clear.

The novel then goes back to look at the childhoods of Dorothy and Justine. Dorothy has already complained about the way the culture distorts what is "real". "One of my first memories is having to deny the concrete truths of my life, of denying the clear pattern of them . . . You were never supposed to discover the way things interlocked."[40] The novel sets out to remedy this.

The differences between the girls was even more marked in childhood. Dorothy—she was called Dottie Footie then—comes from a peripatetic lower-middle class family and is by reason of her weight, a hopeless outcast. In life she has been forced into the masochist's role. Justine, pretty, clever, upper-middle class, is socially successful and indeed overtly sadistic in her dealings with other children. Nevertheless, both are sensitive and feel a great deal of anxiety and alienation amidst the harsh dominance rituals of suburban childhood. These passages are the most evocative and successful in the novel as Gaitskill strips away sentiment from family life and childhood sexuality, but she never takes the sort of risks in her writing that Bret Easton Ellis took in *American Psycho* or that Dennis Cooper takes throughout his work. Even as she leads us into the physical embarrassments and hideous intimacies of family life she maintains a certain subtle politeness. Bathroom ritual, for example, is never exposed as Joyce exposed it with Leopold Bloom, or as Alice Munro did in her stark account of working-class Canadian family life *The Beggar-Maid*. Gaitskill does not really want to offend.

It is when Dorothy's family is living in Painesville, Pennsylvania that the focal event of her life occurs, when her father starts to abuse her. By contrast, the events that form Justine—her sadistic abuse of fellow-children, not her own younger experience of being a victim—occur when she is living in Action, Illinois. People are formed forever by a particular aspect of their past. Dorothy lives forever in Painesville. Justine, less abused, more assertive, is rooted in the events of Action. Despite her dawning masochistic fantasies, fuelled by voracious reading (the "Heathcliff" factor again), Justine has far more control over her life, is far less down-trodden and disadvantaged within the "rigid pattern" of the "adolescent social system".[41] Dorothy is obsessed with the story of Peter Pan and when she is released by joining Granite's cult she assumes the name Dorothy Never. From being Dottie Footie—a "mad", dotty, ugly person kicked ("footed") too quickly into adulthood—she is able, under Granite's kindly auspices to retreat to a safe, "spiritual" childhood. Dorothy's account of her past is more florid and imaginative than Justine's as befits the "character" on whom the authorial imagination is projected. Justine is equally haunted by her past, particularly her abuse of an outsider in school known derisively as "Emotional". It can be seen just how complex are the inter-relationships between the characters of Dorothy and Justine. For all her relative success. Justine is tormented by sado-masochistic impulses and ultimately ends up more of a "victim" than Dorothy who, despite the relentless abuse, is far calmer, stronger and more genuinely "spiritual". The way in which sexism, gross dominance and submission are built into the very fabric of American life, in the family and in school, is also made manifest.

Once back in the present, Justine becomes entangled with a shallow, specious sadist, very like the boy in "A Romantic Weekend". He abuses her; she is "pinned, helpless, exposed."[42] She has dark dreams that suggest Octave Mirbeau's fin-de-siècle masochistic fantasy *The Torture Garden*. Dorothy feels terribly betrayed by Justine's article on Anna Granite in which Justine suggests that Granite is a "Yuppie Grandmother", foreshadowing in her awful novels and aggressive Definitist (Rand's Objectivist) philosophy all the greed and right-wing selfishness of the eighties. This, although fair comment, is really a frantic last minute attempt to integrate Granite, who otherwise functions largely as *deus ex machina*, into the fabric of the book. Dorothy, enraged, arrives at Justine's apartment just in time to free her from what might possibly be a murderous attack by Bryan, the slippery sadist. The two girls end up in bed together, ("I'm not gonna hate Emotional any more"), and the two halves of what might be read as one personality are reconciled. Justine welcomes the rejected outsider in herself and Dorothy receives the validation of her intellectual self. Together they form an impregnable female unity against the misbegotten power of all sadistic Fathers.

It is a powerful book, albeit flawed. The Ayn Rand figure functions very uncomfortably as device, as meeting-point. Gaitskill's view of what she terms "objective reality" is unclear. The denouement is contrived. But Gaitskill, in revealing the bare bones of female upbringing in an abusive and patriarchal society, achieves something of considerable value and without simplistic overtones. The roots of such psychic twisting can lie in women (Anna Granite, Justine's childhood behaviour) as much as in men.

E.Y.

iv. Catherine Texier

Catherine Texier was, with her partner Joel Rose, editor of the seminal Downtown magazine *Between C & D* in which many of the writers covered in this book were first published. Texier is French, born in Brittany and educated in Paris. She moved to America in the late sixties and travelled widely before settling for a while in Montreal. There she wrote, in French, her first novel *Chloe l'Atlantique* and a study of prostitution in Quebec. She now lives in New York, and the city, in common with so much other urban neo-realism, functions more as character than as background in her work.

Her first novel in English, *Love Me Tender*, was greeted with the same sort of warm accolades as was Mary Gaitskill's *Bad Behaviour*. It was similarly praised for being less "trendy" and more "heartfelt"[1] than the other accounts of New York Downtown life. Both these books were actually being contrasted favourably with books by men. The implication in both cases is that these accounts by women were somehow warmer, deeper, more sensitive and eloquent than the books by Jay McInerney and Bret Easton Ellis. That this reinforces sexual stereotypes need hardly be emphasized. *Love Me Tender* and *Bad Behaviour* were never described as sharp, brittle, shallow and somehow threatening because they were considered ... you know ... more womanly. More intuitive, more "natural". Texier makes less attempt than either Janowitz or Gaitskill to eschew the deep, deep well of womanly feelings and desires. She neither apes the boys with the flattened affect of Janowitz's *Slaves of New York* nor does she possess Gaitskill's spiky, slightly irritable edge. Both *Love Me Tender* and her follow-up novel, *Panic Blood*, simply pullulate with female fluids; menses, miscarriages, urine, blood, sweat and tears. Both books are so well-lubricated

—and indeed lubricious—that the reader is in danger of drowning.

Texier is a true child of the sixties. Her primary concerns are sexuality and sexual liberation, overlain with sufficient feminism to justify her emphasis on female myths and just enough independence to propel her heroines from one man as far as the next. She has an extraordinarily visual imagination and her books are as vivid as anything else written about New York during this time, but her concentration on the relentless cycles of female life produces a textual whirlpool pulling the reader further and further towards the black hole, the nothingness at its centre. She makes this clear in *Love Me Tender*: "there is no story. Only cycles repeating themselves ad infinitum. No beginning no end just voices clashing."[2] The voices clash less than one might expect—they are primarily the voices of French expatriate women.

Love Me Tender and *Panic Blood* are very similar novels. They both have a beautiful young French heroine earning her living in the sexual exploitation industry of New York. Each girl has an older Frenchwoman, also an expatriate, as a mentor. They are both pursued by a mysterious and threatening man. They both flirt with the black-magic aspect of *santería*. Each girl fucks a great deal as an antidote to the undercurrent of fear and despair, nothingness, that runs throughout the two books. Both books end with a long and largely pointless journey.

Texier's vision of bohemian life has less to do with female independence than female servitude. The shoddy apartments and low incomes may be one of the few avenues of independence open to women but its freedoms are largely illusory. Bohemian life does not define anyone; rather it sucks them into a dark maw where everything becomes blurred. Mystique, an ageing stripper in *Love Me Tender*, cannot now remember "why she fought so hard against a straight life" although she dimly remembers her "early nightmare: ending up married to a doctor, with three kids in a suburban split-level."[3] In Texier's work bohemian life is merely fate and broken dreams. It may have originated in some far-off spiritual and sexual needs but ultimately it is just drudgery and street survival. It is in no way a romance. This is an elusive and sophisticated point of view. By denying, unlike Mary Gaitskill, that bohemian life offers any freedom, growth or source of strength for women, Texier gains points for a blindingly honest, world-weary, street-smart stance. Simultaneously, however, she presents women whose undeniable glamour and beauty—not to speak of their gorgeous boyfriends —undercuts this pragmatic, cynical viewpoint and resurrects all the ancient, seductive myths of bohemian life—sex, drugs, hedonism and fantastically individual clothes.

Texier also has considerable nostalgia for an older *Vie Bohème*: Paris in the Twenties, Berlin in the Thirties. The heroine of *Love Me Tender* is called Lulu, which instantly evokes the prostitute heroine of Frank Wedekind's play *Pandora's Box*. German film director G.W. Pabst made a film of the play in 1929 with the capricious, wayward American actress Louise Brooks in the role of Lulu.[4] Texier's Lulu works as an erotic dancer at The Blue Night Lounge which in its turn evokes further decadence, the perverse appeal of Marlene Dietrich in *The Blue Angel*.

Lulu is employed by an older, richer Frenchwoman, Salvine. She too, as Lulu was to do so many years later, fled provincial France for the vast promise of America. Salvine is now a wealthy widow, a dilettante, something of a sexual dominatrix. She is extraordinarily beautiful and elegant, although her composure hides "a deep terror cleverly camouflaged".[5] She employs Lulu to reminisce on tape about her, Lulu's, early life, hoping to receive some illumination about the nature of her own flight and expatriation. We learn that both Lulu and Salvine are having an affair with the same boy, a masochistic little junkie poseur called Julian. Lulu is also terrorized by a series of phone-calls to her sub-let apartment. She eventually meets their instigator, a handsome, street-wise Puerto Rican with whom she promptly begins another affair. Lulu seems utterly subservient to her own sensuality and pursues at the same time another liaison with a rich, up-town artist. "He fucks her in the elevator going up to his loft, he fucks her on his king-size bed with a view of New Jersey sunsets, on the beach at the Hamptons at 2 a.m."[6] Lulu seems addicted to sex, to men "a smell, a presence, a movement . . . life running through them and flickering in odd shapes and moods."[7] The third woman in the trio is Mystique, another dancer at The Blue Night Lounge. Younger than Salvine, she is still much older than Lulu who is only twenty-five. She too is a sort of expatriate, from the privations of Middle America and she too seeks to dull her anxieties with casual sex. All three women assume the gaudy plumage of the sexually available which both flaunts and conceals their interior selves: Salvine as the courtesan and dominatrix, Mystique as the tarty stripper and Lulu, dressed as a parody bride for a Halloween party or as a sexy street punk. Although they seem to play with these stylized roles, yet we learn little of the women beneath the self-dramatization beyond their formless fears and fragmented memories. They are subsumed by their sexuality and by the price they must pay for their beauty and hedonism—the dreadful fear of ageing, the "near-panic at time closing door after door every day".[8]

Besides female sensuality, the novel explores two other major themes. Texier seeks to understand expatriation, particularly in the case of Salvine and Lulu whose experiences are so very similar despite the age gap and whose dislocation involved the loss of a language. The three women are linked in an even more fundamental way by the loss of their mothers. Lulu's mother either died in childbirth or was removed to an asylum and Salvine and Mystique both lose their mothers during the course of the novel. Disease and ageing hover over the book as the women perform a Masque of the Red Death, desperately dancing and fornicating in the teeth of their on-rushing physical decay. Their interior emptiness and desolation is explicitly linked to their motherless state and each seeks to replicate a mother-daughter relation and by implication to create a happier family situation than the one they experienced. Salvine hires Lulu to be, in essence, her daughter, Lulu and Mystique respond to each other like siblings and Lulu fantasizes constantly about older mother figures. For all their beauty and desirability the men in *Love Me Tender* are even slighter and function even more as dressed-up props than the women. It is the cycles of woman-hood, the never-ending story of female birth, sexuality, motherhood and ageing that are the well-springs of life and within the depths of all that fecundity and suffering, little enough changes down the generations. When free-thinking, free-loving Lulu rejects her Puerto Rican lover Mario it is for the most rock-solid of *petit bourgeois* reasons, class prejudice. "His hands betray him, coarse skin, sores, cuts, thick nails . . . hands skillful at tuning a guitar, beating a drum, rolling a joint, changing a tire, but uncomfortable with a pen or a demitasse . . . She reads ignorance and peasant heritage and unfinished high school."[9] And we read snobbery: Lulu remains a good daughter of the French middle classes who will probably marry for money as Salvine did before her.

These three women are all refugees who have left one illusion—the happy family—for the plethora of illusions on tap in New York: "You have to know how to play with signs," says Lulu, "but instead of offering well-established codes New York demands that you be ahead of constantly changing ones."[10] Here, with "worlds/words slipping against each other"[11] they have to forge a new language of survival which involves a manipulation of their sexual charms, partly as a way to enjoy their new-found freedom but partly because they have little alternative. Everyone in their world is "alienated from parents, siblings, their own culture, their country, the rest of the world, hanging onto Manhattan by their fingernails for fear of falling back into America's wasteland."[12] They must make do as best they can; Lulu makes clear that a "feminist stance" is far less important than "economic necessities".[13] And if each of the three women is aware of the void, the emptiness within them— "I am a hole. I am completely hollow inside"[14]—well, is that not perhaps part of the bargain they have made? They will stupefy themselves with memories, photographs, romance, clothes and lust to try and subdue their existential anguish and blind themselves to the harsh and inescapable realities of their position as women, their lowly servitude as daughters in past generations and as sexual playthings in the bright new world. Ironically it is in the very act of writing a novel (not the most economically sensible thing to do), that Texier confronts and up-ends the patriarchal hierarchy. In *Love Me Tender* fundamentally it is the men who are secondary, who are weak, who are the playthings and it is the women who, despite their butterfly glamour, are empowered and foregrounded by this recital of their histories. The act of writing here is genuinely subversive in that it gives a voice to these women and all those like them. They become archetypal, a dramatic chorus speaking to us from out of the shadows and neon of the city, telling of that long, strange trip down the Boulevard of Broken Dreams.

Texier's elliptical, imagistic style is closer to poetry than to prose and in *Panic Blood* she ranges over the same themes in the same highly evocative language. Eva—another archetypal name—is a gorgeous French nightclub chanteuse. Texier's astonishingly vivid visual imagination creates an unforgettably alluring woman; Eva croons at the microphone at a club called the Angel's Follies. She wears an emerald green bustier, her black hair is twisted untidily into a bun, her mouth painted carmine. She wears a black Bakelite bracelet. "Her skin, dead white of the night. Do you know she powders her thighs, her breasts? To give them this pearly effect?"[15] Eva has a "cappuccino coloured daughter", Mimi, child of the long-vanished Frank Jackson, a sinister, unpredictable musician. Mimi lives much of the time with Albertine, an older Frenchwoman, a dressmaker. She, in her turn, had deserted her own daughters back in France when she fled to America. Thus the patterns, the cycles of neglect and damage continue again, spiralling down the generations. Albertine is a semi-alcoholic and perhaps not always a fit childminder, but Mimi must be sacrificed to expediency and necessity. Eva must earn. She must spend long days fucking her lover Johnny at his downtown loft. Johnny is a pure sex object with his soft, floppy hair, limpid eyes and generous mouth, long, long legs and battered leather jacket. When the pornographic gaze falls on a man it seems it must bleach him of all personality, just as that same gaze, by men, reduces women to ciphers.

In these days of AIDS Eva also operates a sex-phone line from her hotel—"Lola, the Fantasy Queen". She is being pursued by one of her callers who has tracked her to the hotel. It would seem that he is a notorious criminal, the Times Square Rapist, who has infected several women with the HIV virus. Frank Jackson also turns up again and tries to befriend his daughter, eventually kidnapping her.

The tone of *Panic Blood* is dark, heavy and brooding. It is a lubricious book, sexually very explicit, veering between exploration and exploitation. Texier pursues various intoxicating sexual legends: white woman and black man; the myth of the rapist, cruising like a shark, repellent yet masochistically titillating; the myth of the call-girl, purveyor of sexual fantasies, herself consumed by lust. And in again exploiting the Gallic connection Texier creates a dizzying nexus of desire that combines sweet sluttishness with sophistication. Texier cannot be unaware that much of Lulu's and Eva's allure comes from their nationality, that their high-style French chic and lewd sexual abandon constitutes a cliché. The age-old promise of Gallic sensuality has long proved irresistible to Puritan prudery—the snap of a garter, the silken frou-frou of lingerie, the lazy post-coital Gauloise, paint, beauty-spots, scented orifices—all of this has long denoted a physicality and lust for life generally deemed absent from more repressed races. All these sexual legends, the stuff of fantasy, give the book a powerfully erotic charge. Does Texier mean to deconstruct them, to demythologize them? Certainly Eva is just another suffering girl, trying to get by. Frank Jackson ultimately wishes no harm to either Mimi or Eva. The rapist is apprehended and proves to be as mild, cowed and ordinary as they always are—hardly the stuff of fantasy. However, in setting up all this sexual danger within these well-worn parameters Texier cannot altogether escape their consequences, their potent force. These are the sort of fantasies that the politically correct indulge in secret and despair of in that they reinforce stereotypes of race, sex and class. Austrian novelist Elfriede Jelinek has said that she attempted to write pornography "of, by and for women" but found it was impossible. The structure of language precluded such writing because it served male needs and perceptions.

Texier seems to have exactly the same problem here; she attempts to reveal Eva's erotic depths and sensual needs and ends up writing something that sounds, at times, like a lingerie advertisement, that plugs straight into an array of fantasy clichés and that leaves the eroticized woman—Eva—as devoid of personality, as much of a sex-doll as her lover Johnny. The sexual gaze of our culture, encoded in language, is a dehumanizing one. It is only the non-sexual or pre-sexual characters, Albertine and Mimi, who have any animation. In this respect the book is divided against itself as was *Love Me Tender*, which seemed to want to show the gritty reality of Downtown life but evoked a vision that would enthral any alienated small-town teenager. Similarly *Panic Blood* may seek to demystify Eva's life but produces instead elegant and beautiful pornography. Texier is perceptive about states of desire—"like all lovers they are making love with their imaginations"[16] she writes in *Love Me Tender* and "You have to tap on the unspoken to really arouse,"[17] in *Panic Blood*—but her readers are inevitably denied these states—they are un-writeable, pre-Oedipal—and directed along the old paths of linguistic arousal, erotic writing being quite distinct from *jouissance* in the Barthesian sense.

Eva is, like Lulu, adrift in a brutal city. There is a sense of doom, of apocalypse. "We are the last ones . . . the last generation. We live in the cracks like rats."[18] Rage, death and sex seem to reach a boiling point as Eva, like Lulu before her, is drawn to the atrocity reports in the newspapers. Eva reacts similarly, using sex as a shield against decay and entropy. "Eva believed men were like drugs. She craves them, but deep down she thought she'd be better off without them."[19] The story splinters and fragments, dreams and memories unfold, time expands and collapses as different characters speak at different points in their lives. Eva's grandmother is dying and much space is devoted to her physical decline. But despite the hellish pressures of Eva's life her insistent sexuality remains a barrier to our sense of her personality. The text seems to turn in upon itself, to *become* Eva to such an extent that the reader lacks an entrée. Frank Jackson says to her: "Stop thinking you're the center of the universe. Still as self-involved as ever, are you?"[20] And she is.

Eva moans that she was a bastard because her father didn't recognize her but makes no attempt to shield Mimi from her own bastardy, introducing Frank Jackson to the child in a notably brutal manner: "that, my dear, is your dad".[21] Texier may have intended a complex characterization but the reader finds it hard to celebrate Eva's loveliness and wanton sexuality alongside her humourless self-absorption. At the end of the book, Eva travels to California to reclaim Mimi and return home. Similarly in *Love Me Tender*, Lulu journeyed to Mexico with Mario. They both return to New York, back to the fear, the emptiness and "the stench of human misery",[22] back to the city whose uncompromising presence has replaced all family, where everything is possible, whether of hope or despair. Nothing has changed. They will grow older, they will neglect their children, their liberation will begin and end in a desirous adolescent sexuality, they will be at the mercy of irresponsible men. They are motherless children, they do not want to grow up and they will only ever really belong in the vast kiddies playground that was the nineteen sixties.

In looking at these writers, Tama Janowitz, Mary Gaitskill and Catherine Texier, it seems clear that what separates them decisively from the women in their books is the act of writing. This has given them status, money and respect. They are recording a world they know very well and have performed a valuable literary service in documenting the lives of girls in contemporary New York. Finally, we are hearing from women who have traditionally been silent: the misfits, the decadents, the bohemian individualists, those who felt uncomfortable with hard-line feminism or utopianism. However it would seem that the considerable freedoms available nowadays to women are expressed almost exclusively in the sexual arena; the emphasis on sexuality is constant and unremitting. However much one might wish to approach these texts without this constant stress on sexuality and on the gender of the authors, feminism itself has rendered this impossible. We now know the ways in which gender is socially constructed and the domination it exerts over every aspect of our lives. Tama Janowitz's books are relatively gender-fluid; the sex of the author is of little importance. Female sexuality is the central theme in the work of Mary Gaitskill and Catherine Texier and one cannot examine their books without an emphasis on gender.

It would seem, looking at much recent women's fiction, that a rampant libido is mandatory for the liberated woman, that it virtually defines liberation, much as it did in the work of Erica Jong or Lisa Alther. Jenny Turner, writing recently in *The Guardian* about two English novelists, Christina Koning and Katie Campbell, says: "Is it really the case that education, travel and all the other privileges that go along with being a middle-class woman these days equip one to think only about where the next lay is coming from?"[23] This is not to decry the importance of sexual freedoms gained in recent decades nor to deny that women's liberation as we know it originated with easily available and reliable contraceptive methods. The sexual freedom had to pre-date any other freedoms. But now surely there *are* a great many other freedoms available to all the women who choose to live on the edge in the big cities? There are many, many other ways of living dangerously, if one so desires. There are intellectual and artistic freedoms available to women as never before in history. There are freedoms in travel, in sport, in every sort of political activity. There are freedoms to be creative in any aspect of life: in personality, in every sort of artistic endeavour, in motherhood and in friendship. There are freedoms to explore any variety of decadent experience. There are a range of choices available to women that would have been unimaginable a century ago. Admittedly all these freedoms have an economic basis and are limited to a privileged minority in the developed countries but this still represents a huge advance in terms of life choices. We have escaped from the grim hegemony of Nature over women's lives and we have access to a hitherto unprecedented range of opportunities, yet many novelists persist in writing as though sex was the single area of interest for women. Admittedly, most of the male writers covered in this book have been able to foreground sexuality in their work—and frequently a very destructive and violent sexuality—without critics suggesting that it wholly dominates their writing. It may indeed be that the language available to women writers imprisons them in exactly the way the French feminist writers have tried to challenge; they cannot mention sex at all without reinforcing patriarchal assumptions about women. The emphasis on sexuality in these books by Gaitskill, Janowitz and Texier is not cynical or commercial in intent. They want and need to answer questions about the sexuality of their heroines, but doing so seems to deliver them into a commercial trap that sexualizes themselves and their work at the expense of the other issues they raise. Writing about sex often seems reductive for women in that it tends to mire them in what they most need to escape from. Within the limitations of patriarchal language it seems to involve them inevitably in a degree of sexual display, the flirtings of a female child. The phantom phallus, the tool of the patriarchy, looms behind all the novels of Janowitz, Gaitskill and Texier. One can sense the Male Artist as in the Parker Junius/Andy Warhol figure in Tama Janowitz's work and the male as Colonizer in all her books. Mary Gaitskill evokes the Janus-faced Good/Bad Father and Catherine Texier a whole range of powerful male archetypes who threaten her heroines from the Rapist to the Mighty Black Phallus, as well as imprisoning them within an endless search for the lost phallus, the perfect Other. Both Gaitskill and Texier have found it necessary to actually stress penile size in their work which could not be a clearer symbol of the Law of the Father.[24] It *is* the Law of the Father, or rather its ever present representative in our lives either as physical actuality—in men—or Holy Grail, for heterosexual women.

Something in the construction of these books, with their phantom appendage lurking around sub-textually seems to reduce the characters and the female world to doll-size, play-size. The books may be lubricious, but they are never gross. They remain dainty, they do not offend. The chances are that Bad Girls don't write novels. Those who do are really nice and good and disciplined and trying hard to please a male archetype: mentor, father, tutor, lover, artist.

In Freudian theory it is at the moment of Oedipal crisis that the girl-child turns from her pre-Oedipal attachment to the mother and takes her father for love-object instead. There are deep flaws in Freud's theory of penis-envy as Luce Irigaray, in particular, has pointed out. Women, at the Oedipal crux, become man's Other—his negative, excluded mirror-image— and, following from this, she argues that patriarchal discourse, language itself, consigns women to an outer darkness. She exists outside representation; she *is* negativity, absence, nothingness and therefore, by definition, lesser than the male. For women as writers to join the male master discourse, involves them, as Irigaray has described, in endless contradictions. She feels that in mimicking male discourse the woman writer is trapped in inauthenticity, or as she calls it, *hysteria*. She is miming her own sexuality, which is all she can do with it in patriarchal discourse. However there is no other way in which we can speak. At the point where we join discourse we have already been inserted into the Symbolic Order and there is no escape. It is our language, our only language, and if women are to speak at all it has to be within this framework of symbolic language. What becomes important, at this point, is what the woman writer does with the language available to her. If she just accepts it as immutable, she will of necessity be mimicking male discourse and, indeed, male representations of women. (I am told that much lesbian erotica in bookshops sells to the dirty raincoat brigade.) Moreover, when she comes to write of primal issues—sex, power, love, dominance, submission—she will inevitably re-enact, uncon- sciously, the Oedipal crisis that provided her with language. Primal issues will revert to the primal point. And this is what happens in all these novels, which gives them a certain stasis in terms of a future for women writing. They are well-written, entertaining, often touching, but in purely formal terms they do not go anywhere new other than in the sense that all the work covered in this book is helping to create a fictional future beyond postmodernism. As Lou Reed said, "Some kinds of love/are mistaken for vision."[25]

Unfortunately there is no space to look at the work of lesbian writers like Jane DeLynn and Sara Shulman, whose writings are set within the same New York milieu, although, from a psychoanalytical point of view it differs less from the fictions already described than one might expect. The most dramatic work so far, in feminist terms, has been by writers like Hélène Cixous, Monique Wittig and Christine Brooke-Rose, all influenced by decades of European theory. But their work remains resolutely uncommercial and I believe it will be from the ranks of the urban postrealists, in the footsteps of Kathy Acker, that we will see more women writing, being successful and adding to what Gaitskill, Janowitz et al have managed to tell the world about the variety of women's lives.

For the time being in America, the most exhilarating women artists are those working in visual or performance art, where all these textual problems need not apply. It is significant that most of this confrontational art occurs without the intervention of language. Cindy Sherman, Jenny Holzer and Barbara Kruger in their paintings and installations, and women like Karen Finley, Diamanda Galás in performance art, and particularly Avital Ronell who manages to stress language deviancy in her performances and essays, are all doing what the novelists should be doing: creating monstrous art.

E.Y.

Silence, exile and cunning

The writing of Lynne Tillman

"I hold, and this is essential, that verbal inspirations are infinitely richer in visual sense, infinitely stranger to the eye, than visual images proper."

André Breton

"These weren't Greek queens and kings whose realms were at stake. These were middle-class white people with problems."

Lynne Tillman, *Haunted Houses*

As we approach the millennium we can look back on a century of trouble and strife in literature. The great nineteenth-century novel, the "grand narrative" was really barely established before writers in the full flush of early modernism started to play around with it, slice it up and deconstruct it. Also, as everyone knows, these were not even original moves; they had been implicit in the origins of the novel form, in the work of Laurence Sterne and Daniel Defoe. And yet the idea of "realism" in fiction has cast an immensely long shadow. The experience of reading fiction or of thinking about fiction is still measured against the achievements of classic realism. Our hunger for narrative, for sequential form, is intense. We crave a mimesis of the tragic narrative of our own lives, tragic in that they must veer inexorably towards closure, or death. The remarkable popularity of biography in recent years attests to this: publishers will offer large advances to biographers in preference to novelists. For many contemporary readers biography offers a happy alternative to the realist novel. Readers find in biography all the qualities that they previously relished in fiction but which have now been banished by inchoate postmodern wispiness—a strong plot line (birth to death), lust, ambition, sexuality and a cast of indisputably solid characters. As the twentieth century progressed the discoveries in quantum theory laid waste to any ideas of a meaningful, ordered universe and these new uncertainties were paralleled by all the immense upheavals and disruptions in the arts. Yet many people have never been able to relinquish this need for stability and order in art, for "realism" in fiction and the visual arts. If neurological advances ever confer immortality upon us will they all suddenly become comfortable with every form of abstraction, experimentation and dissonance—for what are they but attempts to cheat narrative structure or avoid death?

Now, after everything possible has been done to the form of the novel the whole future of fiction seems to hang in the balance. Will anyone, apart from scholars, read at all in the future? Surveys suggest that relatively few people read books even now and that of those, the majority tend towards genre—romance, crime, horror—much of which echoes the conventions of traditional narrative in terms of plot, structure and character. "Serious" fiction seems to belong increasingly to academia and the academics, to the creative writing class and the beleaguered intellectual rather than to the public at large. It has become too frail and etiolated a plant to survive out there in the world amongst the crashing music, the clamour and the cartoons of contemporary life. Novelists wish to be read but realism in fiction is no longer a device that can animate characters who inhabit this modern world; their desires, their love affairs, their very selves are now so muddied by commodity fetishism, consumer homogeneity and a chaos of contemporary cultural imperatives that it is now almost impossible for authors to animate and illuminate character in the ways that they were once able to do.

The novelists under consideration in this book have all been searching for a way to deal with the problems of writing fiction, readable fiction, at this point in time when all the old strategies seem played out. They have succeeded, largely, by concentrating on aspects of contemporary urban life which are commonly experienced but frequently ignored in other fictions: urban breakdown, sexual and narcotic experimentation, street-life, crime and the melodrama of metropolitan adolescence. Additionally they have treated fictional conventions, both traditional ones and the knowing devices of postmodernism, as *bricolage*, to be assumed and discarded as convenient. This comprises the postrealism that can engage a reader whilst continuing to be aware of the fictionality of the processes it assumes.

At first glance Lynne Tillman's career and work would seem a perfect representation of every observation that could be made about this group of writers. She would seem to embody every cliché of the Lower East Side artist. She has been involved in the visual arts and in film. Her fiction first appeared in the many small magazines that emerged from the East Village during the eighties. She too documents bohemian sub-cultures, city-life and media saturation. And yet her work conspicuously lacks the nervous glitter and frantic pace so prevalent in that of her contemporaries. Her writing has a stately, courtly quality that seems to anchor it far away in a slower, more questioning space, despite the contemporaneity of her themes. She makes few concessions to popular success and continues to write books that require thought, patience and time. They seem to be the product of pure will. Her commitment to reasoned enquiry lies in direct opposition to the moral vacuum that underlies so much fast-paced postmodernist thought.

As a woman writer she faces all the additional problems that have bedeviled the other women writers already discussed. Tillman is a self-confessed feminist[1] but in common with other of the New York women writers is disinclined to focus on the more obvious aspects of feminism in her work. She fears that "feminism" as it is currently understood tends to ignore issues of style and form in writing and to dwell solely on content and on a fairly narrow definition of content at that. The desire to resist the label of "feminist" writer is understandable in that it is such a paradoxical label. On the one hand, it seems to many people to denote precisely this narrowness of focus and interpretation. On the other, as Tillman rightly says, "There are so many feminisms."[2] Linda Hutcheon takes up this point in her discussion of those she defines as being "ex-centric, on the border or margin". She says, "Feminist theory offers perhaps the clearest example of the importance of an awareness of the diversity of history and culture of women: their differences of race, ethnic group, class, sexual preference." Hutcheon goes on to speak of all the different orientations that are subsumed under the feminist label. She speaks of: "Canon-charging and women's literary history . . . separatist or women-centred gynocriticism . . . psychoanalytic studies of female subjectivity . . . theories of *écriture feminine* . . . deconstructive interrogations of cultural concepts"[3] and many many more, lesbian feminisms, Marxist feminisms, post-colonial feminisms, so many in fact that one can see clearly that a feminist of Tillman's persuasion, that is someone who is aware of all this intense multi-culturalism, is going to be dealing with an almost unimaginable complexity in their work.

This remains the central problem of Tillman's work. It *is* very complex. Only a lengthy study could do justice to all its shifts and nuances, its references and subtleties. She takes immense risks. She works right on the edge of pointlessness, of silence, of not writing at all and in this respect her work is reminiscent of that of Samuel Beckett. The short story "To Find Words" begins: "I have nothing to say. There is nothing to say is another way to say it. Or still, in another way, there is so much to say . . ." and continues: "I don't know about you but I feel like hell. The country is falling apart, what does anything matter, people are dying, starving, being blown out of the sky, people are suffering, and what does anything matter, what difference does this nothing make, what matter do words make?"[4] Any writer located on this edge, where language is pared down to its roots, needs immense resources of will and stubbornness. They must have the impulse to continue against all odds, to illumine, to reveal. Tillman lacks Beckett's vast pessimism and his remote, deistic tenderness towards his characters. Her own impulse to continue lies in something more opaque.

Tillman has published two books in Britain, a collection of short fiction entitled *Absence Makes the Heart* and a novel *Motion Sickness*. She has published stories in various British anthologies. She also writes as a critic and this familiarity with theory is partly what gives her work its density. Much of her fiction anticipates the critic. It is highly controlled and pretty much certain to out-manoeuvre critical conjecture or alternatively to impel the critic to re-trace the theory that she has already put into practice.

Her tone is grave with moments of wry, self-deprecating humour. Although this style remains constant, her aims and intentions differ enormously from one work to the other as if she sets herself a number of problems to be solved in each endeavour. Her commitment is essentially to the novel of ideas and this is what gives her work its somewhat stately old-fashioned qualities despite the postmodern insistence on the primacy of language. The ghosts of Henry James and Edith Wharton—other intellectual anglophile Americans—are never very far away. The underlying tension in her work is philo-sophical, an oscillation between the need for language to contain and communicate thought and the abyss of postmodern nihilism in the fact of its limitations. This tension, which is both problematic and animating in her work can be seen in an early novel, *Haunted Houses*. *Haunted Houses* intends, rather as Mary Gaitskill does in *Two Girls, Fat and Thin*, to illuminate the dynamics of growing up female in America, to show the ways in which gender is thrust upon us and our pitiful attempts to outrun its implications. Tillman, along with Mary Gaitskill and Tama Janowitz, is very aware of the lack of literary myths for women. Robert Siegle in his *Suburban Ambush* records Tillman as saying: "One of the things I was thinking about when I first started writing *Haunted Houses* was that there was no *Catcher in the Rye* for women, not that I think that *Haunted Houses* is like *Catcher in the Rye*. But there was nothing that took early female experience and allowed readers to go through it in a more or less unadulterated way."[5]

Haunted Houses traces the lives of three girls, Jane, Emily and Grace, as they move from childhood into womanhood. It is a densely textured, richly allusive novel, curiously circular and sinuous in structure. The three girls encounter all the rites and rituals of adolescent femininity: "Glowing with artifice and anxiety"[6] they attempt to take their places within the treacherous discourses of female maturity only to find that the unresolved churnings of their unconscious selves constantly erodes their hesitant forward steps. There is an insistent undertow of psychoanalysis and myth which claims each girl through the seductions of literature. Jane, trapped within an Electra complex, the habit of "loving madmen"[7] in the wake of her father, is explicitly identified with, and splintered upon, the oppositions of *King Lear*. Grace, haunted in her turn by her mother is drawn to "the dark side, the B side, the bad and the beautiful".[8] She is an Imp of the Perverse, fascinated by the ambiguous, deadly fictions of Poe and Wilde. Emily is the one who wishes to be a writer and she finds herself up against the patriarchal canons of literature, particularly American literature and culture. "Call me Ishmael," writes her friend and "perverted suitor", Jimmy; "Call me Tom Sawyer. Call me Adam. Call me Roy Rogers. Call me Tarzan. Call me Dick Tracey. Call me Dick."[9] This could hardly be more succinct.

Tillman's use of intertextuality appeals, in the most obvious sense, to the like-minded reader. Otherwise *Haunted Houses* illustrates very clearly the constant struggle between text and context that underlies all her work. Her attitude to characterization remains unresolved. Grace, Emily and Jane cannot be said to function as "characters" in any classic sense. They are not distinct. They are intentionally fluid and can easily be read as three aspects of one psyche, or as the archetypal components of a certain female American identity: intellectual, questing, alienated. Tillman's reservations about the construction of characters are in some ways no more than the usual postmodern suspicions about the trickery of fictional process, a disinclination to invest in what Barthes has described as the "illogicality . . . incongruity", the "logical contradiction" of text.[10] We have seen Bret Easton Ellis's adamant refusal to participate in traditional characterization and to a greater or lesser extent all the writers we discuss share this uneasiness. Inevitably so. One needs extraordinary innocence, extraordinary obsession or extraordinary disregard for the poisoned cup of postmodern critical insight to create "character" nowadays without some knowing indication of one's collusion in fictionality. In her recent story "To Find Words" Tillman coldly strikes the final blows in describing her central character Paige Turner (*Paige Turner!*): "Paige Turner is a tall woman with bright red hair. She is a petite woman with jet black hair. She is of middling height, has blonde hair and is known to diet strenuously and laugh loudly."[11] Right, that's it! She is nothing. She is anything the author wants her to be. In another way Tillman's flattening out of character is another not-uncommon testimony to postmodern lack of effect. But, at yet another level, Tillman's barely differentiated characters testify to something that seems absolutely personal—the sense of fear and distrust of imagination itself, its duplicity, its fundamental immorality. This becomes clearer in later work.

The sketchy characterization in *Haunted Houses* also attests to Tillman's understanding of patriarchal discourse. Participating in fiction, setting forth character, traps women, according to Luce Irigaray, in the role of mimic or hysteric. Within language, women are the non-sense, a confluence of negatives that exist only as lesser representations of, or the other side of, the male. For a woman to describe female identity or female sexuality is merely to mime it, clothed in the cast-off rags of patriarchal language. To find ways around this is the task of every woman writer and throwing oneself into full-fledged representations of womanhood in "traditional" language is not one of them. Luce Irigaray writes: "In her statements—at least when she dares to speak out—woman retouches herself constantly . . . One must listen to her differently in order to hear an *'other meaning' which is constantly in the process of weaving itself, at the same time ceaselessly embracing words and yet casting them off to avoid becoming fixed, immobilised.*"[12] It is this *'other meaning'* that we encounter in Tillman's work. Lastly, in *Haunted Houses* it is the constant questioning that is significant. Grace wants to know "Why she thought one thing rather than another. Why she was heterosexual. Why here rather than there." Her views are, she realizes, "predicated upon what she had or had not been given, a set of things, facts, conditions over which she had no control."[13] Jane asks: "What did I think about BEFORE, when I was young?"[14] Grace in her turn wonders, "Where does a thought come from?"[15] What they seek is truth of course, and it is this frustration, this matter of the author being a philosopher *manqué*, cognizant of the instability of language and its inability to answer her questions that lies at the heart of Tillman's work. Robert Siegle attempts to deal with this in his analysis of *Haunted Houses*. Of the characters, he says, "Given secondary or dependent gender roles, they cut out the givens and find themselves not liberated into utopic freedom, but empty, listless, occasionally even nostalgic. Given cultural coding rather than Nature or Truth, they undermine every verity and find mainly irony or silence. Given institutions that discipline and normalize rather than nurture and sustain, they live in one kind of exile or another—counterculture, foreign culture—and find only other customs, other norms, other laws. Given language rather than knowledge, they find not presence, but absence. Given roles rather than identity, they find otherness within."[16] This is the clue to Tillman's work, the imponderable, awful realization that we are "given language rather than knowledge." This is why her urge towards understanding is constantly poisoned by her being entrapped in the late twentieth century. Might she have been happier as a Victorian bluestocking, a rectory daughter with her botany kit and Latin dictionaries, or as an early Girton scholar? Perhaps.

When Tillman's collection of short fiction *Absence Makes the Heart* was first published in Britain it became clear that many critics approached her work as if it were autobiographical rather than, as was more often true, an attempt to deal with certain formal and technical problems associated with the experience of being a woman writer. The book contains her earliest work written for publication, "Weird Fucks" and "Diary of a Masochist". Tillman has said; "What I wanted to do there was to take different kinds of 'experience' and write it differently. I felt that the novels written about women's sexual lives were inadequate and that I was writing against a certain sentimentality, a certain over-emotionality in 'women's fiction'. I also felt that I wanted to take on writers like Jack Kerouac whose road was never a female one. I felt that I was writing about how we write about sex. 'Weird Fucks' is definitely as much about narrative style as it is about sexual content."[17]

It is in these early pieces that we encounter a narrative voice that was to become very important in Tillman's fiction and that was ultimately to function as a bridge between the elusiveness, the "unknowability" of experience and the difficulties of expressing this in language. This is the voice of the exile, the traveller, someone distanced from her own homeland, her own culture, her own socially constructed gender, someone for whom journeying becomes narrative itself and whose context is the construction of a "self" which is itself a foreign country. This vision of people as nation states had already surfaced in *Haunted Houses*; one character remarks: "I'm a displaced person, a country without a man."[18] As for Emily, the writer, "Being an occupied country obsessed Emily . . . Love is like that, an occupation, being occupied by."[19] In the early stories in *Absence Makes the Heart*, as the narrator drifts about Europe and America, making love and suffering with various men, one can see her taking the first steps into this exile, into a narrative flow which is constantly, inconsequentially, disrupted by "events" and "characters" and whose destination is that far-off country, a new self, the new found land. This is living fiction, fiction in process, mirroring ourselves as Kristeva's fluctuating "subject in process". Joan Didion wrote: "We tell ourselves stories in order to live,"[20] and stories are what happen along the way, along the journey. Even in *Haunted Houses* people are "just around, the way many people were in Grace's life. The connections were fragile, short-lived." Grace feels, "She was a story. (There were) . . . hundreds of stories."[21] This sense of the narrator as traveller, recounting and representing fragments of hundreds of stories along the way becomes omnipresent in Tillman's work. In "Diary of a Masochist" the narrator reads a quotation: "but also all journeys have secret destinations of which the traveller is unaware."[22] "Language follows change," she says.[23]

This idea of the journey, the traveller and the psychic nation state is absolutely central to Tillman's work. It is her answer to the problem of language, truth and knowledge. Psychically it seems extraordinarily apt. It is, for one thing, a charmingly old-fashioned concept in some ways, almost a Victorian one. The vision of the "Grand Tour", that legendary bid for freedom available to privileged young men and women, American and British, of the last two centuries is enshrined in fiction and travelogue. It was their one chance of escaping the stuffy conventions of middle-class life at home and as we see particularly in the work of Henry James and E.M. Forster, often their only chance to encounter older, less puritanical cultures. Additionally the idea of oneself as a country or an "occupied country" seems entwined with nineteenth and early twentieth century notions of colonialism, exploitation, suffering and an obscure patriotism, that sense of one's very self being bound up with the soil of one's native land. It is also an obvious metaphor for the experience of being a woman. Tillman has been able to annex such ideas, which accord so well with her anglophilia and her need for enquiry and exploration and combine them with our contemporary understanding of language, and our location within our own "mother-tongue". Tillman has stated: "I work within the American English language as a white, middle-class second-generation American woman, at a particular moment in history, with my own particular biography . . . So I must wrest this language and its forms away from or out of 'the majority' (of which I am part, in some ways and at some times, to others), to un-man it, to un-American it, even to un-white it, to inconvenience the majority language, to unconventionalize it, even to shame it, in an odd sort of way, to question privilege, my own too of course."[24] She explains that her concern is with "essentialisms of all kinds (and the construction of identity generally), that questioning national identity—how the nation state is inscribed in our different psyches, how each of us may be the repository of a national history and culture, how identity is inflected by nationality."[25] What is interesting is the way in which Tillman is able to use the concepts of nationality, colonialism and cultural identity, old concepts inscribed deep within our selves, and is able to "detourn" them, to subvert, decentre and destabilize them in the interests of "new narratives to replace the old ones",[26] new narratives of sexuality and identity. Tillman acknowledges her debt to Bakhtin, to the idea of the world as "a multiplicity of voices, a heteroglossia."[27] Postmodernism has been described as "language put into action"[28] and in Tillman's work we see language used as a conduit, as a means of communication between the old and the new, the old world and the new world, the old self and a new self, language engaged in constructing an identity, one which is not constrained by repressive, stultifying patriarchal conventions.

In addition to establishing this characteristic method of working, Tillman's other significant achievement in *Absence Makes the Heart* is the creation of Madame Realism. She originally appeared as a playful critical voice, particularly useful in art criticism, and was later adapted to fiction as it became clear that she was an exceptionally strong and flexible persona who could be sent into any kind of text as a sort of undercover agent. Madame Realism is not directly autobiographical: indeed, as time passes she seems to accrue more and more of a fearful and distinct personality of her own. Tillman has commented, memorably: "I say, 'Madame Realism got her period much like getting a statement from the bank.' Well, in fact I, Lynne Tillman, don't get her period like that."[29] Tillman goes on to describe how, in this instance, she was writing about not being tied to the body, foregrounding and playing around with the way the body exists in representation but what is particularly striking here is how true to Madame Realism's curious "being" the description of her getting her period is and indeed, how far it must be from Tillman's own experience. It is as if in defiance of all Tillman's reservations about personality in fiction Madame Realism has insisted on acquiring an increasingly disturbing character all her own.

Madame Realism is an astonishingly flexible figure. Tillman

has described her as: "a vehicle, a critical voice, a conduit for ideas, a way of thinking, someone who is usually changing."[30] She is all these things and more. She is the ghost in the machine, the spectre at the feast. In any piece in which she appears, walking around, observing, musing, going to parties she is a constant, forcible reminder of the shadow that must always fall between ourselves and the text. She is the language barrier. "After all," writes Tillman, "doesn't she exist, like a shadow, in the interstices of argument?"[31] Madame Realism knows that "my boundaries shift . . . like ones do after a war when countries lose or gain depending on having won or lost."[32] She really is an extraordinary creation, an embodiment, in text, of the problems of art. Her very name, with its connotations of bondage and discipline, helps to empower an author normally so suspicious of the privileges of the authorial voice, who subscribes to the Barthesian notion of contesting the idea of an original and originating author. Madame Realism *is* a persona—she goes to the parties, she pets her cat, she does all the things that a literary character might do but her name is a constant reminder of the impossibilities of fiction. Madame Realism tells us that she is not realism, that realism in literature is impossible, that words do not represent life any more than does paint on canvas. Madame Realism returns us constantly to the source of modernism—the point at which artists understood that their medium was their message and that it bore no relation to "life". "The phrase 'life drawing' popped into her head almost like a cartoon,"[33] Tillman writes in "Madame Realism's Imitation of Life". The piece is set at an art opening where a women observes: "I think that is Madame Realism but can a fictional statement ever be true?"[34] Madame Realism is pure signifier, the word that floats free of object and yet paradoxically she seems to take on weight and substance, all the forbidden tricks of "character". There is a pathos to her too, the feeling that, well, one cannot hope to reproduce life in words, but I, as author, through Madame Realism am doing the best that I can—I am bringing you as close as I can, even though I know all this is impossible. Similarly Dennis Cooper in his novel *Closer* tries to evade the lies of pornography and bring us "closer" to lived erotic experience. Madame Realism exists as near to pointlessness as a literary creation can. She is there in each sentence, in each arrangement of words but as meaning in language must continually elude us, so Madame Realism eludes us. Who is she? She stubbornly resists categorization outside of language: she is not muse, or mystic, or femme fatale. She is possibility and she is despair.

Tillman's writing is pure postrealism. Nothing pretends to be other than linguistic—an elliptical moment in which we may glimpse something only to have it torn away from us by the next moment in language and the next. Madame Realism is "subject in process", never formed, never final, eternally fluid—language itself. She is irretrievably flawed by the frustrations of language. When writing of Madame Realism, Tillman is writing on a knife edge. Everything she writes about Madame Realism—her thoughts, the continuity in the stories—is compromised by the impossibility of Madame Realism's "being". Every sentence is a permanent monument to a continuing impermanence. She is a "life drawing" that tells us all fictional characters are "life drawings" and that they must all fail. They pretend to be other than what they are. They impersonate life even though they are merely frail constructions of words. Madame Realism changes her clothes, she disguises herself, she even turns into a museum catalogue[35] and in her guise of admonitory reminder of the duplicities of art she is terrifying. She implies void. She suggests that words whirl above a terrible abyss of nothingness, unknowableness. "MADAME REALISM REVEALED AS A HOAX, she wrote in her notebook."[36] Madame Realism can hang around anywhere imparting her own terrible inauthenticity to anything that is being described. We participate breathlessly in a tour-de-force, a fictional high-wire act that forces the reader hard up against the limitations of the reading experience. She strips all hope, all romance, all dreams from the reader. She is an inexorable reminder of fictionality and the seductions of language games. She is equally poignant in fiction or non-fiction. In "The Museum of Hyphenated Americans", Madame Realism visits the museum at Ellis Island that remains now as a reminder of all the tidal waves of immigrants that swept into New York and where "each station of the immigrant's Via Dolorosa" is presented in "images, objects and words—many words."[37] Madame Realism forces honesty into the journalistic experience. Tillman's own family—as with so many in America—were immigrants. Madame Realism is not an autobiographical voice. Yet, for a writer whose main subject is identity and *faute de mieux*, her own identity as a white, middle-class American woman, Madame Realism is possibly the most personal voice that can emerge, a deviant autobiographer born out of theory, experience and art. This is what is most paradoxical about the Madame Realism voice—forced to be so little, a repeating, disciplinary lash that says "artifice, artifice", she ends up being so much: a hybrid personality, a mutant being that proclaims, "I am still here, I go on, I survive. Ignore me at your peril."

In her novel *Motion Sickness* Tillman brings together many of her feelings about fiction, identity and exile to provide a perfect miniature map of a psyche. Again, as in all her work Tillman establishes her own rhythm; the reader must adapt to her pace. It is rather like studying a painting. The book reveals itself slowly in a leisurely, sometimes barely perceptible manner. It is a fully realized novel which, unlike the writing in *Absence Makes the Heart* does not rely on epigrams, *aperçus*, and dizzying flashes of theory. An unnamed narrator, an American woman, is travelling, randomly it would seem, around Europe and North Africa. She lives modestly, relying on her steadily dwindling savings. She travels in a very ordinary, unpretentious contemporary manner. She reads a great deal and is particularly interested in art and cinema. She appears to be open and friendly. She has occasional affairs and makes a great many friends along the way. She buys and writes postcards to send to all her friends, new and old, but somehow, these postcards, although we read them, do not seem to get sent. She calls them "my playing cards that mark absence and presence" [38] and they are literally, playing cards, cards with which a game is being played. This is the first clue we have that the novel may be quite unlike what it seems, that its small daily pleasures and careful descriptions—the sunny, dusty streets of

Bayswater, the old gold light of Amsterdam—conceal a tortuous interiority.

Tillman is recounting the (w)rite of passage already mentioned —the spirited American girl, so familiar to us from the fiction of Henry James, who comes to the Old World in search of culture, civilization and possibly love. Tillman implicitly deconstructs the epistolatory style on which many such novels depend by not allowing her heroine to establish "communication" in sending her postcards. The cards can only refer to herself, who is the subject of the novel and they can only ever be read by the reader of the novel, as they are here. They are, she writes, "Postcards from the imaginary into the impossible real."[39] The postmodern novel is self-referential; its characters cannot "communicate" with one another. They do not need to—they do not "exist" and there is no plot.

The journey is the narrative and in travel Tillman finds the perfect metaphor for language. Being a traveller in this sense is random or "meaningless", yet at the same time it constructs an identity, the identity of the traveller. Tillman continues to think of people as places, both in an abstract sense and in the sense of their national identities. "A person without a past is like a nation without a history. It's impossible" . . . "Perhaps I should think of her as a nation with a multiethnic and complex religious character that would account for her seeming contradictions."[40]

Other than escaping from the contradictions of language by establishing the literal narrative "flow" of the traveller, *Motion Sickness* plays a complex game with character. As the narrator meets different people in different cities, they often turn out to be connected or to know one another. It is a "small world"—the world of the novel where characters are connected per se—they all belong to the author. This is used to comic effect: by the end acquaintances are popping up everywhere the narrator goes, however obscure, linking each other in long tales of murder and melodrama: "I may be in a melodrama, not a tragedy, white middle-class young woman from yet another dying empire, who dreams that change is possible but will remain unaware always of her fate, because she believes there is no fate, no history she can be tied to . . ."⁴¹ Some characters seem more "real" than others; Sal the rogue cop or criminal killed in Amsterdam and his waif-like girlfriend Sylvie seem to belong to a different genre, a cartoon or a comic, from Paul and Alfred, the staid English brothers, or Clara, the old lesbian, with her haunting memories of Europe after the rain, when the golden bowl was broken in the wars. Charles, obsessed with spy stories and encountered randomly in Istanbul, turns out to be the estranged husband of Jessica, alone and pregnant in London. And so it goes on, all the endless fragments of lives which the traveller observes in the same way that the novelist observes and recounts stories. The novelist is what Jim Morrison called "a spy in the house of love" and the narrator observes, "the unconscious is a spy and makes everyone a double agent."⁴² Towards the end of the novel the narrator begins to draw her themes, or her self, together. She is reading *My Gun is Quick* and quotes from it: "You pick up a book and read about things, getting a vicarious kick from people and events that never happened. You're doing it now, getting ready to fill in a normal life with the details of someone else's experiences."⁴³ She is reading *The Quiet American*, another book in which people stand in for their countries. The many sent or unsent postcards, each one a particular juxtaposition of image and text, are made available to the reader. She envisages "all the people I've ever known" as if in a film, coming in one by one "silently, like the dead in 'Our Town'." She sees all the characters from the novel passing by, "A personal demonstration protesting nothing. Though each might be carrying a placard. The placards might have nothing on them at all, or be mirrors, and when I looked I'd see my own face."⁴⁴

Motion Sickness gives an impression of buoyancy and freedom as if in this account of exile and expatriation the author has some success in uniting language with meaning through motion, through action. Freed from cultural imperatives and the expectations of family and friends the narrator has some chance of achieving a less fettered, less fragmented identity. The role of the writer may always be a compromised one—Sylvie in *Motion Sickness* comments that "writers are voyeurs" and the narrator agrees: "I'm a paranoid voyeur."[45] Tillman may worry about this, feeling in common with a surprising number of other novelists that she lacks imagination and is unable to fantasize. She may even continue to distrust imagination a little—her mind inclines to reason rather than romanticism—but for all this she succeeds in writing fiction in the teeth of every intellectual opposition. We live in a time where theory is chic and fiction seems fatally compromised, when to write fiction at all requires an act of faith and imagination. Tillman's fiction, in common with that of other writers who are themselves critics and theorists such as Kathy Acker or the French *écriture féminine* writers may not be particularly accessible. She is writing on the edge, in the vanguard of theory and having to evade, duck and weave numerous contemporary insights about the act of writing in order to write at all. She bequeaths what she can, which is a sort of map or blueprint of the contemporary mind, a mind drenched in movies, books and Americana, the mind of the liberal humanist who is also a woman and who has to deal with all that these positions imply within a still patriarchal culture. As she travels she writes guide books. Inevitably the mind she reveals is her own and in this sense, ironically, Tillman does produce a sort of autobiography but an autobiography paranoically aware of all autobiographical pitfalls which in the end becomes detached from any single person to form the map of another country, of how we might be.

In *Haunted Houses* she wrote: "If you're going to write a story, why would you write the same story again and again?" The response is: "Maybe you'll finally get it right."[46] Emily, in "seeking" some basic structures that would guide her comes to feel "Words fail me. Words fail me". The mirrors that Tillman holds up reflect her own face. Words fail her. It is always, as Beckett wrote, "I can't go on. I must go on."

E.Y.

Crashing in the fast lane

Gary Indiana

"Fear of sexuality is the new, disease-sponsored register
of the universe of fear in which everyone now lives."

Susan Sontag

"These are peculiar times."

Gary Indiana

The literary theorist Todorov once argued that the short story
was not as popular as the novel simply because readers cannot
immerse themselves in them. The brief duration of their
narrative, so he suggested, does not allow the reader to forget
that there is life outside of literature. If we reverse Todorov's
argument then we come close to understanding the appeal of
Gary Indiana's collection of short stories *White Trash Boulevard*.
For Indiana's prose addresses the issue of defamiliarization—
small snap-shots of life which flicker rather than linger,
constantly throwing us back into an awareness of their own
artifice. His slices of hyper-(ventilated) reality evoke a world
dominated by images rather than fact, a style that invites
comparisons to photography rather than fiction. Trapped as his
characters are within the tyranny of image, *White Trash
Boulevard* responds by incorporating the language of surface
into its struggle to surpass it: "Note: as in many films of this
genre, an inanimate object assumes the role of a major character.
Brandy's Cuisinart, like the picture of Dorian Gray, functions as
a symbol of all that is to follow."[1]
What we have here then is self-referentiality as a means of

escape. We impose scripts on a world that is already scripted, add images to a society whose very drive is to saturate us with them. Indiana's stories are thus a strangely naive response to a consumer-hungry society, suggesting both a sense of senti-mental loss as well as throwing down an insolent challenge. This is precisely the *suspense* of the book—its attempt to steal post-modernism's plunder, whilst simultaneously surrendering to its strategies. It occupies exactly the kind of schizoid nihilism that Susan Sontag has described in *On Photography*: "As we make images and consume them, we need still more images, and still more . . . The possession of a camera can inspire something akin to lust, it cannot be satisfied: first, because the possibilities of photography are infinite; and, second, because the project is finally devouring. The attempts by photographers to bolster up a depleted sense of reality contribute to the depletion . . . Cameras are the antidote and the disease, a means of appropriating reality and a means of making it obsolete."[2]

What then does Indiana's writing represent? The tattered remnants of postmodern excess, the ruinous vacuity of mediated burn out? Certainly he points to the impossibility of ever reclaiming the innocence of the past, or of ever indulging in the luxury of nostalgia: "With your dark glasses, which have deep blue lenses, you see the pornographic movie of a dead, nostalgic time." His narratives do not so much represent our personal past so much as they represent our ideas or cultural stereotypes *about* that past. Our only access to the nostalgic is through the lenses of pop images which go into creating that very notion. If *The Big Chill* took a longing look at the sixties, *White Trash Boulevard* looks with even more envy at the film itself—for a time when ideals could afford the luxury of being lapsed.

It is in this problematic relationship to the past that these short stories provide a framework for Indiana's explosive debut novel, *Horse Crazy*, a book that manages to contextualize and dramatize the socio-sexual climate of his earlier world view. If *White Trash Boulevard* provides fragments of fast-lane casualties, *Horse Crazy* brings these pieces together, and, with a perverse inevitability, insists upon them falling apart.

The very title of the novel presents a mischievous reversal of American key-notes, taking the "natural" ethos of the most famous native American and standing it on its head. If Neil Young lay claim to the primitive chic of *Crazy Horse*, Indiana places himself at the other end of the spectrum—the alienated and estranged, the junkie angel rather than the "noble savage", the horse-crazed Indiana not the red-skinned Indian.

Indiana portrays New York as a world of commodities and erratic communication, deluged by junk mail, populated by junk males. The glare of neon dominates the cityscape, encasing its inhabitants in a jungle of slogans and de-sign. The novel's hero is an eternally struggling writer, an aesthete and homosexual whose promiscuity has dwindled under the relentless pressure of post-AIDS paranoia. The book traces his frustratingly platonic relationship with a would-be photographer, Gregory Burgess— their unsatisfactory celibacy colliding with their emotional inter-dependence.

It would seem from such a summary that it is their relationship itself that works as the governing metaphor for the panic-stricken frigidity of contemporary sexuality. Their fears of consummation, their (excessive?) reliance on masturbation, their points of contact and those of departure all appear to speak to a sadly recognizable conflation of despair and desire: "After all, he says he wants me to be attracted to him. But then again, knowing I want him physically, he should give me what I want or leave me alone, if he does care about me, because I don't want just a friendship. It's too frustrating that way. This feels like a movie I've seen before."[3]

Whilst such a reading certainly has its validity—their celibate solitude is obviously bound up with an AIDS-phobic society—it is also possible to view Indiana's writing itself as emerging directly out of this climate. Critics have pointed to his insistence upon detail, his circumlocutive detours into specifics, and it is precisely this *style* that allows Indiana to suggest language's participation in the reality that he describes. Consider the following passage, which is worth quoting at length in order to convey its full effect: "I raced back to my original spot, trying to recall exactly what corner we'd agreed on. I knew it was Seventh. But it could also have been Eighth. The corner of Eighth and Second is such a typical corner for meetings of this kind, perhaps we had settled on Eighth after all, having at first rejected it in favour of the less frequented corner of Seventh and Second. But should I venture up to Eighth, I wondered, in the certainty that I could see the corner of Seventh and Second from the corner of Second and Eighth, or stay put in front of the drug store, confident in my ability to view both the corner of Second and Eighth and the corner of Sixth and Second, which suddenly seemed another possibility, from my vantage point at Seventh and Second? I now felt less confident."[4]

And so he goes on. And on.

The point that needs emphasizing about this technique is that the prose mimes and mirrors the uncertain networks and chains of event that are involved with social interaction. Like the domino effect of sexual transmission, this passage acts out the self-doubt and terminal paranoia arising from cross-wired communication. Indiana is not only writing about AIDS, he is writing from *within* it.

The critic Jacques Derrida has written of the notion of "mimetologism"—a pun on the idea of mimesis, extending it to incorporate the peculiar logic of language: "It complicates the boundary line that ought to run between the text and what seems to lie beyond its fringes, what is classed as *the real*."[5] Put simply, Indiana's writing *does* what it describes, mimicking its own creation, resisting any intervention between itself and the world that it inhabits.

Whilst writers like Edmund White and Armistead Maupin have written with compassion and conviction about AIDS, their prose has always *addressed* the issue, speaking *to* a condition never *of* it. If Maupin's *Babycakes* writes about AIDS as a subject, Indiana's novel positions itself in the realm of what Julia Kristeva has called "the abject"—that which cannot be fully contemplated, yet hovers constantly within our beings. As Kristeva puts it:

"There looms, within abjection, one of those violent, dark revolts of being, directed against a threat that seems to emanate from an exorbitant outside or inside, ejected beyond the scope of the possible, the tolerable, the thinkable. It beseeches, worries and fascinates desire, which, nevertheless, does not let itself be seduced."[6]

The relationship between the novel's protagonists may provide the narrative framework for an exploration of AIDS, but it is in the writing's brooding reticence, the fearful imminence of language, that the abject voice of AIDS-speak is to be found:

"We listen to the hum and throb of the hospital and watch the soundless river shatter light into thousands of white drops. It isn't fair. We used to say: How can we live like this? And now the question really is: How can we die like this?"[7]

Far from prioritizing this intersection of illness and language over the reality of actual suffering, Indiana suggests the ways in which language affects our understanding of and attitudes towards people who suffer from it. When going to see a friend with AIDS in hospital, the narrator worries about his status as visitor being transformed into that of patient: "Paul passes over into the territory of no-longer-quite-alive, and I calculate that if he got it five years ago, the general incubation period, he must have been infectious on each of the fifty or sixty occasions when we slept together, giving me a much better than average chance of being infected . . . The worst thing is, I can't feel anything for Paul, I'm too scared for myself."[8]

The narrator's consciousness both enacts and foregrounds the importance of identifying the person with the disease as well as acknowledging the fact that they are separate entities. The people with AIDS in *Horse Crazy* may be carriers, but they are always characters, inextricably linked in the sexual chain yet with their own histories and narratives that enable them to stand outside of the role of "victim". Susan Sontag has written: "The fear of AIDS imposes on an act whose ideal is an experience of pure presentness (and a creation of the future), a relation to the past to be ignored at one's peril."[9]

Indiana neither ignores his characters' past nor inscribes them into it. They suffer from AIDS, they do not act as the signifiers of it. Sontag's warnings about the dangers of using *Illness as Metaphor*, is answered by Indiana's presentation of illness as *metonomy*—a process of combination that operates within a chain, yet constantly works to resist being enclosed within it.

Such writings from the AIDS-zone can have no hope of closure. The usual loose knots of fiction cannot be tied up or reconciled, but at present must continue to remain suspended, frozen in fictional cryogenics. The tone inevitably becomes one of entropy rather than apocalypse, wearied indifference, the perpetual erosion of expectations and potential. Indiana's novel obviously does come to an end, but with a note of such self-doubt and burn-out that the writer himself relinquishes his status of author-ity:

> "This story, if it is one, deserves the closure of a suicide, perhaps even the magisterial finality of what is usually called a novel, but the remnants of that faraway time offer nothing more than a taste of damp ashes, a feeling of indeterminacy, and the obdurate inconclusiveness of passing time."[10]

Time passes, people die, and the best a novel can hope for is to convey a sense of horrified paralysis. As I write, William Buckley has called for the branding and tattooing of people with AIDS. The British government refuses to provide condoms in prisons, needles for users and limits funds for research: all the while their message screams out from the billboards—"Don't Die of Ignorance."

G.C.

On the road again

David Wojnarowicz's Close to the Knives: A Memoir of Disintegration

"Patronizing sympathy is revolting."
Diamanda Galás*

"Some people left for Heaven without warning."
Shane MacGowan*

David Wojnarowicz is a New York artist and writer whose central concerns go right to the heart of many of the issues raised by the other works discussed in this book. It is possible to see in his work a stark apprehension of the fundamental life/death struggle that underlies all the hard-edged urban living, deviance and alternative sexualities one encounters in contemporary urban (post)realism. Wojnarowicz presents all this in its most raw and unpretentious form. His book *Close to the Knives* differs significantly from other urban fictions in a variety of ways and yet could act as an underlying map or blueprint for all the writers who have found themselves perilously alienated from the mainstream of American life and fiction in the past two decades.

Wojnarowicz is little known in Britain and has, unlike some of his more adaptable contemporaries, never made much money from his art. He has had a notably harsh life. An abused child and high-school drop-out he, probably alone of the writers in this book, had to literally live on the streets of New York and sell himself as a rent-boy on 42nd Street. Although much of *Close to the Knives* deals explicitly with his own homosexuality and the AIDS crisis, it completely avoids any narrow-focus ghettoization; the emphasis on sexuality in this case tends to lead us away from any crude definition of people in sexual terms and towards an engagement with basic moral issues and human values. Oddly enough, in this he is perhaps closer to Bret Easton Ellis than any of his other peers. Ellis's apparent vapidity and abnegation of moral issues tends to conceal a harsh, stony-faced puritanism whereas Wojnarowicz's moral stance emerges from a much gentler and more optimistic view, which nevertheless speaks of a wearing away of the spirit in close, daily observation of the unbearable. Wojnarowicz lacks something of the sense of cleansing fire occasionally perceptible in Ellis's work but that sort of scourging is a luxury that Wojnarowicz has never been able to afford. His own moral rage is a less complex, more pared-to-the-bone and ultimately much more humane mani-festation of values forged in daily adversity. Whilst one is more than reluctant to concede to Wojnarowicz any of the patronizing praisings of "authenticity" that often greet works of art by anyone who has manifestly suffered—as if the mere fact of such knowledge guarantees artistic credibility when those resonances must obviously lie in the force of the writing itself, regardless of lived experience—nevertheless it has to be admitted that Wojnarowicz's evocations of street-life come far closer to our own experiences of the under-privileged, desperate realities of life on the streets of European capitals than many of the more soft-focus, college-kid urban fictions of Ellis, McInerney or Gaitskill. However the differences between Wojnarowicz and these other writers are more subtle than just those of directness and reportage, although *Close to the Knives* remains an extremely direct book.

Firstly *Close to the Knives* completely lacks any overly self-conscious postmodern fictional trickery and this leads into the first of the curious oppositions within Wojnarowicz's work: most of the writers we are concerned with have at some level intended to reject the academic intricacies of high-postmodernism and return to some more direct "story-based" representation of experience. In doing so, many of their books have remained "literary" but without overt manifestations of a literary past or literary influences. This has tended to give their books a strangely suspended "disposable" feel as if the conjunction of college education and popular culture has caused them to retain literary form without any concomitant "literary" values in the sense of Grand Narrative with its moral imperatives and in-depth characterizations. Their books knowingly simulated and were treated as consumer artefacts, art works, which, in the Pop art tradition, blandly reflected emptiness, and a cool, non-judgemental lack of involvement. *Close to the Knives* resembles these novels not at all. It is not even a novel: it is a memoir. Yet, ultimately it becomes far more traditionally "fictional" than many works presented as novels. It evokes a literary past—the suffering and alienation of Jean Genet, the broad American sweep of Walt Whitman. Wojnarowicz's ostensible ("I never had enough of an education"[1]) disregard of "literature", his very unselfconsciousness, creates something which is far closer to the passionate concerns of modernism, moral and political concerns inherent in the language used, than to the empty rhetoric of much playful postmodernism. Wojnarowicz's writing is less sophisticated, more open and naive than that of his peers and this allows him to embrace political issues which are precluded by the frozen cool of his literary contemporaries. Although he recounts a life that is almost certainly more traditionally "self-destructive" than anything experienced by the other New York novelists, he is simultaneously far less jaded and empty, far less interested in producing any mimesis of a spiritually etiolated society and far more concerned with confronting its appalling failures in terms of humanity, decency and honesty. In this political and confrontational stance, Wojnarowicz is closer to the work of performance artists such as Diamanda Galás or Karen Finley and closer, I believe, to a literary future when passionate engagement and humanitarian issues will no longer continually dissolve into apathy and the labyrinthine ways of language theory.

The fact that *Close to the Knives* does not present itself as fiction raises a number of interesting issues that have never really been satisfactorily addressed. It has escaped no one's attention that most of the urban postrealists, the Downtown novelists covered in this book, have drawn extremely heavily on their own experiences in writing their novels. Early novels by young writers have of course always tended to do this but it is a tendency particularly marked in all of the writers discussed herein and in a great deal of recent contemporary fiction. This is partly a reaction to the period of high-postmodernism and magical realism, when it was customary to approach the process of fictionalization from every *other* possible angle, to deconstruct the history of fiction, to play endlessly with the "I" persona and in general to exhibit an intellectual virtuosity fuelled by academic concepts of the death of meta-narrative and the possibilities of post-structuralist language theory. The eventual postmodern paralysis encouraged younger writers to revert to a flat representation of the events of their own lives, which, they often felt, were so heart-stopping in their extremes and in what these extremes implied about the prevailing culture that they needed no amendment. All the writers covered in this book had been observing closely the urban carnival of the seventies and eighties and saw, within their own lives, events and experiences that barely needed fictionalization. It is fair to conclude that many of the writers discussed herein had witnessed at first—or at least second-hand—many of the experiences they described. However, as readers tend not to be interested in autobiography or memoirs by ambitious young punks, they call it fiction and hope someone will read it—and very often the titillating undercurrent of implied "authenticity" ensures that they will. This takes us to a point upon which some of Wojnarowicz's work turns. All these writers are describing "extreme" lives—well, extreme when contrasted with the quaint byways of much contemporary English fiction—lives that include bisexuality, drug-use, sado/masochism and the whole walk on the wild side mythos. However, it is safe to conclude that all their experiences stop far short of our ultimate taboos; child-abuse and murder. Part of the opprobrium that greeted Ellis's *American Psycho* lay in the tacit understanding that many of the original brat-pack books were, roughly speaking, autobiographical, something which Ellis evidently wanted to escape but which the critics were reluctant to let go in their attempts to identify Ellis with the attitudes of Patrick Bateman. His choice of what was apparently a murderer as protagonist in *American Psycho* served the purpose of wrenching his novel into fictionality—and of revenging himself, in numerous wry ways on this tacit "autobiographical" understanding. (Contemporary author-murderers are, as far as I am aware, unknown apart from Gerard J. Schaefer, serving two consecutive life terms in Florida State Prison for mutilation slayings, who writes snuff-porn fiction with titles like *The Sex Beast Caper*, and who can, I think, be safely discounted.) Now Wojnarowicz, whose experiences have been even more extreme than those of his New York contemporaries certainly doesn't claim to have killed anyone but, in his best piece, "The Suicide of a Guy Who Once Built an Elaborate Shrine Over a Mousehole," he writes of someone who did and it is in this piece that he, Wojnarowicz, in quite a different way from Ellis, also seems to escape from autobiography into fiction. In this piece, in attempting to understand the profound death wishes of his friends, contradictorily manifested against the background of those others with AIDS, struggling to live, Wojnarowicz achieves an ordering of experience that transcends memory and, in contemplating death, illuminates life in the most classic fictional tradition. There is little point in pursuing this interaction of autobiography and fiction further at this time. Even Paul de Man had to conclude that while all texts are autobiographical, simultaneously none of them are. ("But, just as we seem to assert that all texts are autobiographical, we should say that, by the same token, none of them is or can be . . . the specular moment is not primarily an event that can be located in a history but that it is the manifestation, on the level of the referent, of a linguistic structure."[2])

Close to the Knives, like so much great American fiction, describes a journey. William Burroughs accurately describes it as "the age old voice of the road, the voice of the traveler, the outcast, the thief, the whore . . ."[3] It is precisely on the fault-line where fiction and autobiography, or, as Wojnarowicz calls them, "vision and memory"[4] meet that *Close to the Knives* reveals its meanings. As autobiography it is painful and wrenching to an unbearable degree; during the book Wojnarowicz is diagnosed as having the AIDS virus and *Close to the Knives* becomes a journey straight into darkness, straight into death—real, literal inescapable death. However, as Wojnarowicz continues to write there is a curious transformation. Initially, in the early pieces, the act of writing seems like a sort of death, a sort of small, cramped death, the death that art always holds within itself when contrasted with all the variety and physicality of life. Wojnarowicz muses on this in the early parts of the book where he dwells on the intimacy and sensuality of gay lives and whilst in a bath-house considers "the eternal sleep of statues" and a possible "face beneath the sands of the desert, still breathing".[5] This is oddly prophetic because, whilst aware of the little death inherent in art, Wojnarowicz during the writing of the books finds that his art indeed embodies death; it comes to record his own death-sentence. Yet, as he struggles on, writing of all the terrible sadnesses and losses of AIDS and continues, in the long final piece of the book, to eulogize the memory of a friend, there occurs that shift in perception that has always been the essence of fiction and that is always as mystical as transubstantiation or any other awesome and mythic occurrence. As Wojnarowicz evinces an extraordinary empathy with his dead friend, and as he magically animates his friend's lost life, Wojnarowicz loses the consciousness of his own "self" that naturally propels a memoir. In achieving identification with his lost friend he achieves fiction and therefore achieves in art not only that part of it that must always signify corporeal death but that part that has always signifed permanence and immortality. Wojnarowicz, through an act of great compassion, bequeaths to us, forever, the book, his art. The "face beneath the sands" continues to breathe.

The early pieces in *Close to the Knives*, although they largely describe gay life on the streets of New York, convey a very different impression of New York from any given by the other Downtown writers. This is not some fragmented postmodernist hell, not some poseur's dream of nightlife, nor even a city more animated and "real" than ever a modern human being could be.

Wojnarowicz uses New York as a microcosm for America, for its size, its mystery, its unknowableness. Here, New York has an *On the Road* potential for mythic journeys; it holds our childhoods, our memories and our most secret desires. There are echoes here of much classic American writing; Hart Crane's *The Bridge*, William Carlos Williams's *Paterson*, Walt Whitman's visionary America and Nelson Algren's street-wise compassion. There is also that sense of loss and nostalgia that occurs in such writing, the loss of something that can never be articulated, Jack Kerouac's sense of "all that road going, all the people dreaming in the immensity of it . . ."[6] the gentle pain that comes in America with dusk and that far-off whistle blowing and in Wojnarowicz's own writing: "Late this evening I was sitting by the dock's edge, sitting in the rain remembering . . . the quiet deliciousness of walking through coal-gray streets where trees leaned over and by the fields where nuns in the cool green summers would hitch up their long black skirts . . . a kind of memory slow motion,"[7] and again: "at dusk after a clear hot summer's day when the ships are folding down into the distance . . ."[8] Much of this writing is set by the docks where the river and seas begin their endless journeys, and in waterfront bars where he listens "to the horns of ships along the river" then turns a corner and "headed towards town".[9]

The piece entitled "In the Shadow of the American Dream Soon All This Will Be Picturesque Ruins" describes an actual journey across America, and makes it clear that Wojnarowicz fully understands the mythical-lyrical literary tradition towards which he is naturally inclined—the John Rechy *City of Night* cruisings—and the way in which he feels he is right at the end of that kind of vision, that he is passing into its outer limits and that "these are strange and dangerous times".[10] He finds himself lost, in stasis between the tensions of sensuality and "interior abstractions", between life and death, language and silence, "hooked into the play between vision and memory".[11] There is a dawning sense that it is no longer possible to escape through mythic, psychic or sensual journeyings: "I feel that I'm caught in the invisible arms of government in a country slowly dying beyond our grasp".[12] On this last journey in the old sense, these last literary wanderings of an outsider, there is an increasingly claustrophobic sense that the old America of hopes and promises and dreams and endless travellings and last frontiers is slowly shutting down, becoming small and mean, pinched and cruel. The range, the vastness, the visions have died as surely as the Indian legends and the buffalo and the great quasi-fictional wanderings of his literary precursors. He sees the traditional "images of poverty . . . like the gray shades of memory"[13] and he begins to rail against "research centers" and the governmental dream of "laser warfare from the floating veil of outerspace".[14] Wojnarowicz is forced to confront this closing-down, this closing in of hopes and dreams as they become ground down to rat-like city living and unfocused rage. "I thought of the neo-nazis posing as politicians and religious leaders and I thought of my genuine fantasies of murder and wondered why I never crossed the line. It's not that I'm a *good* person or even that I'm afraid of containment in jail; it may be more that I can't escape the ropes of my own body, my own flesh, and bottom line in the pyramids of power and confinement one demon gets replaced by another in a moment's notice . . ."[15]

Wojnarowicz looks helplessly at the "zombie" tribes of contemporary America; the government tribes who "sell the masses a pile of green-tainted meat; i.e. a corrupted and false history . . .": the tribes "that suckle at the breast of telecommunications".[16] He sees too the outsiders those, like himself, "who understand the meaning of language" and he sees how easily they could one day find themselves running amok with a handgun or lobbing a grenade at the president—"Or that person can end up on a street corner, homeless, hungry and wild-eyed, punching himself in the face or sticking wires through the flesh of his arms or chest."[17] It is too late. Corruption has gone too far. Everything has been tried and failed. "I'm gasping from a sense of loss and desire."[18] And it is with these lonely, bitter realizations that Wojnarowicz continues onwards into "Being Queer in America" which is the beginning of his "Journal of Disintegration" wherein, with desperate courage, he charts the AIDS crisis.

"So I'm watching this thing move around in my environment, among friends and strangers; something invisible and abstract and scary; some connect-the-dots version of hell."[19] It is impossible, within Wojnarowicz's book, not to see AIDS as having an apocalyptic edge, as seeming to arise from the corruption and mind-rot and dying of dreams in America that he has described in the early part of the memoir, as seeming to arise inevitably from his words to form a new language of pain and disaster. In its very existence, its preying upon the vulnerable, the disenfranchized, the outsiders, the disease seems directly aligned to the currents of hate and deception and the "fake moral screens"[20] that dominate the country and whose emanations are now tearing and shredding at the very bodies of those Wojnarowicz has seen as most helpless, lost and haunted. Wojnarowicz may not have intended to summon this image of a vengeful, ravaging plague, a shadow on the land, but it is as though, shamanistically, in his pre-AIDS writings about the loss of the best of his country's art and dreams, he himself produced, through language, this terrible shade that once given linguistic form so interestingly parallels all the moronic, homophobic, fundamentalist rantings about an apocalyptic plague. It may be that this sense of AIDS as the real and malignant form of all the foulness and loss of hope he has already documented, has in fact empowered him and allowed him to continue to counter and confront with such passion and integrity the inhumane filth about it being a quasi-Biblical punishment for the unworthy. Wojnarowicz writes: "When I was told that I'd contracted this virus it didn't take me long to realize that I'd contracted a diseased society as well."[21]

As Wojnarowicz writes about visiting hospitals and the death of friends and other friends being beaten up by queer-bashers in the street, and writes about visions of disease, pain and death and writes hopelessly, helplessly about memories and desire and homosexual encounters both violent and tender, he tries to conserve tiny fragments of love within his text. But a rage begins to build from within his stunned narrative and from within his dreams and finally his friend dies ("how quietly he dies, how beautiful everything is . . .") and at the end all Wojnarowicz knows is the dimensions of his own body and "all I can feel is the pressure is the pressure all I can feel is the pressure . . ."[22]

In the subsequent piece, "Close to the Knives", he describes a visit made with a dying friend to some sort of quack doctor who is injecting the patients with a vaccine developed from human shit. Knowing the toxic properties of faeces, Wojnarowicz figures that the doctor would at least make a vaccine for each patient of their own shit, but no. "Later we found that one person's shit served as a base for all treatments."[23] The patients get more ill of course and the analogy is clear: Shit—any old shit—is good enough for AIDS patients and who cares if they die? Someone will profit, of course. As they travel home, Peter, his friend "looked tired and sad". He was staring out of the window and saying, "America is such a beautiful country—don't you think so?"[24] There is no need to emphasize the unbearable pathos and poignancy of such moments, re-enacted in one form or another, thousands upon thousands of times over the past few years. It is very hard to read Wojnarowicz's descriptions of his friend's death. It is far harder to deal with the anguish and love twisted within the text (in that we are far more threatened by tenderness than fury) than it is to read of Wojnarowicz's rage when he begins to have to inure himself to all the deaths and to turn outwards towards the injustices: "and I'm watching a group of people die on camera because they can't afford the drugs that might extend their lives."[25] He hears some Texan on TV say, "If I had a dollar to spend on health care I'd rather spend it on a baby or an innocent person with some illness or defect not of their own responsibility; not some person with AIDS . . ." and Wojnarowicz says, "I reached through the television screen and ripped his face in half."[26] Later, Wojnarowicz goes on to indict by name individuals who have withheld funds and help from AIDS patients, or fanned the flames of hatred towards homosexuals, or have discriminated outrageously against the poor, or uneducated, or communities of colour or the homeless suffering from the disease. ("If you want to stop AIDS shoot the queers," they say.) Wojnarowicz calls these men "walking swastikas" and they include Edward Koch, Cardinal O'Connor and Jesse Helms, names notorious even in Britain.

In "X-Rays from Hell" Wojnarowicz documents his own diagnosis and details conversations with his suffering friends. "There are no more people in their thirties. We are all dying out,"[27] says one. Wojnarowicz describes the anxious interchange of symptoms, the surges of hope over the rumour of a new drug and his continued faith in the power of words. "Describing the once indescribable can dismantle the power of taboo."[28] In the middle of all the furore and drama and psychic terror surrounding AIDS Wojnarowicz, in this book, asks, quietly, pitifully: "What exactly is frightening about the human body?"[29]—a still, small voice which goes right to the heart of nearly everything written on the subject of AIDS and indeed on the subject of sexuality itself. What, exactly *is* so frightening about the human body?

The last piece in the book, "The Suicide of a Guy Who Once Built an Elaborate Shrine Over a Mousehole", concerns the death of his friend Dakota. At the beginning Wojnarowicz is still sadly, bemusedly contemplating his situation: "Death comes in small doses," he says and goes on to realize that most of the fixtures in his apartment, the sinks, lampshades, shower-stall, "and even the drinking cups"[30] will all probably outlive him. Changing tack, he begins to concentrate upon Dakota and to raise a number of fundamental questions about him, about Wojnarowicz himself and his friends from his own generation, the punk kids of the seventies.

At the beginning of this essay Wojnarowicz recounts how he had originally included segments of letters he had received from Dakota, letters that allowed Dakota "to speak on his own behalf about his humanity, his animal grace, his own spirituality"[31] in the essay. In applying to Dakota's family in Texas for permission to use these letters he was told that the parents had destroyed all Dakota's life work; writings, screenplays, paintings, drawings, collages, photographs and recordings and that they had absolutely no intention (as was their right under Texas law) of allowing Wojnarowicz to publish letters that their son had written. Dakota was gay and he committed suicide. Wojnarowicz concludes that, "his entire identity has been murdered by his folks."[32] This is the first indication we have of what Wojnarowicz is able to do in his homage to his dead friend: Dakota immediately becomes representative of all the outsider voices choked off and silenced by the strictures of a judgemental mainstream. Wojnarowicz talks of his own pain in having to deny Dakota his voice in the piece but struggles on to achieve via his own memories and in interviews a stunning sense of both an individual and a generation to such an extent that it really doesn't matter whether Dakota was ever a "real" individual or not. He is emblematic.

Initially, as he writes, Wojnarowicz is preoccupied with the seven people he knows in that particular month who have died of AIDS. One of whom, a junkie, "ran every scam imaginable on his friends," all of which in retrospect becomes "charming" as evidence of *survival*, "such a lovely thing, such a transient thing".[33] A basic tension is thereby established between the death-wish romantic nihilism of Dakota and the frantic struggles of other friends—once equally self-destructive—for life when confronted with the AIDS diagnosis.

Wojnarowicz includes a great deal of autobiographical material in his memoir of Dakota. He describes his own early personal shrinking from the social structure and his feelings that if he were to embrace its illusions and lies he would "suffer a death more terrifying than physical death: an emotional and intellectual strangulation".[34] We don't know if he has re-assessed this—is anything more terrifying than physical death?—but such details help us understand why Wojnarowicz felt such a close empathy with Dakota, who felt similarly. In describing his own past, the repression he had suffered as a homosexual and his memories of the televisual violence of the Vietnam War, he begins to establish a context within which he can approach his memories of Dakota's—and Wojnarowicz's own—generation and their activities during the punk years: "The youth of the urban centers of America, as well as their dislocated counterparts in the suburbs, began slowly warming up for a dance of social death by firstly quietly and then publicly tracing all the outlines of taboo and violent activities and forms of nihilism they came across."[35] Wojnarowicz describes the process by which Dakota "with his dime store scissors and glue", and thousands of similarly minded punk activists and writers began "to turn the WORD in on itself like a psychic snake swallowing its own tale."[36] Having internalized the violence and schisms of their society, writers, artists and singers tried to subvert and decontextualize it in a multitude of ways, some of which were triumphant and some of which rebounded, like a vicious curse upon a shaman. ("For a period of time I entered a circle of people who were attracted to forms and expressions of violence and bloodletting because these things contained some unarguable truth when viewed or experienced against a backdrop of America."[37])

Dakota was one of these people, as was his friend Johnny, a geneticist who put out a xerox magazine called *MURDER*. ("Two centimeters beneath Johnny's curiosity about murder exists one of the sweetest heterosexual guys I've ever come into contact with."[38]) It was through Johnny that Wojnarowicz met Dakota and felt a kinship with his energy and also that there was a bond between people like themselves who didn't fit in or were "not attractive in the general societal sense".[39] Wojnarowicz also meets Joe, a sexually ambiguous and attractive guy, a writer. Joe too puts out a xerox magazine which explores drugs, sex, guns, boredom, obscenity and madness and in which Dakota publishes regularly. In this "Dakota" memoir, "The Suicide . . .", Wojnarowicz "interviews" Joe and Johnny at length for their recollections of their friend. Dakota, says Joe "was really into death and stuff"[40] and this is the essential point that Wojnarowicz is trying to clarify in the piece. What attracted all these people— including at times Wojnarowicz himself—to varieties of murder, mutilation, medical deformities, nazi regalia and drugs? "What was it about 'dark things' that attracted people back then?" he asks. ("It breaks up the boredom," says Joe . . .[41]) As Wojnarowicz pursues this question one sees, yet again, how profound and central it is. From the laissez-faire rich kids of *Less Than Zero* to the street-wise punks of *Close to the Knives* this obsession with sickness in all its forms defined most of the alienated (white) youth of the seventies. None of the answers from Wojnarowicz himself, or from the people he interviews here, are really sufficient, as he is all too aware. There is a certain glibness to all the suggestions: that it was the response to a hugely duplicitous and corrupt society, that it indicated a vast impatience with what was presented as "normal" within a crudely over-simplified, media-dominated national moral framework, or that "at least in the 60s some of our parents had a momentary idealism they shared as a reference point" and that the loss of this reveals a gaping moral and spiritual void—and all these factors certainly played their part. But there is still, in Wojnarowicz's writing the sense of something elusive and mysterious moving below the surface, as if, as previously suggested, there were layer upon layer of psychic ugliness that eventually manifested itself as AIDS. Was the ugliness of a corrupt society possibly even eventually *absorbed* by those who most opposed this society so that they themselves focused insistently upon every variety of hatred and ugliness?

This question reaches its climax in the character of Dakota, a guy so sweet and sensitive that he couldn't kill cockroaches and built "an elaborate shrine over a mousehole", a boy of great intelligence and creativity, who was himself obsessed with ugliness, murder and death. He also subscribed to the older artistic myths that have surrounded these issues: "He was really into Harry Crosby, you know—the Black Sun and all that shit."[42] Dakota's personality embodies all the tensions and oppositions of the young artists of his generation and yet he also exists for us in a purely pitiful and ordinary sense—"Dakota was short and ugly", says Joe, "let's be blunt here."[43] He had difficulty getting laid. He attempted suicide several times. As well as bearing all the weightier artistic preconceptions of his peer group, Dakota was also, says another friend, just the sad "school geek" type. "Too kind for this world." "He thought he was really ugly." "He was just a very unhappy person." After his suicide the words of his friends have a painfully drab, gentle and ordinary ring to them. Wojnarowicz has managed to make manifest in Dakota's being, in his soul if you like, all the forces that flashed through his being as an archetype, the representative of a particular generation at a particular time in history without ever losing sight of the very average, un-selfconfident worries and doubts that such a boy could have suffered at any time. There is a particular point at which Dakota comes to life and this is the point at which he, to all intents and purposes, passes into fiction.

Poor Dakota "skidding through the grainy black pall that surrounds addiction and life in America",[44] claimed at one point to have fought back. He claimed to have practised on a padded coat with a knife and then to have actually gone out and stabbed a dealer who had been ripping him off and to have read later that a body was found in that place. Dakota then knows that he has actually murdered someone. There is however "a pall of grey from the stabbing incident surrounding him";[45] a degree of uncertainty about the whole event, obscured as it is with rumour. It is at this point, as I suggest, that Dakota passes irretrievably into "fiction". The stabbing incident may or may not have happened; it is a characteristic street story, or fiction. Also Dakota in crossing the final barrier or last taboo for those who live on the edge—"the line," says Wojnarowicz "was always there to cross,"—achieves a larger-than-life, a "fictional", quality. In turning, in acting, in resisting victimization, in claiming, owning and "becoming" death, Dakota ironically comes to life. He becomes utterly distinct, more of a "character" than any of the other "real" characters in the essay. Joe and Johnny are both sympathetic towards Dakota over the stabbing: "It all came from that powerlessness that comes from being a human being."[46] "He finally stood up to it all,"—even though by that time Dakota was ripping them off for drugs. It is Wojnarowicz who writes: "I don't think there was even a fragment of judgement coming from those he knew,"[47] and Wojnarowicz is referring not just to the alleged stabbing but to Dakota's entire, by then almost wholly wretched, existence. It is a curious sentence. It almost seems to contain a plea. There is an edge which suggests that perhaps someone *should* have made a moral judgement, that they might then have cared enough to say

231

to Dakota that he was ruining his life on drugs and worthless obsessions and that it was wrong of him to have wanted to kill someone that badly and possibly to have done so. Wojnarowicz, Joe and Johnny were his friends, they "cared" about him but only within the loose, cool carelessness of that milieu where you let anyone go their own way, whichever way it is, and you joke with them about their horrendous, gory suicide attempts. Joe says of hearing one of Dakota's stories about his failed suicide attempt: "I was laughing my head off . . . he was laughing too. I just thought it was such an incredible story."[48] Nothing is ever quite real in this world. Survival and cool freeze us into a rictus grin of acceptance however bizarre or demented the behaviour in question. Wojnarowicz understands that within a world that has been morally polluted by the greed and venality of religious and political leaders one *has* to accept, one *cannot* judge, one is in no position to, being no better than one's friend. And yet . . . and yet, there is the faintest of implications that someone *should* have cared for Dakota as if he were what he really was, a helpless, spoilt, confused, irresponsible, lost baby. And somewhere within that brush of angel's wings there is, even more faintly, the tiny shadow of an idea, inarticulated, that maybe not absolutely all of the serious ugliness and sickness lay in the opponents, the straight, corrupt world, but that some of it, at a much deeper level than the one that is always easy and cool to acknowledge, actually lies in us ourselves, the traditional victims, the outsiders, the persecuted.

By this point in the narrative Wojnarowicz's closest friends have started dying of AIDS and he tells Johnny that: "I couldn't hang out with him (Dakota) any more because, emotionally, it was too ugly to be taking care of a guy who was battling to live and then hang out with people who were jamming shit into their arms or throwing themselves into the various arms of death."[49] Dakota is not the only person in this narrative who comes to "own" death. Wojnarowicz devotes the rest of the memoir to trying to understand the central paradox between those who pursued death and those—sometimes the same persons—who found the diseased reality thrust upon them. He tries to trace the correspondences and closeness between himself and Dakota and that whole death-fixed romantic agony and at the same time chart more deeply what has always been within him, Wojnarowicz, as a writer but has been forced into sharp relief by the AIDS deaths and his own diagnosis, that is, his own personal inner resistance to the amoral druggy death-worship culture. He feels like "I was in the middle of wartime", a sensation similar, he says, to when he first came off the streets in his 'teens and "the weight of image and sensation wouldn't come out until I picked up a pencil and started putting it down on paper."[50] Wojnarowicz continues to do the same thing now, trying to resolve the tensions as he writes. He continues using the same natural uninflected language throughout the book, a language with its roots in Kerouac's attempts at transcribing thought and speech and in Charles Olsen's idea of the natural "projective" voice where the rhythms of breathing—of life—provide pauses, stresses and emphases and help to generate unforced emotion.

Wojnarowicz reproduces telephone conversations wherein AIDS symptoms and medications are endlessly discussed. He wonders if it was his realization of the AIDS epidemic that "woke me up and helped me draw back from the self-destruction that other friends found themselves spinning into uncontrollably."[51] He re-asserts his political commitments to "those who have died from the way this disease was handled by those in positions of power." He goes back into his own scared, frightened childhood. He describes how he receives the news of Dakota's suicide ("I felt like my soul was slammed against a stone wall"[52]) and he transcribes the conversations he has with Dakota's friends after his death. Eventually his empathy with Dakota becomes so complete that, although he really wasn't all that close to him in life, it is as if Wojnarowicz transcends himself—his own singularity and unity which was all he felt he owned at the start of the AIDS crisis and he actually *becomes* Dakota, having seen in him, or in the Dakota persona that Wojnarowicz has built in language, such a density of endlessly refractive, reflecting issues and questions pertaining to all these lives, such an absolute archetype that Wojnarowicz cannot help but be absorbed by it.

He *is* part of it. And Wojnarowicz passes beyond the particular, beyond the self, into this fiction, this immortality, this sense of the many in the one and is empowered by it. Compassion for a friend has freed him into a larger compassion and into an intensely moral and direct humanity: "Oh, love is wounding me and I'm afraid death is making me lose touch with the faces of those I love . . ."[53]

The "Postscript" is a highly organized account of a trip to Mexico with his boyfriend Tom—and the ghost of Dakota. They attend a bull-fight (the sense of literary history in the first part of the book has come full circle and now claims the author for its own) which Wojnarowicz intercuts with his own memories. He becomes infused with pity for all living—and dying—things. In this final stand-off with death, animated by Dakota's sad ghost, Wojnarowicz confronts all frailty and transience and if language sometimes fails him here in his intensity, his soul is intact. In undergoing the hardest journey possible, in considering so deeply so much of our pain and in reaching such pity, such forgiveness, Wojnarowicz returns to us in this book a great deal of what we have lost under mountains of panic and trivia in the past decades: eternal verities, unfashionable goodness, deep emotion, and the prospect of hope.

E.Y.

Postscript: David Wojnarowicz died in New York 22/7/92.

Death in Disneyland

The work of Dennis Cooper

"Applaud me but no one applauded. Instead in the
distance a child screamed."
  Joe Orton and Kenneth Halliwell, *The Boy Hairdresser*

"Alors, o ma beauté! dites à la vermine
Qui vous mangera des baisers,
Que j'ai gardé la forme et l'essence divine
De mes amours·décomposés!"
                    Charles Baudelaire, *Une Charogne.*★

There is a famous self-portrait by the late photographer Robert
Mapplethorpe. Entitled "Self-Portrait (The Whip)", once seen
it is never forgotten. It was part of a Mapplethorpe exhibition,
"The Perfect Moment", which opened in April 1990 at the
Cincinnati Contemporary Arts Center. Seven of the photographs, including "Self-Portrait (The Whip)" featured in the
ensuing obscenity trial, which found the Arts Center not guilty,
although the furore testified to the growing number of attacks on
artistic freedom by right-wing demagogues in the States.

In the self-portrait, Mapplethorpe, dressed only in thigh-high
boots and oddments of leather paraphernalia, presents his naked
buttocks to the camera. His ass★ is stretched open by his stance

---

★ I am using the American slang word "ass" for buttocks rather than the English
equivalent "arse" throughout this essay. "Arse" is more confrontational and
coarse, with a suggestion of the comic or farcical about it, the saucy postcard,
whereas "ass" is a smoother, easier, cooler word which does not disrupt linguistic
flow in the same way.

and he holds a large bull-whip which is inserted into the dark crevice. The upper part of his torso is twisted around so that his face looks into the camera. The entire pose is initially suggestive of the statues of classical antiquity—the virile, eroticized male body denoting action and aggression, with veins and tendons in relief, frozen in the moment of artistic stasis. Careful lighting with heavy black and white contrast leads the eye inexorably up the length of the bull-whip, into the anus, round the body to the face and back down to the whip; any art professor could trace the contours. The impression of classic male beauty gradually begins to blur as one becomes aware of ambivalences within the pose. There is an ironic awareness of the unnatural tensions of the "classic" pose. There is doubt, fear and hesitancy as well as defiance, in the lineaments and attitude of the man. This is no simple statement of desires and tastes, but rather one which encodes within the body of the artist a multiplicity of possibilities and blocked possibilities. There is both assertion and denial, courage and fear in the pose. The eyes of the artist, anticipating response, lock onto the eyes of the viewer, which are forced, again and again to shift (in shame, denial, rage, desire?) to the other highlighted area, the globes of the buttocks.

This constant oscillation between face and buttocks provides a commentary of sado-masochistic practice—the fluctuation between the human being and the ritualized sex—as well as mirroring the oppositions within the pose itself. And every time our eyes trace the buttocks we run the risk of being drawn—forever?—into that forbidding, heavily shadowed cave between them, where the whip leads us into darkness, into ultimate taboo.

It is precisely at this point of sado-masochistic anal taboo that Dennis Cooper locates his work. All that Mapplethorpe means to convey in the self-portrait lies in Cooper's work which is similarly clear and aesthetically beautiful, and at the same time, dense, threatening and impacted with meaning. Cooper's work too has the courage to defy prurience and reject obscenity in favour of clarity and understanding. He too operates against the murmurous clamour of all those who would prefer to shut the "box", to "pull the plug" on the excremental vision, to flush away the shit, the perversity, decay and rot and, if at all possible, death. America! To old, dirty Europe, America has always seemed aglow with toothpaste, Gleem and deodorizers for every intimate inch. Showers seem to gush constantly. And Hollywood—every image has been dry-cleaned. We know that America is pathologically, obsessively, fanatically obsessed with hygiene. This fear of contamination seems to be part of the psychic pulse of the nation. Pity the frail, lone artist who like Cooper or Mapplethorpe tries to say, "Dirt and desire and shit and disgust and fear are all mixed up together—in you! And in you!"

Recently there have been an increasing number of artists, particularly visual and performance artists, who have shown themselves to be explicitly concerned with the body—with its limits, its boundaries, its encoded meanings. One thinks of Andres Serrano and his totemic bodily fluids, Damien Hirst trawling the morgues, Joel Peter Witkin and his deathly neo-classicism or Karen Finley hoping to rub people's faces in their own physicality. The reasons for this drawing-in, this narrowing-down, this focus on the human envelope are all closely inter-twined. The most obvious is the mythic status of AIDS and all that the disease implies in terms of sexual libertarianism. Closely aligned to this is a reaction to the sexual and social mores of the sixties and seventies, in the sense that there was an odd "bodylessness" about the period: although naturally physical attractiveness mattered as much as ever at that time, yet it was as if the free play of careless sexuality plus the amorphous shapes of psychedelia, the unconstrained shapes of hallucinogenic thinking all led away from the individual body, towards more of a group body in the sense of a vast, like-minded, thoughtlessly eroticized community. This permeated the sub-culture, not just the hippie end of it. Both Andy Warhol and his art represented an extreme of "bodylessness"—a denial of the realities of the body which co-existed with an emphasis on its hyper-real, camply over-eroticized, mythic qualities. Gradually, during the eighties as times got harder and sharper and selfishness and self-interest became fashionable all this narrowed down to an intense focus on the individual body, its grooming and exercise. And then of course AIDS added a necessary increase in sexual narcissim and auto-eroticism. Finally, with some of the artists who now emphasize the body there is an element of desperation. It is as if stunned by years of postmodernism and all the endlessly circulating codes and signs and signifiers there is a sense of the body being the last frontier, an actuality that no amount of theory can disperse.

It is against this background that Dennis Cooper works. He is not primarily a New York artist although he has lived in that city. Cooper lives in Los Angeles where he has been involved in a number of art, theatre and dance projects but although these tend to centre around his identity as a gay man, as indeed do his novels, it would be a loss if his work were to receive little response outside the gay community. His writing has an uncompromising exactitude that merits close attention. In this essay I intend to concentrate on two of his novels, *Closer* and *Frisk*. These have some parallels with the work of Bret Easton Ellis. *Closer*, like *Less Than Zero*, is centred on the West Coast teen scene—or at least we can assume it is—and *Frisk* has thematic affinities with *American Psycho*. Cooper's work seems to go further than Ellis's in uniting West Coast laid-back vapidity with the urban nihilism of much New York fiction and indeed *Frisk* takes wing for Europe, some of the action being situated in Amsterdam. This is the only novel, apart from those of Lynne Tillman, to actually leave America for the Old World and the significance of this move is reflected in the work of both these writers. All the books we have surveyed were, so to speak, "born" into postmodernity and they tend to be, apart from the work of Cooper and Tillman, remarkably, even alarmingly free of literary references and influences. They have little sense of literary history. This may be intentional and even inevitable. Postmodernity in fiction, and particularly in the work of this group of writers, has been distrustful of the hegemony of the literary past, has been disinclined to worship at the altar of "great" writers and academic tradition. When Ellis evokes other books, they are those of his peers. Such writers have been reflecting a world in which "literary" values have been eroded and replaced with a media rather than a textual literacy. Additionally, postmodernist fiction has required inventiveness and ingenuity—it has been necessary, in Ezra Pound's words, to "Make It New"—which is possibly why many of the novels we have looked at seem almost blind and stunned in terms of "literary" qualities, as if surprised to have found themselves "written" at all. Cooper's work is quite unlike this. It is so considered and "literary" that were it not for an almost involuntary animation, it might seem mannered. On reading Cooper's novels for the first time, one is reminded irresistibly of the Gothic tradition, the psychoanalytical chasms of Edgar Allan Poe's work and the resolute taboo-baiting of Georges Bataille.

Closer is a very singular book. It functions on at least three distinct levels, all closely intertwined: as a fantasy or fable, as a critique of pornographic writing, and also as the simulation, or coming-into-being in textual form, of a number of unrealized, ineffable psychic states. *Closer* tells of a group of teenage boys, still in high-school whose lives come to converge around the body of the sublimely beautiful George Miles, one of their number.

The fantasy aspects of the story lie in its undifferentiated location—presumably Californian as it is set close to Disneyland (where all good postmodernist theorists send their valentines) and in its sense of timelessness, although this runs us straight into some of the curious ellipses of Cooper's style. It *is* oddly timeless—a chapter entitled "George: Thursday, Friday, Saturday" refers us to no specific days in terms of plot but to all the wistful Thursdays, Fridays and Saturdays of those sad end-of-childhood years, the endless Fridays and Saturdays of high-school when terminal boredom, speculation and a sinister excitement all seemed to coalesce—but at the same time the book is utterly specific in being set in the post-punk eighties. The fantastical element continues in the fact of this group of boys seeming, most of them, to be so very pretty and in their being so endlessly sexually interested in, and available to each other. They have no hang-ups about their homosexuality, there is no mention of AIDS but while these would seem to be the constituents of an erotic paradise the book explicitly positions itself against the lies and distortions of such nonsensical pornographic utopias. And yet this is neither any known high-school society, nor is it the jaded bisexuality of Ellis's Californian teenagers in *Less Than Zero*, which as a novel is very much closer to reportage than Cooper's. Cooper's teenage boys are meant to be as blank and stunned and inarticulate as Ellis's teenagers but they refuse to remain as deadened; they seem to fight their way, almost beyond Cooper's control, into individuality. (Recalling Susan Sontag's assertion that, "Pornography is a theatre of types, never of individuals,"[1] one sees how this tendency towards characterization helps to distance Cooper's work from the pornographic genre.) Despite the similarities in some of their subject matter there are very profound differences between Bret Easton Ellis and Dennis Cooper as writers. Despite his accomplished formalism, Ellis has little imagination. The desires that turbo-charge the creative imagination are too muddied in him to allow the creation of archetypes and he has, for very good reasons, little interest in characterization. Ellis's artistic vision is fundamentally conventional, moralistic and upholds the status quo and it is ironic that he is seen as such a sensationalist literary wild child. He is leaden, rooted in time. Cooper on the other hand is transcendent, timeless. He has extraordinarily clear unconscious drives and these tend to animate and energize every aspect of his text whether he wishes them to or not. His imagination is that of the outsider, the outlaw, or more classically the Prankster. He is an Imp of the Perverse who can create even as he destroys or self-destructs.

Cooper's *fabula* in *Closer*—his story in real time—is disjointed, disrupted, spliced and re-spliced and his *sjuzet*, the story within his discourse, here an erotic one, is located within these gaps and interstices. When Alex, one of the boys in *Closer*, reads a gay porn mag he notices the disjunction between the muscular nude bodies and the "X-rated story line, added on later": "It's these gaps that Alex keeps glancing at."[2] Cooper is writing, as far as is possible, what Roland Barthes termed "a text of bliss" and Barthes refers to Jacques Lacan's contention that bliss "cannot be spoken except between the lines."[3] In writing of erotic sublimity, which by its very nature cannot be articulated or even realized, Cooper's meaning is "doomed" to inhabit such "gaps", one of which lies at the centre of George Miles's body, at the very centre of the text.

Apart from this mystery within the body and within the text, Cooper is able to comment on many aspects of Californian teendom. John is the first boy in the book and "he liked the way punk romanticized death". He feels that "Punk's bluntness had edited tons of pretentious shit out of America",[4] although punk is now becoming passé and bores his schoolmates. John is an artist but will not discuss his work for a school project. "My portraits speak for themselves,"[5] he announces and the critic is uneasily aware that Cooper is speaking here of his own work too. Barthes maintains that, "Criticism always deals with the texts of pleasure, never the texts of bliss."[6] Texts of pleasure are more orderly, less disruptive. Barthes mentions Flaubert, Proust, Stendhal and one could add Austen or Dickens; the text "that comes from culture and does not break with it". Texts of bliss, he says, impose "a state of loss"; they "unsettle the reader's historical, cultural, psychological assumptions."[7] In evoking the unspeakable, Cooper is dreaming the impossible dream, writing the impossible text.

John of course, like everyone else, desires George Miles, but even when they are in bed, where it is "warm and familiar", John is aware that "the kid was just skin wrapped round some grotesque-looking stuff."[8] The reader is from the start face to face with the central mystery and terror of life. Nothing can shield him. Barthes says that the text must "cruise"[9] the reader. Cooper's text goes further. It is, as they say of serial murderers, "trolling for prey".

In this first section Cooper is able to deal with his Gothic literary heritage and the death of punk and to dismiss them both. John and George pick up a battered, suicidal punk boy in a gay bar and have sex with him. Later they visit the neighbourhood "haunted house" once so redolent of myth but when John reached his teens he had been inside and found it to be "nothing, an empty thing".[10] At this point in the narrative George's meaning, his seductivity, is displaced onto the body of the punk. It is as if the author is blinded by the light and cannot turn his gaze directly upon George's physical irradiation. The punk yells, "Hurt me . . . I really fucking love violence."[11] John despises this "me-generation angst from the seventies". He bites the punk in what is a textual comment on the vampire myth which along with haunted houses and horror films comprises so much of the media fall-out around teenagers. The experience causes John to feel that "A bleeding punk kid was so much more horrific and ridiculous and sort of moving too"[12] in comparison with more self-destructive activities. John is tentatively considering moving towards the outer limits, towards focusing his desire and rage upon the bodies of others, rather than self-destructively, self-reflexively—and worst, old-fashionedly—upon his own. He arranges the punk's ass into a sort of gift box, "I'll make his ass a gift,"[13] and "decorates" it with "red ribbon(s)" of whip marks. In this book George's body—perfect young male flesh—is the ultimate Object of Desire and quite literally within that, his ass is the fetish object. ("The text is a fetish object,"[14] intones Barthes.) The punk, the displaced Object of Desire here, has by now become a "silhouette", a ghost.

Closer takes a break at this point for a dramatic monologue, delivered in "numbers" like the songs in a pop concert, by David, another cherubic beauty. David, consumed with teen yearning, so longs to be a pop star that he has convinced himself—almost—that he actually is one. Cooper allows David to muse on the tragedy and pathos of the pop process. David realizes that, for example, Fabian, "my 1950s equivalent" who "seems like heaven on earth in old film clips," is today "a stooped, sagging child". Pop stardom is an all-engrossing, infantilizing myth and the singers "lure children into adulthood by mouthing inanities like 'I love you' when what they actually mean is 'You'll die someday'."[15] David is also nervous of his own beauty. He too knows that he is only "a bunch of blue tubes inside a skin wrapper" or perhaps "a shiny thing crammed with blood, guts and bones."[16] David is self-confessedly delusionary, "I lie all the time"[17], but he is allowed, in the text, to speak truth. The reader is trapped in the Liar's Paradox. David too has a crush on George.

George Miles. So beautiful that he is almost out-of-focus "like a badly tuned hologram".[18] Again the sublime evades language. His name certainly suggests distance and journeying but it may be fanciful to recall Robert Frost's lines: "The woods are lovely, dark and deep/ But I have promises to keep/ And miles to go before I sleep."[19] The woods are certainly dark and deep for George. George at this stage in the narrative is still a child, almost a baby. He is inarticulate, frustrating; he speaks in "squeaks" or "whispers", and is constantly close to tears. He is polymorphously perverse. George is, in fact, explicitly pre-Oedipal. When we meet him his mother is dying. George day-dreams constantly and takes a lot of drugs. His room is a shrine to Disneyland. He has scale models of all his favourite rides: "The Haunted Palace, Enchanted Tiki Room, Peter Pan, Space Mountain."[20] He has a map of Disneyland over the bed and keeps his acid in a battered Mickey Mouse cap. "His room was so dazzling it made the rest of the world seem like a parking lot." George's favourite Disneyland ride is a spooky one where a scary voice announces, "Dead . . . Men . . . Tell . . . No . . . Tales."*

After a school dance George meets—as if by magic—a strange Frenchman called Philippe. Philippe wears an ivory skull ring and has crazy eyes. "Perfect" thinks George. Philippe is Death's messenger. George goes home with Philippe and fellates him while Philippe explores every inch of his body "like it was covered with braille or something".[21]

---

* The origins of this phrase, so central to *Closer*, are lost somewhere in sub-literary history. It was first used as a book-title by E.W. Hornung, the creator of *Raffles* in 1899. It became a catch-phrase and other authors followed suit with titles including *Dead Men Rise Up Never, Dead Men Leave No Fingerprints* and, my favourite, the classic *Dead Men Don't Ski*, in 1959.

During the sex acts George accidentally shits and Philippe shouts, "that is what I wanted to happen."[22] George, mortified, takes the Warhol route and pretends that what is happening to him is a movie, or, in this case, a scary Disneyland ride through a dark barren tunnel where skeletons fall from the roof. Philippe appears to be saying, "You are dead, baby," as he fucks George.

Philippe would seem to be a paedophile, a coprophile, a necrophile and quite possibly a murderer. We come back to David Wojnarowicz's question: what is it about "dark things or what William James called 'morbid-mindedness' that so attracts people now?" In one sense this is a non-question. "Dark things", strict societal taboos, have always simultaneously attracted and repelled people, often with an erotic undertow. The "forbidden" has, to use Baudrillard's phrase, its own "fatal strategies". Nevertheless, the novels we have studied in this book cover a remarkable plethora of "dark things", including sado-masochism and other sexual perversities, drug-addiction, voyeurism, prostitution, occultism, suicide and murder. "Dark things" lay at the heart of the pleasures of the seventies.

Martin Green's book *Children of the Sun: A Narrative of Decadence in England after 1918*[23] attempted a shaky theory about periods of cultural rebellion and schism in industrial society, periods such as the 1890s and the 1920s. Green suggested that the young rebels of these periods could always be seen to belong to one of three cultural types which were interconnected and indeed could merge and change within one individual. These were the *dandy* or aesthete, heir to Baudelaire and Robert de Montesquieu, the *naif* type who was more idealistic or searching in his impulses and the *rogue* who frequently inclined towards politics. It's a rough thesis, but it is possible to see during periods of rebellion against the dominant order something of these distinct fashions in cultural life. For example, to go far beyond Green's book, during the sixties one could see very clearly the distinctions between the fashion victim or dandy whose concerns were purely stylistic, (Keith Richards, Michael Rainey), the naifs who turned towards mysticism and Eastern religions and the rogues or radical/ political wing (SDS,

Baader-Meinhof). In 1973, Stephen Koch's prescient study of Andy Warhol and his influence, *Stargazer*,[24] explicitly identified Warhol and his concerns with those of the Baudelairian dandy in terms of nihilism, narcotic sense-derangement and stylistic excess. We have seen the vast influence that Warhol has exerted; his stunned postmodern passivity and deliberate emotional inauthenticity virtually defined "attitude" or cool for millions of middle-class white kids. It would seem that for a long time now, style—which *is* culture for the generations we are considering— has merely surrendered to the extremes of the dandy mode: the camp, the black humour, the frozen moments, the rigidly enforced cool. And, as Koch made clear, they all have their origin in a fascination with death.

Additionally, and with particular reference to Cooper and Ellis, murder has come to be very central in our society. There is not just the proliferation of serial killers but all the "murders" inherent in postmodernism: the "murder" of imagination and unselfconscious emotion by the media, the "murder" of the "real" by the simulation, the "murder" of the individual by the type, or clone. Dick Hebdige writes: "the discourse of post-modernism is fatal and fatalistic: at every turn the word 'death' opens up to engulf us: 'death of the subject', 'death of the author', 'death of art', 'death of reason' and 'end of history'."[25] Lastly, with specific reference to Cooper and his prose, Death has become overwhelming in the mind of the literary theorist. Paul de Man states, with a trace of his grim irony, that "Death is a displaced name for a linguistic predicament."[26] The word "Death" has displaced "God" as the ultimate "transcendental signifier". It is now more than the distinguished thing, it denotes the impossible in a world of endlessly deferred meaning; Death means *closure*. Anyone who plays now with language and literature is playing with the (im)possibility of Death. Cooper is clearer than most with respect to the ways text relates to the Grim Reaper.

George's affair with Philippe continues, although it troubles him. He arranges for a friend, Cliff, to observe him having sex with Philippe. Cliff is nauseated by Philippe's coprophilia and his sadistic treatment of George. Cliff confides in another friend/lover, Alex, who is unusually, not particularly attracted to George. ("He reminds me of a cartoon character.") They discuss the situation, although they have some trouble with the demotic. "George's, uh, shit is supposed to be heavy but to me the concept is incredibly lightweight."[27] The word "shit" has of course become ubiquitous and Cooper is carefully realigning it with its . . . source.

Alex is a would-be film director. He is fascinated by sex and violence and is "juggling lots of ideas" for a possible film: "porn scenario, B-movie parody, rock opera, pseudosnuff."[28] Alex reads gay porn and comes upon a coprophile scene. This reminds him of George's situation. Initially embarrassed, Alex is becoming excited by coprophilia and decides to make a porn movie around the subject, starring George. Cliff suggests he films the "real thing",[29] through Philippe's window. Alex does this and, as he observes the scene between George and Philippe, he composes in his head a gay-porn script along the lines of: "He . . . smelled something rich but rancid, like the trace of perfume in a king's tomb . . ." and "Whipping his fierce, swordlike prong into a frenzy, he gulped the abhorrent meal down in one bite."[30] The reader is forced to "see" the scene through Alex's camera and his god-awful prose commentary. Afterwards, in the car with Cliff, Alex prattles about "the mystique of shit": and how "banal"[31] it all was really. Alex and Cliff promptly have a car-crash. Cliff escapes but Alex, the pornographer, will be in a wheel-chair for a year or so. He has been punished for the falsity of pornographic writing. Cooper is not writing pornography. He intends to take us "closer".

The section entitled "George: Wednesday, Thursday, Friday" is the heart of the matter. Firstly we see George, at home, poring over two "crinkled typewritten pages". These are from Philippe and contain detailed descriptions, in French, of how George "looked, smelled and tasted."[32] George takes some acid and listens to The Cramps' immortal "Garbage Man" before hitching to his date with Philippe. There are no pornographers present tonight. Cooper's spare, delicate language probably brings us as close to "realism" as words can in this context. George is introduced to Philippe's friend, an older man called Tom. After visiting the bathroom—where he pops a zit on his back; this is very unlike Alex's purple prose—George, his thoughts in a whirl from the acid, returns and lies face-down on the rug. The two men caress him, slipping their finger up his ass. They talk between themselves; their tone is casual, almost jokily sardonic. They are clinical and detached, but not wholly without tenderness. "Shit, baby," says Philippe, and "George pushed a couple of turds out." The men joke about the fact that he obviously eats typical teenage junk food—french fries and candy bars. Someone spanks him. The conversation becomes more urgent and disjointed and come is "splattered over his ass, back and legs",[33] but it is all very low-key. Tom drives him home and asks him if he has ever thought of killing himself. "If you decide to go all the way, call me."[34] George is puzzled. Does Tom mean he would dissuade him or assist? Back home George examines his ass. With the swelling, "It looked exactly like Injun Joe's cave, his eighth or ninth favourite Disneyland ride at the moment".[35]

Soon after this episode George's father finds Philippe's written pages. "I know a little French. I've never seen such filth!"[36] but they have to go urgently to the hospital. Sitting by his mother George sees that the monitor is running a straight line. "Mom's . . . shit . . . dead".[37] Even at this moment his sexual life, his slangy teenage life and his private emotional life are all mixed up in his language. George's affect may seem blunted. He writes later in his diary: "She really loved me once. Likewise, I guess,"[38] but the effect on the reader is one of terrible pathos. Moreover, his mother's death is cataclysmic in Oedipal terms. Jacques Lacan has explained how the Oedipal crisis represents the entry into the Symbolic Order which in turn corresponds to our acquisition of language. One could say that George with his babyish ways and his acid trips in Disneyland has been located in the Imaginary (as Lacan calls it) or pre-Oedipal period. Now, with his mother's death he decides to clean up his room, "make it look like a normal place,"[39] and to burn all his Disneyland stuff.

His mother's death, the loss of the maternal body, means that George suffers what Lacan terms the "primary repression". From now on the desire for the lost mother must be repressed and it is this that opens up the unconscious. In the pre-Oedipal stage there is no unconscious since there is no loss, no absence, no differentiations, merely subject-identity and perpetual presence. Obvious parallels can be seen here between breasts and buttocks. It is this primary loss of the mother that creates difference, gender-awareness and desire. George now enters human culture and society, that is the Symbolic Order which is dominated by the Law of the Father. He is no longer wholly passive. Had he remained in the realm of the Imaginary he would have been psychotic. George now, on the death of his mother, enters too the realm of the unconscious, which is really desire itself, the eternal driving search for lost unity. Probably Lacan's most famous statement is "The unconscious is structured like a language", and here we see that George has been validated, *signed in* to the world of desire and language through Philippe's letters—which are, tellingly, written in French. Shortly afterwards, in conversation with Philippe, George starts questioning him about the motives behind his erotic perversions. "To Philippe's recollection, George hadn't probed before."[40] George has become aware of the unconscious. In a textbook case of Oedipal crisis George has at last grown up and entered the signifying circles, the marriage of Heaven and Hell that comprises language and desire.

George, still in shock over his mother's death, decides to visit Tom "to say my goodbye to the person I am".[41]

Tom is detached, almost off-hand, but not without a weird tenderness. "Poor baby, school hasn't done you a lick of good, has it?" and "Your beauty is far more profound than the works of our fine intellectuals, don't you think?" (George "chortled nervously".) George tentatively admires the paintings on the wall, executed by a friend of Tom's. "My friend believes corpses dream," says Tom. "Try to imagine each work is the dream of a murdered child."[42]

In creating Tom, Cooper reaches for what is probably the

most violent taboo in contemporary culture, the taboo against child sexual abuse and child murder. Even Cooper, with his intense insight and pity does not attempt to humanize Tom. Tom's desires are to us literally unspeakable. But it should be said that the matter of these paintings provides a direct link with the period from which I have suggested so much of our concern with "dark things" originates. This is the Symbolist and Decadent period of the 1890s. The artists and writers of this period who include Paul Verlaine, Stéphane Mallarmé, Odilon Redon, Felicien Rops and Gustave Moreau, all heavily influenced by Baudelaire, were all deeply, sometimes ecstatically involved with Death—and with dreams and the unconscious and with souls and chimeras. The Decadent obsessions were "opium, death, crime and the ecstasies of sexual pleasure and pain".[43] Sounds familiar? As Cooper writes about Punk in *Closer*, the Decadents too "romanticized death". They dressed it up in intoxicating vapours, clouds of rags and lace, lilies, swans, incubi and succubi, bejewelled skeletons and vampires with moonstone eyes. All this was the corrupt impedimenta of the decadent dream with its overt sado-masochism and its stubborn sub-textual auto-eroticism. There were no perversions that they did not know and no profane ecstasies that escaped them. They looked to "morphine or the whip, to little girls or fairground wrestlers to plunge them into the delirium they had hoped to find in Art."[44] In writing, the Symbolists and Decadents were the forerunners of Modernism. The French writers in particular were much influenced by the works of the Marquis de Sade and Edgar Allan Poe. Oscar Wilde wrote at this time in *The Picture of Dorian Gray*—one of the most culturally prophetic books ever: "There is no such thing as a moral or immoral book. Books are well-written or badly written." But in general, apart from in literature, the very profound influence exerted on twentieth-century culture by the Symbolists and Decadents has been too little understood. Even Jean Baudrillard, with all his deathly brilliance, does little more than refract Decadent strategies through the mirror of the technological media. Excess, extremes, decay, fetishization. They wrote the book. And so, looking at

Tom's creepy pictures we must remember firstly that Cooper's concerns stem directly from the Symbolist/Decadent heritage and secondly that the death of children—and even the murder of children—was somewhat less repellent to the Victorian mind than to our own. It was more common for one thing. Much English Victorian art is lavishly sentimental in its treatment of early death. French Decadent writing and painting is full of dead children, "souls" who are now enchanted. For a brief example look at the central picture in Baron Léon Frédéric's (1856-1940) triptych "Tout Est Mort", its panels entitled *Le ruisseau, Le torrent* and *L'eau dormante. Le torrent* is a sickly pink and blue painting. It depicts hundreds of dead children being swept along a chilly Styx beneath an apocalyptic sky. A tempest of swans accompanies them. The painting is both kitsch and insipid with its pastel colourings but chilling in its mortuary chic and perverse undertones. I know it is overly literal but I see Tom's paintings as being something like this. The poets, especially the bad ones, were not far behind. Consider: "Souls of children who died before the baptismal dew/Weak-winged the frail things could not reach paradise . . ." or: "You alone, posthumous child of serene times/Bear proudly the stigma of beauty."[45] How like Tom they sound.

So perhaps Tom too is a victim of this immensely seductive period. Many of us are, in some more mildly decadent way. Tom burns George's clothes and injects his ass with Novocaine "so I can take you apart sans your pointless emotions". (This is one of the differences between 1890s and 1980s decadence. Hysteria and emotionalism have been replaced by chilly cool.) George is still too stoned on acid and grief to be warned until Tom starts chopping at his ass with some dangerous implement. Even so, he agrees with Tom. He "didn't want to be crying his eyes out and miss the good parts. It was enough to see his blood covering the floor like a magic rug." Tom asks softly, "Any last words?" and George goes "Dead . . . men . . . tell . . . no tales," in his best spooky voice. When Tom doesn't laugh, George bursts into tears. Tom is infuriated. "I said no fucking emotions! Do you want me to kill you or not?"[46] George *doesn't know* and Tom throws him out into the night with a blanket. Of course dead men *literally* do not tell tales, tell stories. Cooper is suggesting that were we really to abandon all restraints and carve any of our murderous desires into the corporeal bodies of others, there would *be* no stories, no books.

The whole scene seems unreal to George with his zombie-ish postmodern personality. He actually saves his life by reverting, briefly, at this moment of crisis to babyhood, to Disneyland and tears. Tom, incredible though it may seem, needs more adult, even consensual participation, to remain aroused. (Another victim who responds more normally, more pathetically at the last minute—"Please don't"—is killed by Tom.) But George is still close enough to pre-Oedipality to not realize his danger as a separate, autonomous being. On the other hand there is also the possibility that humour saved him. Humour is understood to be deeply unerotic in serious, ritualized sex.

George recovers, albeit scarred, and even continues his relationship with Philippe. This does not actually seem totally improbable or fantastical. People can understand, forgive and live with extraordinary extremes of behaviour, particularly in regard to the gratification of desire. George's desires, now that he is beginning to have them, incline towards a need for love and tenderness which he hopes Philippe can provide. This seems unlikely. Cooper tries to tell us a little about Philippe's personality and chicken-snuff obsession but the writing is somewhat half-hearted and it is hard to feel for a man who acts as pimp for Tom. Philippe himself cannot kill although he belongs to a group of paedophiles. "Each participant wanted to kill someone cute during sex," but they lack the strength and just act out scenarios. One night Tom brings a film of his activities and Philippe becomes Death's pimp, Death's messenger. Philippe thinks, "My ideas about death are very beautiful, so I wanted to think about killing a beautiful person." He feels that Death "is too beautiful to explain."[47] Some of this—the desire to kill during sex—seems incomprehensible although it is not apparently uncommon. Otherwise the romanticization of Death completes an entire century of flirtation with the subject which, as it had retreated more from our lives, looms larger in our fantasies.

In the final section of the book, a new character, Steve, sleeps with George. "His ass looks like someone threw a grenade at it. He must get rejected a lot."[48]

Heartbreakingly, George, once so perfect, has survived precariously, violently—barely—into adulthood, his experience a terrifying exaggeration of societal rites of passage. It's nothing too sudden though; George retains much of his shy, sweet immaturity and Steve is falling in love with him. Steve also phones Tom and threatens him with the cops if any of his friends and acquaintances disappear. "He could do what he wants but not in my world."[49] George's friends love him and Steve does not think that death or self-destruction "is a hip place to be." Steve opens a nightclub in his parent's garage but in another cartoonish crash a car ploughs into it. (It's Steve's party and he'll cry if he wants to.) The comic-strip element helps to dispel any notions of one orderly genre—fable, realist, hyperrealist, pornographic. This, along with the constantly changing narrators and tenses helps to create the textual disjunctions wherein Cooper locates sublimity. In the second car crash, David, the aspirant pop star, dies. In the first crash, pornographic inauthenticity was shattered. In this one all the teen pop dreams are demolished. That is over. Steve had fallen for David's gorgeous looks, but seeing him mangled on the floor reveals David's "perfection" now "uglified". Steve feels that his love for George, who is no longer perfect but scarred and marred by his experiences, has become deeper and clearer as a result of his new understanding regarding how very limited is human physical perfection. Skindeep. Steve's loving impulses towards George and his attack on Tom restore balance and humanity to the book. But, still in some part of him Steve feels that "Perfection's like God", and he has to conclude predictably, "Shit, I'm all tangled up."[50]

Closer is an impeccably realized, complex and luminous novel. In reaching for what Roland Barthes calls "Bliss"—*jouissance* or rapture—in trying to speak the unspeakable, Cooper can be numbered among, in Barthes's words: "the very few writers who combat *both* ideological repression and libidinal repression."[51] When it comes to writing "the text of bliss", Barthes mentions only two writers, Bataille and Poe. ("Bliss may come only with the *absolutely new*, for only the new disturbs [weakens] consciousness."[52] The correspondences between their work and Cooper's have already been mentioned in this essay. It is, says Barthes, "the extreme of perversion"[53] which defines bliss. Barthes also points out that in using language, the mother tongue, "The writer is someone who plays with his mother's body . . . in order to glorify it . . . to embellish it, or in order to dismember it, to take it to the limit of what can be known about the body."[54] This is exactly what Cooper wishes to do to the bodies of the boys he writes about. In *Frisk* he writes: "I'm pretty sure if I tore some guy open I'd know him as well as anyone could," and: "You fascinate me so much that in a perfect world I'd kill you to understand the appeal . . . If I killed you I'd be free . . . I think of it as religious."[55] Lynne Tillman has pointed out that the mutilations inflicted upon the boys' bodies in these books is very similar to "making vaginas".[56] "Doesn't every narrative lead back to Oedipus?" asks Barthes.[57]

In Cooper's work the text is the body. Barthes has said that "*Text* means *Tissue*",[58] and in *Closer* George's body which is seen as "covered with braille" and "filled up with hieroglyphs"[59] is the text itself. Bliss, or *jouissance*, the ultimate unspeakable mystery and rapture which Cooper seeks, is located within the fissure or chasm at the centre of the text, that dark "Injun's Joe's cave" so suggestive of child-like pre-Oedipal sexuality, that which is literally fundament(al), the split in George's body that leads to sublimity, unknowingness, unsayableness. Barthes has said that the text of bliss always rises out of our history "like a scandal" and that it is always "the trace of a cut".[60] Here in the text is that cut, that gap at the centre of George's body, at the heart of the text. Bliss approaches "the gratuitousness of death," writes Barthes and "shock, disturbance, even loss" are "proper to ecstasy, to bliss."[61] This is the sense of loss that leads us towards death. In Sontag's words, "The truth of eroticism is always tragic."[62]

*

Frisk continues these themes in denser, more highly structured form. The narrator is called Dennis. This device of the authors using their own name is also employed by Lynne Tillman. It has a curiously distancing effect in that one actually learns far less about the author in this way than one does in less stringently aware and controlled texts where the authors often helplessly, inadvertently reveal far more about themselves than they probably intended. The narrative in *Frisk* is dense, spliced, inter-cut; double and even triple-tracking through time and points of view. Even Dennis's identity is fluid. At one time he was a punk called "Spit"—suitably liquid. Dennis describes himself as a "predator and aesthete", "pretty removed and amoral",[63] although he is more of a victim and far more moral than this might indicate. He is also writing an "artsy murder-mystery novel",[64] fragments of which appear in the narrative. These sections seem, presumably intentionally, slightly more crass and abrupt than the "non-novel" sections.

Dennis was traumatized at the age of thirteen by being shown photographs of what was apparently a dead boy, whose ass had been horribly mutilated. He becomes transfixed by this certain type of boy—"younger, lean, pale, dark-haired, full-lipped, dazed looking";[65] the archetype that was George Miles in *Closer*, and here is called Henry. Dennis meets Henry early in the novel and learns that Henry was the model for those pictures and that they were staged, simulations. This immediately removes any sleazy pornographic suspense or tension from the text. We know the answer. It wasn't "real".

Dennis struggles with his desires to kill and gain access to the ultimate "information" about the human body. He knows murder is obscene and selfish but he is distanced from death. Even when his friends start dying of AIDS he still finds the "idea of death is so sexy and/or so mediated by TV and movies I couldn't cry now."[66] He confides at length in a hustler called Pierre in New York, discussing his tormented desire to kill "someone cute" during sex. "I mean I know there's no God.

People are only their bodies and sex is the ultimate intimacy etc. but it's not enough. I can't get beyond my awe." "I think of it as religious," he says, "I saw God in those pictures."[67] Dennis feels that if he could kill someone of the right physical type it would be "unbelievably profound".[68] He is seeking enlightenment—his urge actually leads away from all that is dark and decadent towards all that is mystical and sublime. He says, "I see these criminals on the news who've killed someone methodically, and they're free. They know something amazing. You can just tell."[69] Pierre's response is, rightly, "It's sort of sad."[70] Do Jeffrey Dahmer or Dennis Nilsen "know something amazing?"

In *Frisk* the focus is on the desirer or "Tom" figure rather than on the desiree, George or Henry. Unlike Tom however, Dennis cannot bring himself to kill. The "Dennis" persona never achieves the luminous intensity of George in *Closer*. Cooper is more adept at describing the dream than the dreamer. He is able to understand and animate archetypes in an extraordinary manner but some sort of reserve or humility prevents him from applying these mythic qualities to his own writerly persona. Dennis goes to live in Amsterdam, in a windmill. Cooper uses the form of the windmill in an old-fashioned fictive manner: it functions as symbol so that one is again alerted to the links that Cooper's writing has with the past. It is difficult not to see something of Dennis's arrested development in the motionless arms of the windmill and not to contrast the circular sweep of an unfettered "free" windmill with the circular structure of the text. Here Dennis appears to flip-out and start killing boys, describing the murders in letters to Pierre. However the only letter we see—the reader is kept destabilized about what is "real" in the text and what isn't—is a lengthy one written to an old-friend and cruising-partner, Julian, whose kid brother Kevin Dennis had seduced many years ago. The letter is grotesquely detailed in its accounts of murder and cannibalism. It is flattened in affect yet simultaneously desperate, urgent. Dennis describes his home in the upper part of the windmill, with its spiral staircase and a room "shaped like a bell" at the top, wherein he stores one of the bodies. He says he has found a "major transcendence" in killing "cute guys" and, crazily, he wants Julian to join him and "participate in this discovery".[71]

Julian and Kevin are living in Paris and, horrified, they rush to Amsterdam. This final chapter, "Wilder", is technically very complex. The points-of-view of the three characters are presented simultaneously as in: "My eyes looked kind of drugged."[72] Narrator and character "response" have merged into this textual dissolve. Kevin has doubted Dennis's letter from the start. Together, as if in a Gothic novel, he and Julian climb the spiral staircase to the top of the windmill, looking for the bell-shaped room where Dennis has supposedly "stashed" a boy's corpse. The Freudian aspects of their search are inescapable in this climb up the "tight", "claustrophobic" vaginal staircase within the phallus of the windmill. (*Doesn't every narrative lead back to Oedipus?*) There is no bell-shaped room. It doesn't exist. The bell has not tolled for anyone. "I knew it," Kevin says, gazing up. "Rooms like that exist only in books."[73]

Kevin—who is reading Tolkien's *Lord of the Rings*, the original work of "dark fantasy"—has an idea of the way to help Dennis over his obsessions. Dennis and Julian have picked up a local kid, Chretien—a name that is certainly no accident—and Kevin decides to re-create the original simulation, the photographs of the boy with the apparently mutilated ass that so disturbed Dennis, by reproducing the same artificial effects on Chretien's body and photographing them. Julian thinks to himself: "Kevin and/or his camera would have to be God . . . to transform a mud-pie on someone's ass into the sort of nightmarish image one spends one's adult life obsessing about."[74] At this point, we, the readers and the writer come close to "finding God", insofar as this is possible. God is the imagination; the imagination that writes books and makes art.

At the end of *Frisk* Kevin is to stay on with Dennis. There is that note of love and hope, as there was at the end of *Closer*. The final section of *Frisk* describes the photographs again, just as the opening paragraphs did, but adds a "Close-Up" telling us that the "wound" is made of paint, ink, cotton, tissue, papier-mâché.

Textually there is both circularity and rupture as we view, close-up, the deceptive, endlessly seductive constituents of art and desire.

Frisk—the title refers to the act of caressing a body. It also suggests a lightness, an elusiveness very prevalent in Cooper's work—*Frisk* was published around the same time as *American Psycho* but received comparatively little attention. Both texts confront the absurdities of reading fiction. The reader, says Barthes, "endures contradictions without shame."[75] He/she accepts every incompatibility, every incongruity, every illogicality by accepting the conventions of reading a fictional text. Ellis and Cooper in these novels both make very clear that descriptions of murder have exactly the same effect linguistically, whether the murders are "realities" or "fantasies" in the book. They cannot be *more* or *less* real according to the plot. It is only fictional convention that makes them seem so. They are all just words. Despite this thematic similarity and despite *Frisk* being a more profound book, *American Psycho* is much better known. Cooper works more in the artistic alternative/underground area than Ellis does. But it should be said that this lack of reaction probably has some homophobic overtones. Horrible though it is to contemplate, it was Ellis's descriptions of attacks on women that bought him notoriety and sales. Violence against women is more accepted, more acceptable and better understood within our society than what Cooper is describing. As Ellis himself said: "If they (young men) were mutilated and tortured in the same manner, would you be boycotting the publisher?"[76]

For all the extremes and grotesqueries of his content, Cooper is a tender, lyrical and very romantic writer. His works cannot be described as pornographic in that they are not intended to excite the reader to orgasm, but he certainly has affinities with the French erotic tradition represented by, among others, de Sade, Lautréamont and Bataille. Susan Sontag writes in *The Pornographic Imagination*. "Tamed as it may be, sexuality remains one of the demonic forces in human consciousness—pushing us at intervals close to taboo and dangerous desires, which range from the impulse to commit sudden arbitrary violence upon another person to the voluptuous yearning for the extinction of one's consciousness, for death itself . . . Everyone has felt (at least in fantasy) the erotic glamour of physical cruelty and an erotic lure in things that are vile and repulsive."[77] Cooper's work can be located at this point and indeed in *Frisk* there are references which seem to evoke the French erotic and artistic tradition. He mentions the furry teacup of Surrealist Meret Oppenheim and another passage about Henry opening "his eyes so wide that Julian had to think about the fact that they were balls"[78] seems to recall Bataille's erotic classic *The Story of the Eye*, with its links between eyes, eggs, buttocks and balls. Bataille describes in his introduction the region of his mind where certain "*completely obscene*" images coincide, "precisely those on which the conscious floats indefinitely, unable to endure them without an explosion or aberration."[79] He describes this "as the breaking point of the conscious",[80] precisely that interstice or crack in the textual body of Cooper's work wherein lies unknowability, the unconscious, the sublime. Bataille's attempts to reach *his* sublime, which is to him a sacred state, pure animal existence, without self-consciousness, involve an attempt to attain the unfettered boundary-less sensation of being "like water in water". This state which can only be glimpsed through violent excess and debauchery, is very different from Cooper's intimations of the same pre-Oedipal sublimity. Bataille's writing seems much more willed, much more of a representation of a certain philosophy than does Cooper's which has a certain *helplessness* and *passivity* about it, an unconscious echo of the postmodern mediatized consumer. This is extremely interesting because one would think that, being such a subversive and anarchic writer, in writing "texts of bliss" or *jouissance*, Cooper would almost certainly write what Barthes called "writerly" texts, that is ones which invite the reader to participate in deconstructions and language games. This is not so. Cooper's weird passivity means that one would have to describe his texts as "readerly", that is, more orderly or familiar or, in one of Barthes's more controversial assertions, "feminine". It is paradoxical. *American Psycho* was certainly a "writerly" text but it was not a text of "bliss". It was not challenging, destabilizing to the culture. Cooper's books are exactly the opposite, they are "readerly" texts from which, most unusually, proceed the "shock, disturbance, even loss" which, Barthes says, "are proper to ecstasy, to bliss."[81] One sees very clearly in Cooper's text what Barthes means when he writes that: "the text itself . . . can reveal itself in the form of a body, split into fetish objects, into erotic sites." Cooper's erotica, besides corresponding so accurately to Barthes's writings, is also extremely close to the perverse romance and abstract fluidities of Jean Genet, as well as having the same sort of courage. William Burroughs writes: "Genet said of a French writer who shall here be nameless: He does not have the courage to be a writer. What courage does he refer to? The courage of the inner exploration, the cosmonaut of inner space. The writer cannot pull back from what he finds because it shocks or upsets him, or because he fears the disapproval of the reader."[82]

By living in the present, by combining erotica with language theory, Cooper is able to add significantly, and in an entirely contemporary manner, to the canon of erotic literature.

It might be asked in what way do Cooper's most gruesome passages differ from the writing of the so-called "Splatterpunk" writers in the horror genre, authors like Wayne Allen Sallee or J.S. Russell? The answer is probably very little in the case of the best writers and, as Sontag points out, there are always a few first-rate books in any sub-genre. Much of this type of horror is concerned with transgressing that ultimate taboo, the interior of the body. Films of this type, "Splatter" films—one of Alex's interests in "Closer"—are sometimes repulsively referred to as "moist" films, and indeed Baudrillard talks of the "excessive wetness" of the obscene, the "spectral lubricity"[83] of the obscene simulation which is always too visceral, too sticky, too wet. Cooper's work however has many other intentions beyond this transgression of basic bodily taboos. He wishes to chart the postmodern sensibility as it engages with extreme taboo and thus conjoin the mediatized personality and erotic literary history. Whilst wishing to avoid the outmoded debate about differences between "high" and "low" culture I think it can be said that Art is found at the point where the intellect falls in love and that this of course can be absolutely anywhere, although it *tends* to happen where it might be expected, in terms of painting, literature and music. In writing it is the arrangement or combination of certain words that can have a magical, or disruptive or violent resonance and such combinations can occur and affect the individual reader, by dint of their very individuality, in any written work at all. That is why literary censorship always seems such a broad and crude response. The murderer's favourite, *The Catcher in the Rye*, testifies to the way that the emotive arrangement of words in any book can fire the imagination.

Most importantly perhaps, Cooper's central concern is something that has obsessed postmodern theorists. Faced with a seamlessly hyperreal society, apparently invulnerable to negation, criticism or political change, theorists have struggled to articulate a "real" that escapes representation. Baudrillard's musings on seduction and secrecy, Michel Foucault's faith in the possibility of counter-discursive recoveries of subjugated knowledges, Gilles Deleuze's nomadic drifts through the territories of codes, Felix Guattari's molecular desires, Julia Kristeva's *signifiance* and Barthes's texts of bliss all testify to the desire for some irrecuparable meaning that is not subsumed in discourse. All of these are reducible to what Jean-François Lyotard calls the "sublime", that which is unpresentable, unrepresentable and to which the avant-garde artist must "testify".[84] Lyotard's theories of the Beautiful and the Sublime are close to Barthes's ideas about the dematerializing of the subject within the pleasure of the text, until the subject moves beyond words. With the loss of a God there is a vast need for transcendence. Cooper's texts are concerned with this sublime, that which is beyond words, but Lyotard's concepts have come under attack. Meaghan Morris has commented on the outdatedness of Lyotard's idea of the sublime and foresees: "a spasm of ersatz transcendentalism with 'sublime' for its buzzword and for its content a re-discovery of the unspeakable, the ineffable, the mystic catatonics of art."[85] She sees in Lyotard's hymning of an avant-garde sublimity merely an "overwhelmingly familiar model of modernism as a sensibility dependent on strong and equivocal emotion, on pleasure arising from pain (or boredom) and on the propulsing force of unresolvably recurrent oedipal seizures."[86] Like many other theorists, she sees in postmodernism repeated moments of "rupture" without the grounding of a legitimizing meta-narrative. One can perceive all this in Cooper's work. However, what Morris dreads in Lyotard's evocation of the sublime is its banal aspects; she fears that the trivial tendencies of his argument might be extrapolated into an art-world vogue for "kitsch landscapes".[87] It is here that Cooper's work, with its easy acceptance of kitsch—note the pathos in this use of the kitsch word "cute"—is able to suggest an *all-encompassing* sublimity, a totality of creative tendernesses that would outlaw nothing.

In linking many of the themes that have obsessed the novelists in this book to a literary past, Cooper has paradoxically provided a future for fiction. It is a future in which the banal and the kitsch, beauty and terror will co-exist simultaneously, as they must do in a wholly mediatized world. He has tried to provide a language for this future, one that will encompass and transcend the language-games of theory.

Looking at all these writers playing in the ruins, "playing with the pieces—that is postmodern,"[88] one has to wonder whether there is any future for art at all. Baudrillard claims that "art no longer contests anything if it ever did," and although it "can parody this world, illustrate it, simulate it, alter it," art can "never disturb the order, which is also its own."[89] Nevertheless we have seen how postmodern philosophy has made enormous efforts to envisage some sort of purity or authenticity, uncon-taminated by hyperreal society. Few writers or artists feel that their own work is wholly compromised by the culture in which it appears; few feel that they themselves are entirely inauthentic and alienated from what they produce. The constant attempts to locate sites of "meaning" or authenticity are a reflection of the artists' own feelings about themselves and their own integrity and the longing to find this mirrored in an audience. These attempts to define some sort of unsullied purity are essentially narcissistic.

On a more mundane level, consumer capitalism badly needs the artistic imagination: someone has to create Mickey Mouse or Treasure Island, Fagin or Hannibal Lecter and all the other fictions represented in simulation. So it seems that art will continue, whether the artist is subsumed by the spectacle like Norman Mailer, or tries to resist it, as did Thomas Pynchon. All the writers covered in this book have had the immense task of trying to reanimate fiction in the wake of high postmodern experimentation. They have had to deal with a fragmented, absurd society, driven by commodity relations and loosely united at various points by sites of resistance such as feminist or gay politics. Faced with this sort of complexity it is an act of courage to write novels at all. The best writers are usually the most subversive: those most critical of the society in which they find themselves. Those writers who are prepared to learn from and evoke past novelists also seem to have extra strength; books provide refuge and comfort as well as inspiration in a wholly bewildering world.

Looking at all the writers in this book, the well-known and the less well-known and the very variable quality of their novels, it still seems that the most animated and original new work is likely to proceed from America and from writers in some way associated with the attitudes discussed in these essays. These authors have found themselves right up against the dizzying excesses of consumer society and they document the symptoms that are creeping up on the rest of the developed world: inner-city decay, extravagant commodity fetishism, sexual and narcotic extremes, information overload, AIDS and always "the pressure, the pressure . . ." There is no comparable group of English-language writers anywhere else dealing with the alienation and distortions of life under consumer capitalism. In Britain there is a good novel here and a good novel there but no coherent literary scene. Everything seems scattered and uncertain. In America there are many interesting new writers, far too many to have discussed in this book: David Trinidad, Dorothy Allison, Blanche McCrary Boyd, Dodie Bellamy, Pagan Kennedy. There is also an increasing sense that all the theories of postmodernity have been played out, that everything possible has been said about consumer stress, urban alienation and the signs and codes of mediatized society and that fiction will be able to move on from here. It is enough to give one hope that there is indeed a future for literature.

In some ways things haven't changed that much. I remember reading Robert McAlmon's description of his drinking bouts with James Joyce in 1920s Paris and the way in which Joyce, in his cups, would sob as he tried to explain "his love or infatuation for words, mere words".[90] As long as there are writers—and readers—who feel this way perhaps we'll all get by.

E.Y.

Notes

Children of the Revolution

1. *Sleazoid Express* 4, no. 1 (1984): 7.
2. The phrase "the life," meaning the underground or counterculture, was first used by Tom Wolfe in his essay "The Pump House Gang," reprinted in *The Purple Decades: A Reader* (New York: Farrar, Straus & Giroux, 1982).
3. Tom Wolfe, *The New Journalism* (London: Picador, 1990), 45.
4. Ibid., 44–45.
5. Thomas Pynchon, *Vineland* (Boston: Little, Brown, 1990); Paul Auster, *New York Trilogy* (Los Angeles: Sun & Moon, 1985); Seth Morgan, *Homeboy* (New York: Random House, 1990).
6. Wolfe, *The New Journalism*, 45.
7. Interview with Kathy Acker in *Gargoyle*, nos. 37–38 (Washington, D.C.: Paycock, 1991): 16–18.
8. Ibid.
9. *Amok Fourth Dispatch* (Los Angeles: Amok, 1991).
10. John Williams, *Into the Badlands: A Journey Through the American Dream* (London: Paladin, 1991), 8.
11. Michael Bracewell, *The Crypto-Amnesia Club* (London: Serpent's Tail, 1988); Martin Millar, *Milk, Sulphate and Alby Starvation* (London: Fourth Estate, 1988); Robert Elms, *In Search of the Crack* (London: Viking, 1988); Oliver Simmons, *Delirium* (London: Weidenfeld & Nicolson, 1989); Geoff Dyer, *The Colour of Memory* (London: Cape, 1989); Kate Pullinger, *Tiny Lies* (London: Cape, 1988).
12. Robert Siegle, *Suburban Ambush: Downtown Writing and the Fiction of Insurgency* (Baltimore: Johns Hopkins University Press, 1989).
13. Ibid., 2.
14. Ibid., 1.
15. Ibid., 2.
16. Ibid.
17. Ibid., 3.
18. Ronald Sukenick, *In For: Digressions on the Art of Fiction* (Carbondale: Southern Illinois University Press, 1985), 3.
19. Raymond Federman, "Surfiction—Four Propositions in Form of an Introduction," in *Surfiction: Fiction Now and Tomorrow*, ed. Federman (Chicago: Swallow, 1981), 11.
20. Linda Hutcheon, *A Poetics of Postmodernism: History, Theory, Fiction* (New York: Routledge, 1988), 38.
21. Fredric Jameson, "Postmodernism and Consumer Society," in *The Anti-Aesthetic: Essays on Postmodern Culture*, ed. Hal Foster (London: Pluto, 1985), 113; Port Townsend, Wash.: Bay, 1983.
22. Bret Easton Ellis, *Less Than Zero* (New York: Penguin, 1986), 189–90.
23. Douglas Coupland, interview in *Time Out* magazine, 1–8 April 1992, 27.
24. Mark Leyner, interview in *Mondo 2000* (March 1992): 48.
25. Joe McGinniss, *Fatal Vision* (New York: Signet, 1984).

26. F. Scott Fitzgerald, "Echoes of the Jazz Age" in *The Crack Up* (New York: New Directions, 1956), 14–15, 22.

Vacant Possession

*The Claes Oldenberg epigraph is from the article "Art in the Promised Land" in *The Independent*, 7 September 1991, 37.

1. Bret Easton Ellis, *Less Than Zero* (New York: Penguin, 1986), 96.
2. James Leo Herlihy, "The Jazz of Angels" in *The Sleep of Baby Filbertson and Other Stories* (New York: Dutton, 1959), 102.
3. Don DeLillo, *Libra* (New York: Viking, 1988).
4. Ellis, *Less Than Zero*, 152.
5. Eve Babitz, *Eve's Hollywood* (New York: Dell, 1974), 127.
6. Mike Davis, *City of Quartz: Excavating the Future in Los Angeles* (New York: Verso, 1990), 86.
7. Jean Baudrillard, *America,* trans. Chris Turner (New York: Verso, 1988), 102.
8. Ellis, *Less Than Zero*, 189.
9. Danny Sugerman, *Wonderland Avenue: Tales of Glamour & Excess* (London: Sidgwick & Jackson, 1989), 165; New York: Plume, 1990.
10. Joan Didion, "Dreamers of the Golden Dream" in *Slouching Towards Bethlehem* (New York: Farrar, Straus & Giroux, 1968).
11. "The story of Betty Lansdown Fouquet, a 26-year-old woman with faded blond hair who put her five-year-old daughter out to die on the center divider of Interstate 5 some miles south of the last Bakersfield exit" (Joan Didion, "The White Album" in *The White Album* [New York: Simon & Schuster, 1979]).
12. Ellis, *Less Than Zero*, 28.
13. Bret Easton Ellis, *American Psycho* (New York: Vintage, 1991), 112.
14. *The Angry Brigade 1967–84: Documents and Chronology* (Seattle: Left Bank, 1985).
15. Baudrillard, *America*, 96.
16. Janet Malcolm, *The Journalist and the Murderer* (New York: Knopf, 1990).
17. The full phrase is "You are born modern you do not become so" (Baudrillard, *America*, 73).
18. See Sadie Plant, *The Most Radical Gesture: The Situationist International in a Postmodern Age* (New York: Routledge, 1992), chapter 1.
19. Raoul Vaneigem, *The Revolution of Everyday Life,* trans. Donald Nicolson-Smith (Seattle: Left Bank, 1983).
20. Baudrillard, *America*, 28.
21. Ellis, *Less Than Zero*, 172.
22. Fred Pfeil, "Makin' Flippy-Floppy: Postmodernism and the Baby Boom PMC" in *Another Tale to Tell: Politics and Narrative in Postmodern Culture* (New York: Verso, 1990). See p. 98 for further attributions.
23. Ellis, *Less Than Zero*, 207.
24. Ibid., 202.
25. Ibid., 61.
26. Pfeil, *Another Tale to Tell,* 112.
27. Dennis Cooper, "Wrong," in *High Risk: An Anthology of Forbidden*

Writings, ed. Amy Scholder and Ira Silverberg (New York: Dutton/New American Library, 1991), 116.

28. Ellis, *Less Than Zero,* 175.

29. Ibid., 48.

30. Ibid., 172.

31. Ibid., 189.

32. Bret Easton Ellis, *The Rules of Attraction* (New York: Simon & Schuster, 1987), 114.

33. Douglas E. Winter, "Less Than Zombie," in *Splatterpunks: Extreme Horror,* ed. Paul M. Sammon (London: Xanadu, 1990), 85.

Psychodrama: Qu'est-ce que c'est?

1. Jay McInerney, Introduction to John Dos Passos, *Manhattan Transfer* (London: Penguin, 1986), 10–11.

2. *Blitz,* no. 68 (August 1988).

3. Tony Tanner, *City of Words: American Fiction, 1950–1970* (London: Cape, 1976), 17–18; New York: Harper & Row, 1971.

4. Ibid., 27–28.

5. *Blitz.*

6. Jay McInerney, *Bright Lights, Big City* (New York: Vintage, 1984), 40.

7. Ibid., 22.

8. Ibid.

9. Philip Roth, "Writing American Fiction," *Commentary* 31 (March 1961): 223–33.

10. McInerney, *Bright Lights, Big City,* 34.

11. Ibid., 39–40.

12. Ibid., 42.

13. Ibid., 14.

14. Ibid., 33.

15. Ibid., 164–65.

16. Ibid., 165–66.

17. Ibid., 166–67.

18. Terry Eagleton, *Literary Theory: An Introduction* (Minneapolis: University of Minnesota Press, 1983), 164–65.

19. McInerney, *Bright Lights, Big City,* 180–81.

20. Ibid., 181.

21. Ibid., 182.

22. Duncan Webster, *Looka Yonder! The Imaginary America of Populist Culture* (New York: Routledge, 1988), 128.

23. Ibid., 134.

24. Gary Snyder, *Turtle Island* (New York: New Directions, 1974).

25. Jay McInerney, *Ransom* (New York: Vintage, 1985), 77.

26. Ibid., 3–4.

27. Pico Iyer, *Video Night in Kathmandu and Other Reports from the Not-So-Far East* (London: Bloomsbury, 1988), 31; New York: Vintage, 1989.

28. Ibid., 17–18.

29. McInerney, *Ransom,* 18.

30. Sigmund Freud, *Group Psychology and the Analysis of the Ego* (New York, 1959), 42.

31. McInerney, *Ransom*, 162.
32. Ibid., 65–66.
33. Sam B. Girgus, *Desire and the Political Unconscious in American Literature: Eros and Ideology* (London: Macmillan, 1988), 39; New York: St. Martin's, 1990.
34. McInerney, *Ransom*, 244.
35. Jacques Lacan, "Les Formations de l'Inconscient," *Bulletin de Psychologie* 2 (1957–58). Quoted in Jacqueline Rose, *Sexuality and the Field of Vision* (London: Verso, 1986), 62.
36. McInerney, *Ransom*, 253.
37. Ibid., 269.
38. Ibid., 270.
39. Jacques Lacan, *Family Complexes in the Formation of the Individual* (Paris: Navarin, 1984), 189. As quoted in Malcolm Bowie, *Lacan* (Cambridge: Harvard University Press, 1991), 4.
40. Jay McInerney, *Story of My Life* (New York: Vintage, 1989), 19–20.
41. Ibid., 9.
42. Eagleton, *Literary Theory*, 190.
43. McInerney, *Story of My Life*, 173.
44. Sigmund Freud, *Case Studies 1: "Dora" and "Little Hans"* (London: Pelican, 1983), 80.
45. McInerney, *Story of My Life*, 30–31.
46. Ibid., 32.
47. Michel Foucault, *The History of Sexuality: An Introduction*, trans. Robert Hurley (New York: Vintage, 1990), 114.
48. Erik H. Erikson, "Reality and Actuality: An Address," in *In Dora's Case: Freud—Hysteria—Feminism*, 2nd ed., ed. Charles Bernheimer and Claire Kahane (New York: Columbia University Press, 1990), 44–55.
49. McInerney, *Story of My Life*, 45–46.
50. Ibid., 188.
51. Jay McInerney, *Brightness Falls* (New York: Knopf, 1992), 3.
52. Ibid., 18.
53. Ibid., 101.
54. Ibid., 245.
55. Ibid., 14.
56. Ibid., 416.

French Kissing in the USA

1. Michael Chabon, *The Mysteries of Pittsburgh* (New York: William Morrow, 1988), 9.
2. F. Scott Fitzgerald, *The Great Gatsby* (New York: Collier, 1992), 5.
3. Chabon, *The Mysteries of Pittsburgh*, 28.
4. Jean Baudrillard, *America*, trans. Chris Turner (New York: Verso, 1988), 73–76.
5. Chabon, *The Mysteries of Pittsburgh*, 46.
6. Ibid., 11.
7. Ibid., 96–97.
8. Ibid., 174.
9. Ibid., 33.

10. Ibid., 40.
11. Ibid., 59.
12. Michel Foucault, *The History of Sexuality: An Introduction,* trans. Robert Hurley (New York: Vintage, 1990), 83.
13. Chabon, *The Mysteries of Pittsburgh,* 240–41.
14. Ibid., 245.
15. Foucault, *The History of Sexuality,* 71.
16. Chabon, *The Mysteries of Pittsburgh,* 295.
17. Ibid.
18. Ibid., 297.

The Beast in the Jungle

*From an interview with Bret Easton Ellis in *The Evening Standard* by Nigella Lawson, 22 April 1991.

1. Roger Rosenblatt, *New York Times,* 16 December 1990.
2. R. Z. Sheppard, *Time,* 29 October 1990.
3. Tammy Bruce, National Organization for Women, December 1990.
4. *New York Times,* 6 March 1991; *Rolling Stone,* 4 April 1991.
5. Norman Mailer, "Children of the Pied Piper," *Vanity Fair* (March 1991).
6. Mim Udovitch, *The Village Voice,* 19 March 1991.
7. John Walsh, *The Sunday Times,* 21 April 1991; Fay Weldon, *The Guardian* (April 1991).
8. Joan Smith, *The Guardian* (April 1991).
9. Andy Warhol, *The Philosophy of Andy Warhol (From A to B and Back Again)* (London: Picador, 1976), 176; New York: Harcourt Brace Jovanovich, 1977.
10. Don DeLillo, commentary to BBC 1 Omnibus program *The Word, the Image and the Gun.*
11. *Rolling Stone,* 4 April 1991.
12. Don DeLillo, op. cit.
13. Naomi Wolf, *New Statesman and Society,* 12 April 1991.
14. *Rolling Stone,* 4 April 1991.
15. John Waters, *Crackpot* (New York: Vintage, 1987), 107.
16. *New York Times,* 6 March 1991.
17. Bret Easton Ellis, *American Psycho* (New York: Vintage, 1991), 3.
18. Ibid., 4.
19. *The Evening Standard,* 22 April 1991.
20. Ellis, *American Psycho,* 5.
21. Ibid., 13, 17.
22. Ibid., 16.
23. Ibid., 17.
24. Ibid., 14.
25. Ibid., 20.
26. Ibid., 24.
27. Ibid., 139–40.
28. *Rolling Stone,* 4 April 1991.
29. Douglas Crimp, "On the Museum's Ruins," in *Postmodern Culture,* ed. Hal Foster (Concord, Mass.: Pluto, 1985), 53.
30. Ellis, *American Psycho,* 248, 343.

31. Blake Morrison, *The Independent on Sunday*, 21 April 1991.
32. Ellis, *American Psycho*, 112.
33. Paul de Man, *Blindness and Insight: Essays in the Rhetoric of Contemporary Criticism*, 2nd ed., rev. (Minneapolis: University of Minnesota Press, 1983), 11.
34. Ellis, *American Psycho*, 381.
35. Ibid., 46.
36. Ibid., 59.
37. Ibid., 60–61.
38. Ibid., 22.
39. Ibid., 61.
40. Udovitch, *The Village Voice*, 19 March 1991.
41. Ellis, *American Psycho*, 80–81.
42. *Rolling Stone*, 4 April 1991.
43. *New York Times*, 6 March 1991.
44. Ellis, *American Psycho*, 103.
45. Ibid., 105.
46. Ibid., 107.
47. Ibid., 157.
48. Ibid.
49. Ibid., 159.
50. Ibid., 141.
51. Ibid., 150.
52. Ibid., 151.
53. Ibid., 177.
54. Ibid., 237.
55. Ibid., 347.
56. Ibid., 135.
57. Ibid., 263.
58. Ibid., 271.
59. Ibid., 337.
60. Ibid., 301–06.
61. Ibid., 328.
62. Ibid., 345.
63. *New York Times*, 6 March 1991.
64. Ellis, *American Psycho*, 350.
65. Ibid., 352.
66. Ibid.
67. Ibid.
68. Ibid., 368.
69. Ibid., 387.
70. Ibid., 375.
71. Ibid., 377.
72. Ibid., 380.
73. Ibid., 395.
74. Ibid., 383.
75. Ibid., 384.
76. Roland Barthes, *The Pleasure of the Text*, trans. Richard Miller (New York: Hill & Wang, 1975), 19.
77. Ibid., 14.
78. Ellis, *American Psycho*, 157.

Degree Zero

1. Joan Didion, "Holy Water" in *The White Album* (New York: Simon & Schuster, 1979), 59–66.
2. Bret Easton Ellis, *Less Than Zero* (New York: Penguin, 1986), 114.
3. Lester Bangs, *Psychotic Reactions and Carburetor Dung,* ed. Greil Marcus (New York: Knopf, 1987), 261.

A City on the Kill

1. Joel Rose, *Kill the Poor* (New York: Atlantic Monthly Press, 1988), 1.
2. Ibid., 61.
3. Ibid., 5–6.
4. Ibid., 4.
5. Ibid., 278–79.
6. Fredric Jameson, *Postmodernism, or The Cultural Logic of Late Capitalism* (Durham, N.C.: Duke University Press, 1991), 118.
7. Ibid.
8. Rose, *Kill the Poor,* 292–93.
9. Ibid., 2.
10. Ibid., 185.
11. Ibid., 139.
12. Ibid., 209.
13. Fredric Jameson, "Postmodernism, or The Cultural Logic of Late Capitalism," *New Left Review* 146 (1984): 53–92.
14. Michel Foucault quoted in Edward Soja, *Postmodern Geographies: The Reassertion of Space in Critical Social Theory* (New York: Verso, 1989). See also J. Nicholas Entrikin, *The Betweenness of Place: Towards a Geography of Modernity* (Baltimore: Johns Hopkins University Press, 1991), 43–59.
15. Rose, *Kill the Poor,* 75.
16. Ibid., 296.
17. Ibid.

Library of the Ultravixens

Tama Janowitz

*Djuna Barnes, "Seen from the 'L' " in *The Book of Repulsive Women* (New York, 1915).

I am grateful to Graham Caveney for his assistance with the theory in the first part of this chapter.

1. *Revue des Sciences Humaines,* no. 168: 480. I am indebted to Toril Moi's *Sexual/Textual Politics* (New York: Methuen, 1985) for much of this analysis of contemporary French feminism.
2. Julia Kristeva, "A Question of Subjectivity," *Women's Review,* 12 October 1986, 19.

3. Roland Barthes, *The Pleasure of the Text,* trans. Richard Miller (New York: Hill & Wang, 1975), 47.
4. Erica Jong, *Fear of Flying* (New York: Signet, 1974); Lisa Alther, *Kinflicks* (New York: Signet, 1977).
5. Erica Jong, *Any Woman's Blues* (New York: Perennial Library, 1991); Lisa Alther, *Bedrock* (New York: Knopf, 1990).
6. Joe Orton, "What the Butler Saw" in *The Complete Plays* (New York: Grove, 1977).
7. Tama Janowitz, *American Dad* (New York: Crown, 1981), 52.
8. Ibid., 31.
9. Ibid., 127.
10. Ibid., 36.
11. Ibid., 37.
12. Ibid., 44–45.
13. Ibid., 83.
14. Ibid.
15. Ibid., 208.
16. Ibid., 210.
17. Alice Munro, *The Beggar Maid (Stories of Flo and Rose)* (New York: Vintage, 1991), 28.
18. Tama Janowitz, *Slaves of New York* (New York: Washington Square Press, 1987), 1.
19. Ibid., 3.
20. Ibid., 2.
21. Ibid., 2, 6.
22. Ibid., 5.
23. Ibid., 125.
24. Ibid., 37.
25. Ibid., 23.
26. Ibid., 24.
27. Ibid., 28.
28. Ibid., 8.
29. Ibid., 58–59.
30. Ibid., 59.
31. Ibid., 7.
32. Ibid., 45.
33. Ibid., 92, 115.
34. Ibid., 28.
35. Stephen Birmingham, *Our Crowd* (New York: Harper & Row, 1967).
36. Tama Janowitz, *A Cannibal in Manhattan* (New York: Washington Square Press, 1988), 19.
37. Ibid., 55.
38. *Vanity Fair* (April 1992): 143.

Mary Gaitskill

1. Madison Smartt Bell and the *New York Times,* both from reviews of *Bad Behavior* quoted on the inside cover of the British edition.
2. Mary Gaitskill, *Bad Behavior* (New York: Vintage, 1989), 114.
3. Hettie Jones, *How I Became Hettie Jones* (New York: Dutton, 1990), 81.

4. Teresa Carpenter, from a review of *Bad Behavior* quoted on the inside cover of the British edition.
5. Gaitskill, *Bad Behavior*, 58.
6. Ibid., 70.
7. Ibid., 107.
8. Ibid., 114.
9. Ibid.
10. Ibid.
11. Ibid.
12. Ibid., 126.
13. Ibid., 127.
14. Ibid., 129.
15. Ibid., 92.
16. Mary Flanagan, *Bad Girls* (London: Futura, 1984).
17. Gaitskill, *Bad Behavior*, 34.
18. Ibid.
19. Ibid., 35.
20. Ibid., 36.
21. Ibid., 34.
22. Ibid., 39.
23. Ibid., 45.
24. Ibid., 47.
25. Ibid., 41.
26. Ibid., 42.
27. Ibid., 43.
28. Ibid., 45.
29. Ibid., 46.
30. Ibid., 48.
31. Ibid., 50.
32. Ibid., 52.
33. Mary Gaitskill, *Two Girls, Fat and Thin* (New York: Poseidon, 1991), 18.
34. Ibid., 33.
35. Ibid., 35.
36. Ibid., 30.
37. Ibid., 35.
38. Ibid., 36.
39. Eve Babitz, *Eve's Hollywood* (New York: Dell, 1974), 131.
40. Gaitskill, *Two Girls, Fat and Thin*, 32.
41. Ibid., 111.
42. Ibid., 248.

Catherine Texier

1. Kathy Acker, cover quote from Catherine Texier, *Love Me Tender* (New York: Penguin, 1987).
2. Texier, *Love Me Tender*, 185.
3. Ibid., 15.
4. Frank Wedekind, *Pandora's Box*, written 1904, performed 1918. Filmed by G. W. Pabst, 1929.
5. Texier, *Love Me Tender*, 36.

6. Ibid., 10.
7. Ibid., 80.
8. Ibid., 20.
9. Ibid., 206.
10. Ibid., 182.
11. Ibid., 67.
12. Ibid., 95.
13. Ibid., 164.
14. Ibid., 86.
15. Catherine Texier, *Panic Blood* (New York: Penguin, 1991), 15.
16. Texier, *Love Me Tender*, 19.
17. Texier, *Panic Blood*, 19.
18. Ibid., 66.
19. Ibid., 137.
20. Ibid., 119.
21. Ibid., 94.
22. Ibid., 308.
23. *The Guardian*, 5 March 1992.
24. Texier, *Panic Blood*, 107.
25. Lou Reed & The Velvet Underground, "Some Kinda Love."

Silence, Exile and Cunning

1. Letter from Lynne Tillman to the author, 22 April 1992.
2. Ibid.
3. Linda Hutcheon, *A Poetics of Postmodernism: History, Theory, Fiction* (New York: Routledge, 1988), 67–68.
4. Lynne Tillman, "To Find Words," in *Serious Hysterics*, ed. Alison Fell (New York: Serpent's Tail, 1992), 113–14.
5. Robert Siegle, *Suburban Ambush: Downtown Writing and the Fiction of Insurgency* (Baltimore: Johns Hopkins University Press, 1989), 179.
6. Lynne Tillman, *Haunted Houses* (New York: Poseidon, 1987), 12.
7. Ibid., 9.
8. Ibid., 60.
9. Ibid., 99.
10. Roland Barthes, *The Pleasure of the Text*, trans. Richard Miller (New York: Hill & Wang, 1975), 3.
11. Tillman, "To Find Words," 115.
12. Luce Irigaray, "This Sex Which Is Not One," in *New French Feminisms*, ed. Elaine Marks and Isabelle de Courtivron (New York: Schocken, 1980), 103.
13. Tillman, *Haunted Houses*, 63.
14. Ibid., 82.
15. Ibid., 97.
16. Siegle, *Suburban Ambush*, 195.
17. Lynne Tillman, interview with the author, 5 November 1991.
18. Tillman, *Haunted Houses*, 90.
19. Ibid., 179.
20. Joan Didion, "The White Album" in *The White Album* (New York: Simon & Schuster, 1979), 11.

21. Tillman, *Haunted Houses,* 146.
22. Lynne Tillman, "Diary of a Masochist" in *Absence Makes the Heart* (New York: Serpent's Tail, 1991), 52.
23. Ibid., 59.
24. Lynne Tillman, "Critical Fiction/Critical Self," in *Critical Fictions: The Politics of Imaginative Writing,* ed. Philomena Mariani (Seattle: Bay, 1991), 99.
25. Ibid., 102.
26. Ibid., 103.
27. Ibid., 98.
28. Emile Benveniste, *Problems in General Linguistics,* trans. Mary Elizabeth Meek (Coral Gables, Fla.: University of Miami Press, 1971), 223.
29. Lynne Tillman, interview with the author, 5 November 1991.
30. Letter from Lynne Tillman to the author, 22 April 1992.
31. Tillman, *Absence Makes the Heart,* 107.
32. Ibid., 105.
33. Ibid., 112.
34. Ibid., 111.
35. Lynne Tillman, "Madame Realism: A Fairy Tale," in *Silvia Kolbowski: XI Projects 1987–1990* (New York: Border Editions, 1992).
36. Tillman, *Absence Makes the Heart,* 113.
37. Lynne Tillman, "The Museum of Hyphenated Americans," in *Art in America* (September 1991): 57.
38. Lynne Tillman, *Motion Sickness* (New York: Serpent's Tail, 1992), 88.
39. Ibid., 115.
40. Ibid., 17, 32–33.
41. Ibid., 127.
42. Ibid., 129.
43. Ibid., 181.
44. Ibid., 157.
45. Ibid., 97.
46. Tillman, *Haunted Houses,* 93, 191.

Crashing in the Fast Lane

1. Gary Indiana, *White Trash Boulevard* (New York: Hanuman, 1988), 34.
2. Susan Sontag, *On Photography* (New York: Anchor, 1990), 179.
3. Gary Indiana, *Horse Crazy* (New York: Grove, 1989), 52.
4. Ibid., 15.
5. Jacques Derrida, *Dissemination,* trans. Barbara Johnson (Chicago: University of Chicago Press, 1981), 41–42.
6. Julia Kristeva, *The Kristeva Reader,* ed. Toril Moi (New York: Columbia University Press, 1986).
7. Indiana, *Horse Crazy,* 98.
8. Ibid., 35, 37.
9. Susan Sontag, *AIDS and Its Metaphors* (New York: Farrar, Straus & Giroux, 1989), 72.
10. Indiana, *Horse Crazy,* 217.

On the Road Again

*Diamanda Galás interview in *Angry Women,* ed. Andrea Juno and V. Vale (San Francisco: Re/Search Publications, 1991).
*Shane MacGowan, from the song "Sally MacLennan."

1. David Wojnarowicz, *Close to the Knives* (New York: Vintage, 1991), 25.
2. Paul de Man, "Autobiography as De-Facement" in *The Rhetoric of Romanticism* (New York: Columbia University Press, 1984), 70–71.
3. William S. Burroughs, cover quote from *Close to the Knives.*
4. Wojnarowicz, *Close to the Knives,* 27.
5. Ibid., 23.
6. Jack Kerouac, *On the Road* (New York: Penguin, 1976), 309.
7. Wojnarowicz, *Close to the Knives,* 14.
8. Ibid., 16.
9. Ibid., 22.
10. Ibid., 58.
11. Ibid., 27.
12. Ibid., 28.
13. Ibid., 31.
14. Ibid., 30.
15. Ibid., 33.
16. Ibid., 37.
17. Ibid., 38.
18. Ibid., 39.
19. Ibid., 66.
20. Ibid., 62.
21. Ibid., 114.
22. Ibid., 83.
23. Ibid., 94.
24. Ibid., 98.
25. Ibid., 105.
26. Ibid.
27. Ibid., 112.
28. Ibid., 153.
29. Ibid., 157.
30. Ibid., 165.
31. Ibid., 163.
32. Ibid., 164.
33. Ibid., 168.
34. Ibid., 170.
35. Ibid., 171.
36. Ibid., 185.
37. Ibid., 172–73.
38. Ibid., 178.
39. Ibid., 183.
40. Ibid., 191.
41. Ibid., 202.
42. Ibid., 214.
43. Ibid., 210.
44. Ibid., 209–10.

45. Ibid., 217.
46. Ibid., 220.
47. Ibid., 217.
48. Ibid., 215.
49. Ibid., 225.
50. Ibid., 228.
51. Ibid., 230.
52. Ibid., 241.
53. Ibid., 254.

Death in Disneyland

*Charles Baudelaire, "Carrion" (trans.: "O my beauty, tell the vermin who will devour you with kisses how I have immortalized the form and divine essence of my decayed loves").

1. Susan Sontag, "The Pornographic Imagination" in *Styles of Radical Will* (New York: Anchor, 1991), 51.
2. Dennis Cooper, *Closer* (New York: Grove, 1989), 75.
3. Roland Barthes, *The Pleasure of the Text,* trans. Richard Miller (New York: Hill & Wang, 1975), 21. Barthes quoting from Lacan.
4. Cooper, *Closer,* 3–5.
5. Ibid., 6.
6. Barthes, *The Pleasure of the Text,* 21.
7. Ibid., 14.
8. Cooper, *Closer,* 7.
9. Barthes, *The Pleasure of the Text,* 4.
10. Cooper, *Closer,* 9.
11. Ibid., 10.
12. Ibid., 11.
13. Ibid.
14. Barthes, *The Pleasure of the Text,* 27.
15. Cooper, *Closer,* 26.
16. Ibid., 22, 35.
17. Ibid., 24.
18. Ibid., 4.
19. Robert Frost, "Stopping by Woods on a Snowy Evening."
20. Cooper, *Closer,* 65.
21. Ibid., 49.
22. Ibid., 50.
23. Martin Green, *Children of the Sun: A Narrative of Decadence in England After 1918* (New York: Basic Books, 1976).
24. Stephen Koch, *Stargazer: Andy Warhol's World and His Films,* rev. and updated (New York: Marion Boyars, 1991).
25. Dick Hebdige, *Hiding in the Light: On Images and Things* (New York: Routledge, 1988), 210.
26. Paul de Man, *The Rhetoric of Romanticism* (New York: Columbia University Press, 1984), 81.
27. Cooper, *Closer,* 62.
28. Ibid., 72.

29. Ibid., 78.
30. Ibid., 80.
31. Ibid., 81.
32. Ibid., 87.
33. Ibid., 89–90.
34. Ibid., 90.
35. Ibid., 91.
36. Ibid., 94.
37. Ibid., 96.
38. Ibid., 97.
39. Ibid.
40. Ibid., 104.
41. Ibid., 98.
42. Ibid.
43. Jennifer Birkett, *The Sins of the Fathers: Decadence in France 1870–1914* (New York: Quartet, 1986).
44. Philippe Jullian, *Dreamers of Decadence* (London: Pall Mall, 1971), 192; New York: Praeger, 1971.
45. "Weak-winged," Saint-Pol-Roux; "posthumous," Catulle Mendes, quoted in Ibid., 252, 237.
46. Cooper, *Closer,* 99–100.
47. Ibid., 108, 110.
48. Ibid., 117.
49. Ibid., 130.
50. Ibid., 128.
51. Barthes, *The Pleasure of the Text,* 35.
52. Ibid., 40.
53. Ibid., 52.
54. Ibid., 37.
55. Cooper, *Frisk* (New York: Grove, 1991), 53, 70.
56. Lynne Tillman in conversation with author, 5 November 1991.
57. Barthes, *The Pleasure of the Text,* 47.
58. Ibid., 64.
59. Cooper, *Closer,* 105.
60. Barthes, *The Pleasure of the Text,* 20.
61. Ibid., 35, 19.
62. Georges Bataille quoted in Sontag, "The Pornographic Imagination," op. cit., 62.
63. Cooper, *Frisk,* 59.
64. Ibid., 40.
65. Ibid., 44.
66. Ibid., 59.
67. Ibid., 70.
68. Ibid., 74.
69. Ibid.
70. Ibid., 70.
71. Ibid., 107.
72. Ibid., 113.
73. Ibid., 122.
74. Ibid., 126.
75. Barthes, *The Pleasure of the Text,* 3.

76. Bret Easton Ellis, interview in *Rolling Stone*, 4 April 1991.

77. Sontag, "The Pornographic Imagination," op. cit., 57.

78. Cooper, *Frisk*, 10.

79. Georges Bataille, "Coincidences" in *Story of the Eye*, trans. Joachim Neugroschel (San Francisco: City Lights, 1987), 92.

80. Ibid.

81. Barthes, *The Pleasure of the Text*, 19.

82. William S. Burroughs, "Technology of Writing" in *The Adding Machine* (New York: Seaver, 1986), 33.

83. Jean Baudrillard, "What Are You Doing After the Orgy?" *Artforum* 22, no. 2 (October 1983).

84. Jean-François Lyotard, "Presenting the Unpresentable," *Artforum* 20, no. 8 (April 1982).

85. Meaghan Morris, *The Pirate's Fiancée: Feminism, Reading, Postmodernism* (New York: Verso, 1988), 215.

86. Ibid., 231.

87. Ibid., 215.

88. Jean Baudrillard, *L'Effect Beaubourg: Implosion et Dissuasion* (Paris: Editions Galilee, 1977), 24.

89. Jean Baudrillard, *For a Critique of the Political Economy of the Sign* (St. Louis: Telos, 1981), 110.

90. In Robert McAlmon and Kay Boyle, *Being Geniuses Together: 1920–1930* (San Francisco: North Point, 1984). Also quoted in Humphrey Carpenter, *Geniuses Together: American Writers in Paris in the 1920s* (London: Unwin, 1989), 79.

Bibliography

Source Texts

Chabon, Michael. *The Mysteries of Pittsburgh*. New York: William Morrow, 1988; rpt. Perennial Library, 1989.

———. *A Model World and Other Stories*. New York: William Morrow, 1991; rpt. Avon, 1992.

Cooper, Dennis. *The Tenderness of the Wolves*. Trumansburg, N.Y.: Crossing, 1982.

———. *Closer*. New York: Grove, 1989.

———. *Frisk*. New York: Grove, 1991.

———. *Wrong*. New York: Grove, 1992.

———, with art by Nayland Blake. *Jerk*. San Francisco: Artspace/Serpent's Tail, 1993.

Ellis, Bret Easton. *Less Than Zero*. New York: Simon & Schuster, 1985; rpt. Penguin, 1986.

———. *The Rules of Attraction*. New York: Simon & Schuster, 1987; rpt. Penguin, 1988.

———. *American Psycho*. New York: Vintage, 1991.

Gaitskill, Mary. *Bad Behavior*. New York: Poseidon, 1988; rpt. Vintage, 1989.

———. *Two Girls, Fat and Thin*. New York: Poseidon, 1991; rpt. Bantam, 1992.

Indiana, Gary. *Scar Tissue and Other Stories*. New York: Calamus/GPNY, 1987.

———. *White Trash Boulevard*. New York: Hanuman, 1988.

———. *Horse Crazy*. New York: Grove, 1989.

———. *Gone Tomorrow*. New York: Pantheon, 1993.

———. *Rent Boy*. New York: High Risk/Serpent's Tail, due out in 1994.

Janowitz, Tama. *American Dad*. New York: Crown, 1981.

———. *Slaves of New York*. New York: Crown, 1986; rpt. Washington Square Press, 1987.

———. *A Cannibal in Manhattan*. New York: Crown, 1987; rpt. Washington Square Press, 1988.

———. *The Male Cross-Dresser Support Group*. New York: Crown, 1992.

McInerney, Jay. *Bright Lights, Big City*. New York: Vintage, 1984.

———. *Ransom*. New York: Vintage, 1985.

———. *Story of My Life*. New York: Atlantic Monthly Press, 1988; rpt. Vintage, 1989.

———. *Brightness Falls*. New York: Knopf, 1992.

Rose, Joel. *Kill the Poor*. New York: Atlantic Monthly Press, 1988.

Texier, Catherine. *Love Me Tender*. New York: Penguin, 1987.

———. *Panic Blood*. New York: Viking, 1990; rpt. Penguin, 1991.

Tillman, Lynne. *Haunted Houses*. New York: Poseidon, 1987.

———. *Absence Makes the Heart*. New York: Serpent's Tail, 1991.

———. *Motion Sickness*. New York: Poseidon, 1991; rpt. Serpent's Tail, 1992.

———. *The Madame Realism Complex*. New York: Semiotext(e)/Native Agents Series, 1992.

——. *Cast in Doubt.* New York: Poseidon, 1992; rpt. Serpent's Tail, 1993.
Wojnarowicz, David. *Close to the Knives.* New York: Vintage, 1991.
——. *Memories That Smell Like Gasoline.* San Francisco: Artspace/Serpent's Tail, 1992.

Critical Bibliography

Barthes, Roland. *The Pleasure of the Text.* Translated by Richard Miller. New York: Hill & Wang, 1975.
——. *A Lover's Discourse: Fragments.* Translated by Richard Howard. New York: Hill & Wang, 1978.
——. *Image-Music-Text.* Translated by Stephen Heath. New York: Noonday, 1988.
Bataille, Georges. *Story of the Eye.* Translated by Joachim Neugroschel. San Francisco: City Lights, 1987.
Baudrillard, Jean. *In the Shadow of the Silent Majorities.* New York: Semiotext(e), 1983.
——. *America.* Translated by Chris Turner. New York: Verso, 1988.
——. *Selected Writings.* Edited by Mark Poster. Palo Alto, Calif.: Stanford University Press, 1988.
Davis, Mike. *City of Quartz: Excavating the Future in Los Angeles.* New York: Verso, 1990.
de Man, Paul. *Blindness and Insight: Essays in the Rhetoric of Contemporary Criticism.* 2nd ed., rev. Minneapolis: University of Minnesota Press, 1983.
Debord, Guy. *Society of the Spectacle.* Rev. ed. Detroit: Black & Red, 1977.
Derrida, Jacques. *Of Grammatology.* Translated by Gayatri Chakravorty Spivak. Baltimore: Johns Hopkins University Press, 1976.
——. *Writing and Difference.* Translated by Alan Bass. Chicago: University of Chicago Press, 1978.
——. *Positions.* Translated by Alan Bass. Chicago: University of Chicago Press, 1981.
Eagleton, Mary, ed. *Feminist Literary Criticism.* New York: Longman, 1991.
Eagleton, Terry. *Literary Theory: An Introduction.* Minneapolis: University of Minnesota Press, 1983.
Eco, Umberto. *Travels in Hyperreality: Essays.* Translated by William Weaver. San Diego: Harcourt Brace Jovanovich, 1986.
Foucault, Michel. *The History of Sexuality: An Introduction.* Translated by Robert Hurley. New York: Vintage, 1990.
Foster, Hal, ed. *Postmodern Culture.* Concord, Mass.: Pluto, 1985.
Freud, Sigmund, *Introductory Lectures on Psychoanalysis.* Translated and edited by James Strachey. New York: Norton, 1977.
——. *Case Studies 1: "Dora" and "Little Hans."* London: Pelican, 1983.
Girgus, Sam B. *Desire and the Political Unconscious in American Literature: Eros and Ideology.* New York: St. Martin's, 1990.
Green, Martin. *Children of the Sun: A Narrative of Decadence in England After 1918.* New York: Basic Books, 1976.
Hebdige, Dick. *Hiding in the Light: On Images and Things.* New York: Routledge, 1988.

Hutcheon, Linda. *A Poetics of Postmodernism: History, Theory, Fiction.* New York: Routledge, 1988.

Iyer, Pico. *Video Night in Kathmandu and Other Reports from the Not-So-Far East.* New York: Vintage, 1989.

Jameson, Fredric. *Postmodernism, or The Cultural Logic of Late Capitalism.* Durham, N.C.: Duke University Press, 1991.

Koch, Stephen. *Stargazer: Andy Warhol's World and His Films.* Rev. and updated. New York: Marion Boyars, 1991.

Jullian, Philippe. *Dreamers of Decadence.* New York: Praeger, 1971.

Lacan, Jacques. *Ecrits: A Selection.* Translated by Alan Sheridan. New York: Norton, 1977.

Lyotard, Jean-François. *The Postmodern Condition: A Report on Knowledge.* Translated by Geoff Bennington and Brian Massumi. Minneapolis: University of Minnesota Press, 1984.

Marks, Elaine, and Isabelle de Courtivron, eds. *New French Feminisms.* New York: Schocken, 1980.

Moi, Toril. *Sexual/Textual Politics.* New York: Methuen, 1985.

Moore, Suzanne. *Looking for Trouble: On Shopping, Gender and the Cinema.* New York: Serpent's Tail, 1992.

Morris, Meaghan. *The Pirate's Fiancée.* New York: Verso, 1988.

Pfeil, Fred. *Another Tale to Tell: Politics and Narrative in Postmodern Culture.* New York: Verso, 1990.

Plant, Sadie. *The Most Radical Gesture: The Situationist International in a Postmodern Age.* New York: Routledge, 1992.

Rose, Jacqueline. *Sexuality and the Field of Vision.* London: Verso, 1986.

Siegle, Robert. *Suburban Ambush: Downtown Writing and the Fiction of Insurgency.* Baltimore: Johns Hopkins University Press, 1989.

Sontag, Susan. "The Pornographic Imagination." In *Styles of Radical Will.* New York: Farrar, Straus & Giroux, 1969; rpt. Anchor, 1991.

———. *On Photography.* New York: Farrar, Straus & Giroux, 1977; rpt. Anchor, 1990.

———. *Illness As Metaphor.* New York: Farrar, Straus & Giroux, 1978.

———. *AIDS and Its Metaphors.* New York: Farrar, Straus & Giroux, 1989.

Sugerman, Danny. *Wonderland Avenue: Tales of Glamour and Excess.* New York: Plume, 1990.

Tanner, Tony. *City of Words: American Fiction, 1950-1970.* New York: Harper & Row, 1971.

Webster, Duncan. *Looka Yonder! The Imaginary America of Populist Culture.* New York: Routledge, 1988.

Williams, John. *Into the Badlands: A Journey Through the American Dream.* London: Paladin, 1991.

Wolfe, Tom. *The New Journalism.* London: Picador, 1990.

Index